I0150629

THE CASE FOR THE PROSECUTION

In the Trial of Silent Reading "Comprehension" Tests, Charged with the Destruction of America's Schools and Two Other Papers

By Geraldine E. Rodgers

"The Case for the Prosecution," by Geraldine E. Rodgers. ISBN 978-1-58939-995-2.

Published 2007 by Virtualbookworm.com Publishing Inc., P.O. Box 9949, College Station, TX 77842, US. ©2007, Geraldine E. Rodgers. All rights reserved. No part of this publication may be reproduced, stored in a retrieval system, or transmitted in any form or by any means, electronic, mechanical, recording or otherwise, without the prior written permission of Geraldine E. Rodgers.

Manufactured in the United States of America.

PREFACE

The Case for the Prosecution was written in 1981, *The Wary Reader's Guide to Psycholinguistics* was written in 1982, and *The Flat Earth of American Reading Instruction* was written in 1983. They are out of date to some extent because they do not incorporate additional information which I developed through further library research. However, they do contain a great deal of useful background information which I did not repeat in later books. This useful information is not at all readily available, but would require the same heavy library research which I had to do in order to obtain it.

Therefore, since this background information may be helpful to others who are working on the illiteracy problem, all three works have been republished in this volume.

TABLE OF CONTENTS

THE CASE FOR THE PROSECUTION

In the Trial of Silent Reading "Comprehension" Tests, Charged with the Destruction of America's Schools

By Geraldine E. Rodgers
July 27, 1981
Revised December 8, 2006

Introduction

It Is These Fake Reading Comprehension Tests That Have Caused Our Reading Problem.

T he *New York Post* editorial of June 15, 1981, asked despairingly for the TRUTH about reading tests. Well, here IS the truth: All these silent reading comprehension tests are a massive fraud. Back before 1911, when Binet of France originated the FIRST real intelligence tests, he used oral reading comprehension to test native intelligence, which is itself un-teachable. Binet's reading comprehension paragraphs are STILL used to test intelligence. So reading comprehension scores are really IQ scores!

Binet's associate, Simon, said in 1924 that they had found many children who could pass the reading comprehension part of their IQ tests when adults listening to the children could not understand what they were saying because they missed so many words. So, obviously, such "reading comprehension" tests are a totally inadequate test of reading *accuracy.*

But the American experts from 1912 to 1930 did not care about reading accuracy. They were interested in "reading comprehension." Even though they agreed with Binet that reading comprehension was a function of IQ, they believed IQ itself was just a bunch of splintered potential abilities, each of which had to be developed independently

1

on its own little stimulus-response printed circuit.

There was no such thing as "transfer of training." Their pseudo-scientific ideas make quite a story. Because of their notions, in 1930 and 1931, they sneaked into America's schools, under false labels, to protect "reading comprehension," a method which had been used for almost two hundred years to teach language to deaf-mutes. Gates and Gray, who introduced this method, did not, most naturally, say that it was based on a centuries-old method used to teach the deaf. Now, in 1981, FIFTY YEARS LATER, Americans STILL do not know what was put over on them!

As long ago as the 15th century, Rudolph Agricola saw a deaf-and-dumb man who was able to talk to others by writing. Girolamo Cardano in the 16th century said, "The deaf can hear by reading, and speak by writing." A Spanish Benedictine monk, Ponce de Leon, in the 16th century, taught his deaf-mute pupils to write, before teaching them to speak. A contemporary of his, Francesco Valles, said that Ponce de Leon's method proved that, though we learn to speak first and then learn to write, the opposite was true for the deaf--the reverse order.[1] With this remark about the reverse way, he anticipated the path on a stimulus-response printed circuit of the psychologists of 1912-1930 which would be the basis for their "new" method of reading. But their stimulus-response printed circuit has been kept carefully hidden for almost 70 years, and is part of an incredible story.

---

[1] After this was written, research showed that early teachers of the deaf did not really use a reverse order. Since they taught words by careful finger spelling of the letters, they were not setting up a conditioned reflex to read words initially as MEANING-BEARING WHOLES. However, the Abbe de l'Epee after 1760 did do that as he gave his pupils so very many words at one time to finger-spell that it was manifestly impossible to learn them except as whole words.

CHAPTER 1

OUR READING MESS IS ROOTED IN THE DIFFERENCES BETWEEN PHONICS AND SIGHT WORDS.

I t was Samuel Blumenfeld in his book, *The New Illiterates*, who brilliantly identified the origin of the American sight-word method for normal children. It began with a primer written by the Reverend Thomas H. Gallaudet in 1835. In pure sight-word methods, a child learns a printed word as a whole, like a Chinese character, without any reference to letter sounds. Gallaudet was the founder of deaf-mute instruction in the United States, having studied in France at the school founded in Paris about 1760 by the Abbe Charles Michel de l'Epee. The sight-word method Gallaudet used in his primer was known from the comments of Gallaudet's contemporaries, but, as Samuel Blumenfeld has pointed out, copies of Gallaudet's once popular *Mother's Primer* have strangely totally disappeared from libraries in the United States. Blumenfeld said that HOW the approach of Gallaudet's primer entered the "mainstream" in American education was a mystery, but he felt the missing link must be in Gallaudet's primer itself, which he had been completely unable to locate. Now, after four years of research, I can answer Blumenfeld's question, "How?" and my own question, "Why?" Most of the background I will present to answer these questions has been either totally unknown (or ignored) by our education "experts," which fact is a massive indictment of their abject incompetence.

But the price of understanding our reading problem is to make the effort to understand its background, so it is necessary in this chapter to walk the reader over some rather rough terrain.

Unlike Gallaudet's pure sight-word primer, the earlier American sight-word primer by Samuel Worcester, published in 1826, included a phonic approach, or the teaching of letter sounds. It was like the many sight-words-plus-varying-phonics approaches prevalent in Europe at the time, both in Great Britain and Germany. They cannot be compared to Gallaudet's. [Inserted note in 2006: The preceding is incorrect but grew out of the literature available to me in 1981. When I actually saw Worcester's 1826 primer for myself, I found it was a pure sight-word approach. Furthermore, although Germany did have some phonic materials before 1826, my further research indicated Great Britain did not but did use the syllabary.]

My library research indicates that the sight-words-plus-phonics approach grew out of the famous Philanthropinum School, founded in 1774 in Dessau, Germany, by Johann Bernhard Basedow, at which time Basedow moved the teaching of reading up from Level 1, syllables, where it had always been, to Level 2, words-in-syntax.

Concerning these levels, as I have called them, I believe that a true model of the reading act concerns three consecutive levels. Level 1 is syllables, which can be distinguished even in a foreign language. Level 2 is syntax-generating-words, which can be distinguished in one's native language. Level 3 is consciousness of meaning, the level of life itself. Consciousness is a reality as observable as magnetism and gravity, and just as unexplainable.

By contrast, the first two levels of reading can be duplicated by machine computers, but the third level, consciousness, is possible

4

only to a living creature. Stroke victims sometimes lose the capacity to handle the first two levels, or the power of speech, and look, consciously but painfully, at their relatives, trying to communicate their conscious thought. In speaking or listening, we can be said to hold computers in our heads, as we can hold them in our hands, because our brains can automatically process syllables and syntax-generating-words, to produce the stream of language which is then presented to our consciousness, Level 3, or the essence of life itself, but only IF Level 3 happens to be paying attention. Attention, as S. Jay Samuels of the University of Minnesota said research has determined, can be on only one thing at a time. So, in other words, consciousness is indivisible (which brings us back to Rene Descartes and his, "I think, therefore I am.") So, as Samuels points out, we may listen, or read, in a distracted fashion. That is to say, there can be no "reading comprehension" without attention, regardless of IQ.

Since before the time of the Etruscans in 600 B. C., beginning reading had been taught on Level 1, the syllable. But the method of Basedow in Germany in 1770 began instead first at Level 3, consciousness, before dropping to Level 2, words-in syntax, and finally down to Level 1, the syllable. A devotee of John Locke, Basedow believed, with Locke, that instruction should always begin with real things or objects, and only afterwards move on to words. So, obviously, the ancient practice of beginning with syllables would be unacceptable to Basedow.

But Basedow and others did not see that there was an internal contradiction in Locke's thought. In Locke's magnificent ideas on liberty and personal responsibility, he enshrined the sanctity of the human will. Yet in his totally unrelated ideas on the subject of epistemology (the study of how the mind obtains knowledge), he stated the ONLY possible source of knowledge was the human senses. Undeniably, they are the major source, but not the only source. This idea became the basis for the materialistic philosophy that ultimately denied the existence of the human will. So, two currents of educational thought flowed from his teachings. One supported TRUE progressive education, and its respect for human will with its corollary, personal responsibility. The other supported the philosophy which eventually resulted in materialistic psychology and its denial of the existence of the human will. The two wires crossed in Columbia Teachers College in the early 20th century. That short circuit has almost destroyed American education.

In 1770, Basedow's assistant, Christian Henry Wolke, taught Basedow's infant daughter, Emilie, by Basedow's methods. Emilie may be presumed to have been named after Rousseau's *Emile*. Rousseau's famous book, published in 1762, was also based on Locke's ideas, as expressed in Locke's book, *Some Thoughts Concerning Education* (1693). Rousseau's close friend, Pere Condillac, a devotee of Locke, had published his own book in 1746, touching on education. It is through his association with Condillac that Rousseau may have developed his own interest in education. Rousseau's *Emile* was a stupendous success, and provided the public support for Basedow's earlier ideas, which Basedow had covered in his own book, *The New Method,* in 1752. After 1762, Basedow capitalized on that enormous public support for the ideas expressed in Rousseau's *Emile* by raising a huge sum of money from the "great" of Europe (Catherine of Russia, the King of Denmark, Emmanuel Kant, and hosts of others), using it to write his own school text, the *Elementary Work*, finally published in 1774, and to found his school, the Philanthropinum, also opened in 1774. It was to help Basedow by writing the mathematics and science portions of the *Elementary Work* that Wolke joined him at New Year's, 1770.

Wolke told of his experiences teaching Emilie, in his own

words, reported in the article in the *American Journal of Education*, 1857, "Johann Bernhard Basedow and the Philanthropinum," translated from the German of Karl von Raumer . After starting little Emilie with "object teaching," or the teaching of things through the senses (Level 3), Wolke then taught things as described by words (Level 2). After this, he taught little Emilie sounding-and--blending phonics on words in sentences (using Level 1), long before Emilie had learned to read. Wolke said only the isolated phonemes to Emily (such as in. "D-r-o-p th-a-t d-i-sh", for instance). Emilie would blend them together to say, "Drop that dish." In 1773, when Emilie at the age of three was finally given material to read, she learned with startling speed. Wolke said he was only following Basedow's directions in this method. Basedow discussed his method of teaching reading in his 1774 *Elementary Work* and also in a book he wrote in 1785 specifically on the teaching of reading. Basedow spent the last few years of his life before his death in 1790 concentrating on beginning reading, after he left the Philanthropinum. Ex-teachers there, Wolke, Olivier, Campe and Trapp all wrote beginning readers later, and all used Level 2, words-in-syntax, to some degree, as did Basedow's supporter, Gedike, who also wrote an ode to Basedow, rather a reliable indication of support:

> *Thou North-Albion's son, lighted the sparkling torch,*
> *Flung'st it aloft with a Hercules mighty arm,*
> *Many ran toward thee, kindled their lights from thine...*

What was kindled from Basedow's torch, besides progressive education and the teaching of "object lessons," at Level 3, was the teaching of phonics AFTER having used the level of words-in-syntax, Level 2.

This is what Horace Mann saw years later in Germany and

misunderstood as a true sight-word method. A schoolmaster drew a picture of a house on the blackboard, and wrote the German name for it, "haus," next to it. The schoolmaster then ran over the forms of the letters with his pointer as the children wrote them in the air with their fingers. Next, the children copied the word on their slates. Then they were drilled on the sounds of the individual letters in the word, but WITHOUT using their names: The schoolmaster gave the "h" sound, the "au" sound, and the "s" sound, using letter blocks as he did so. (That was the "analysis".) Then came the "synthesis," when the schoolmaster placed the letter blocks he had shown to the children: "h" and "au" and "s" side by side, to build the word he had started with: "haus." So, after starting with the meaning of the word by using a picture, on Level 3, he had then moved to Level 2, the word that named the picture, and finally down to Level 1 itself, the sounds in the syllable (this word having only one syllable) . He then put the phonemes together to make the word again, on Level 2, and finally moved back to Level 3, when the children ended by discussing houses in general and drawing pictures of them.

This is the German analytic-synthetic method, and, of course, an excellent way to teach reading, but not the only way. Synthetic phonics programs like Alpha One are also excellent, and the choice is simply a question of personal preferences, since both work superbly well. However, synthetic phonics programs START at Level 1, demonstrating sounds blended together to make syllables, BEFORE moving to Level 2, words.

It appears self-evident that it was Basedow who originated the word method in Germany, yet Gedike is commonly credited as its originator, with Gedike's book of 1779. J. Guillaume in his article, "Reading," in the 1887 *Dictionnaire de Pedagogie*, Paris, said that in 1778 Campe, Basedow's disciple, had already used the analytic-synthetic word method. However, it should be evident from the history that it was Basedow, himself, who was the primary source of those methods which use Level 2, words-in-syntax first, before using Level 1, syllables and phonics, as a starting point in teaching reading.

The ideas of some of Basedow's followers, however, by the beginning of the 19th century, became strangely mixed with the ideas of the Abbe de l'Epee, the teacher of the deaf, (the Abbe having been a very famous man). Yet it seems apparent that the present highly successful German analytic-synthetic method, starting with words and then immediately using phonics, was the invention of that erratic genius, Johann Bernhard Basedow, and has no connection whatsoever with what became our exceedingly unfortunate sight-word method. This, instead, can be traced directly back to the 18th century Abbe de l'Epee, the teacher of the deaf, through Thomas H. Gallaudet, who attended in 1815 the school the Abbe had founded in Paris. (It is an interesting sidelight that Gallaudet was professor of the philosophy of education in New York University during 1832 and 1833, the first professorship of education in the United States, and was also active in the movement which established the first normal schools in America. These sidelights can be found in the 1911 *Cyclopedia of Education*, plus the information that Gallaudet wrote "several text-books, including the popular *Mother's Primer* and the *Child's Picture Defining and Reading Book*," being called popular as late as 1911).

[Added correction in 2006: Later research identified the origin of the sight-word method with Abbe Bertaud in France in 1744 who wrote *Quadrille des Enfants*, discussed in my *History of Beginning Reading*, 1995, 2001. The 1887 *Dictionnaire de Pedagogie et d'Instruction Primaire* article on Abbe Bertaud and his method by A. Demkes reported, "This method had a great vogue..." in the 18th century and was used in Prussia in what is now Germany to teach the prince royal, Frederick William, to read. Therefore, most probably, the *Quadrille* method which started with whole words was known to Basedow since he lived in what is now Germany. However, Basedow used whole words in order to demonstrate isolated letter sounds but Bertaud used whole words only to teach parts of them, what Demkes' article called "86 syllables". As his *Dictionnaire* article on Bertaud's method commented, "Like all reading methods without spelling, it succeeds only with those pupils who have, as has been said, the memory of the eyes." It would not be possible to give a clearer definition of the sight-word method than Demkes gave with that remark on "the memory of the eyes." It is probable that the Abbe de l'Epee, about 1760 in France, just like Basedow in Germany about 1770, was familiar with Bertaud's 1744 *Quadrille* program. Unlike Basedow, de l'Epee used it to teach his deaf mutes by sight-words with "the memory of the eyes."]

Phonics itself, however, REAL phonics, whether used with or without the German analytic-synthetic method, was invented in 1655 by Blaise Pascal for the Port Royal school in France, in which Pascal's sister Jacqueline taught. Until then, only regularly formed strings of syllables had been taught to children in beginning reading, since antiquity: such as ba, be, bi, bo, bu and so on to more complicated ones, which the children spelled and then memorized, to learn the printed syllables of their own language. The syllable was still the "atom" of reading up to the 17th century, just as it had been in the 3rd century, B. C., as shown by the O. Gueraud and P. Jouguet papyrus, [*Un Livre d'Ecolier du IIIe Siecle Avant Jesus Christ*, Publications de la Societe Royal Egyptienne de Papyrologie, Textes et Documents, II, Cairo, 1938] a teacher's guide which was dug up from the sands in North Africa, shortly before World War II, where a Greek language school's wastebaskets had been emptied over two thousand years before.

Some people, notably Ickelsamer of Germany in the 1500's, tried to analyze these syllables, so that children could distinguish the letter sounds in them (as in the syllable "ot," without breaking it apart). This, of course, is analytic phonics of whole syllables, without breaking them apart as Basedow did later.

But the French scientist and mathematician, Blaise Pascal, in 1655, was the first to split the syllable atom. He taught his sister Jacqueline, a nun at the Port Royal school, to make abbreviated sounds for the letters, instead of naming them, and then to try to blend these new abbreviated sounds together to form syllables or words. Pascal, of course, was using synthesis, as opposed to Ickelsamer's analysis.

A letter Jacqueline Pascal wrote her brother on October 26, 1655, quoted in the *Dictionnaire de Pedagogie et d'Instruction Primaire*, makes it clear that Jacqueline had a hard time understanding what her brother, Blaise, meant. In modern terms, instead of having a child say the letters, "see, aye, tee," after which the teacher has to tell the child he has spelled the word, "cat," the child is taught to say the sounds "kuh-ah-tuh" and to try to blend them together himself to discover that he has produced the word, "cat." Letter names are NOT clues to unknown words, but letter sounds are. Pascal's was the first recorded use of sounding-and-blending phonics in history, and it was the first successful challenge to the syllable method of teaching alphabetic reading which had been used apparently without interruption since before the days of the Etruscans in 600 B. C.

As a presumed exception to the syllable method, H. I. Marrou of France, in *History of Education in Antiquity*, referred to the practice in 6th century Christian schools where the master was presumed to have had his pupil learn to read by memorizing written Psalms. [Marrou apparently misunderstood the teaching sequence. Other sources confirm that the syllabary was taught first, and it was then used to decode the Psalms. The memorizing came AFTER the decoding. In Andew W. Tuer's *History of the Horn Book*, 1897, 1979, he referred to two papyrus fragments surviving from the third and seventh centuries, A. D. The first from the third century A. D. was a written-out syllabary, and the second from the seventh century A. D. was a Psalm with the syllables carefully separated, which obviously had to have been done either by or for a beginner.] Since in the 6th century A. D. to which Marrou referred, words were generally run together without any separation or any punctuation, just as they had been in Greek and Roman times, the method to which Marrou referred could not have been a word method, but had to have been a syllable method. Marrou also referred to the reportedly modern Moslem methods in which students memorized the Koran. In Arabic, letter names are said to be as close to their sounds as Pascal's abbreviated letter sounds are. So this would, in practice, be an analytic phonics method like Ickelsamer's. It is almost certain that those students of the Koran would have learned the sound-bearing Arabic alphabet first.

But the syllable was the atom in teaching reading generally as late as the 15th century, and syllables were memorized in regularly formed patterns (ba, be, bi, bo, bu, etc.). Leonardo Da Vinci made miniature illustrations for such an ABC book in Milan in the late 15th century, and Shakespeare referred to an ABC or horn book in *Love's Labors Lost.* It was Blaise Pascal who split this syllable atom in 1655 by the invention of synthetic sounding-and-blending phonics.

Pascal's method, however, was largely lost after the Port Royal community was effectively suppressed by Louis XIV and, much later in 1710, the last few religious dispersed and the buildings razed to the ground. After hearing garbled reports on the nature of the phonic method, a man named Delauney tracked down its source in the Port Royal book, *Grammaire generale de Port Royal.* 1664, and published his own reading materials based on Pascal's method in 1719 (*Methode du sieur Py-Poulain de Launay ou l'art d'aprendre lire le francois et le latin*). Pascal's method, plus the use of letter cards to set up spelled words, from layers of boxes each holding a different letter sound, was also used by Dumas in his bureau typographique (described both in Dumas' *La bibliotheque des enfans* (1733) and in Rollin's *Supplement* to *Traite des etudes* of 1734). Both Pascal phonics and Dumas' bureau typographique were used by Herbault, the director of the Child Jesus charity school in Paris in 1747, plus the idea of monitor instruction, having older pupils teaching younger ones, later attributed to Bell and Lancaster in England, and praised in America in the 1820's.

Karl von Raumer, who wrote the article on Basedow translated for Barnard's 1857 *American Journal of Education*, referred to the "pedagogical simoom, which at that time [in the 18th century] blew from France over Germany."

One possible and very famous source for ideas on education coming from France to which von Raumer may have been referring was the *Correspondence Litteraire*, by Baron Friedrich Melchior Grimm, published every other week in France from 1753 to 1773, to which Denis Diderot contributed. It was a subscription newsletter to the royalty of Europe (and, presumably, to others.) Another was the *Encyclopedie ou Dictionnaire Raissonne des Sciences des Arts et des Metiers*, published in France between 1751 to 1772 in 28 volumes, on which Denis Diderot was the principal editor.

Diderot was a close friend of both Rousseau and Pere Condillac, dining weekly with them at the Panier Fleuri in Paris during the 1740's. In Diderot's 1749 book, *Letter on the Blind*, he showed an interest in reading, proposing that the blind learn to read by their sense of touch. In 1751, Diderot wrote, *Letter on the Deaf and Mute*, which, according to the *Encyclopedia Brittanica*, studied "the function of language." His interest in the use of the senses, of course, parallels that of his friend Pere Condillac, the follower of Locke, but it is equally interesting that Diderot showed an interest in the use of senses for teaching reading, though the record only shows what he suggested for the blind, and not the deaf.

Von Raumer with his remark about the "pedagogical simoom" confirmed that the Germans in the 18th century were heavily influenced by French ideas on education. It seems apparent that Basedow read about and then combined Pascal's sounding-and-blending phonics from France with his own idea of teaching reading through words. [Note: As stated, that idea also was almost certainly not original with Basedow but probably also came from France, originating with Abbe Bertaud in 1744]. Basedow's use of Pascal phonics seems particularly apparent since Basedow also used in his school the Frenchman Dumas' idea of the bureau typographique [also, as stated, based on Pascal phonics]. Basedow's work, combining Level I, syllables and phonics [using Pascal's idea], with Level 2, words-in-syntax [using Bertaud's idea], eventually resulted in the German analytic-synthetic method, which is a highly successful approach to teaching beginning reading.

The Abbe de Radonvilliers of the Academie Francaise in Paris in 1768 published *De la maniere d'apprendre les langues* recommending a *pure* sight word method strikingly like that used by the deaf. Since the Abbe de l'Epee's school for the deaf opened in Paris about 1760, it seems reasonable to assume a possible connection between the two. Obviously, the Abbe de Radonvilliers' method had no connection with Basedow's word method in which phonics was an integral part. Nicolas Adam wrote a book in Paris in 1787, *Vraie maniere d'apprendre une langue quelconque*, in which Adam outlined a pure sight-word method, conceivably inspired by the Abbe de Radonvilliers' earlier book in 1768, and also, obviously, having no connection with Basedow's approach.

Concerning Pascal's phonics, however, voice prints show conclusively that it is really absolutely impossible to blend such imaginary letter sounds together to produce syllables because "letter sounds" themselves, no matter how quickly sounded, are

THEMSELVES syllables. The whole idea of sounding-and-blending phonics is only an abstraction meant ONLY to assist in the very beginning stages of reading when a child is learning the printed syllables of his own language. It was only for this purpose that Pascal invented it, to make the previously almost unending memorization of regularly formed syllables (ba, be, bi, bo, bu, etc.) unnecessary. But phonics WORKS, and has since 1655. So it is not surprising that it was invented by one of the most towering mathematical and scientific geniuses in history, Blaise Pascal, and is the route of all the sciences, analysis and synthesis.

But this also shows what was wrong with the American J. McKeen Cattell's 1885 conclusion that adults read "words" as quickly as they do isolated "letters," so children should be taught whole words, and not letters. By flashing words at high speed to adults in Germany, Cattell found that a typical adult could in ten milliseconds read about four random letters, two random words (totaling about twelve letters) or a short sentence of four words (totaling about twenty-four letters) . But I conclude that he was presenting a choice between pure words and pure letters, things which simply do not exist. Words cannot exist outside of syntax, any more than letters can exist outside of syllables. Voice prints show conclusively that there IS no such thing as a pure letter sound, except for vowels. Words can have no existence outside of their function in syntax, which is why the dictionary defines them in terms of nouns, verbs, and so on. (It would appear from H. I. Marrou's remarks on page 376 of *Education in Antiquity* that the ancient Roman, Priscian, did not call them "words" but "parts of speech" in a school treatise he wrote).

The reality is that syllables-in-syntax generate words, not that words generate syntax. What about this sentence, understandable to any American: "Ya gonna go?" What are the "words"? Computers have been made which are able to translate languages, but they have not been able to do so using pure "words" but have had to go another route. Also, research has shown that little first graders have no concept of what is meant by "words," both of which facts would seem to confirm that "pure" words outside of syntax are unnatural.

In presenting adults with a choice between "pure" words and "pure" letters, Cattell was really giving them NO choice, because, in each case, what was being read were simply syllables "letter" syllables versus "word" syllables. The fact that four letter syllables take less ink to write than four word syllables does not change this reality. What about the TWO syllable word, "per cent," and its sign: %? Is one way shorter than the other because it takes less ink to write it?

Not surprisingly, Cattell found that the four isolated letters (something like BGXQ) were read in about the same time as four six-letter words in a sentence (something like "George thought Claire jumped.") But the two random words, read OUTSIDE a sentence , adding up to about 12 letters, such as the words, "found, thought, " he showed took the same time to read as the four letters or four words-in-syntax. Therefore, he actually proved it took TWICE AS LONG to read the isolated words as to read the disconnected letters or words-in-syntax. I conclude that what he actually proved is that, for the readers he tested, the reading of isolated pure words was an unnatural act.

So Samuel Blumenfeld discovered when he wrote *The New Illiterates* that the Gallaudet primer had disappeared. But that has to be amended now to, "almost disappeared," because a copy turned up recently in the library of the Gallaudet College for the deaf in Washington, D. C. I obtained a photocopy and found, as Blumenfeld had suggested, that Gallaudet was using the same method in his primer for normal children as he did in his method for the deaf, most of all, obviously, sight words. I also found, as Blumenfeld suggested, that the primer IS the missing link! Because

Gallaudet was using something else which must, logically be part of ANY method to teach deaf-mutes pure sight words: constant repetition of sight words, a controlled vocabulary, and context guessing! Furthermore, Gallaudet was using what must be used to help deaf-mutes tell printed words apart, if they have not been taught by the oral method: whole word "visual" analysis, in which sight words like "pl - ate" are compared to words like "g-ate".

It was this controlled vocabulary, context-guessing approach, with constant repetition of known sight words, and visual analysis of known sight words natural to deaf-mute instruction by the method which does not use lip reading, and which was almost two centuries old, which was introduced to the world with much fanfare by William S. Gray and Arthur I. Gates in 1930 and 1931 as the new, improved method of teaching reading with "intrinsic phonics".

Nobody had ever heard of "intrinsic phonics" until Gates (and Gray) invented it. But it was only the visual analysis of known sight words, used to teach the deaf, in new trappings. As a child is reading his sight-word story, he comes across an unknown word, the meaning of which is suggested by the context. He checks the sight-word guess he makes, from the meaning of the story, against his remembered store of sight words, to see if they have a like part or parts that confirm his guess. For instance, he may be reading, "The man opened the *gate*," but he cannot read the word, "gate." He guesses that the word is "gate" from the context, and then checks his sight-word "bank" and turns up "pl-ate" and "g-un," and, putting together parts from each of these known words, confirms his guess, "gate."

Honestly! The method is precisely that atrocious. That is why rhyming "phonics" is so necessary to the sight-word basal textbooks, because the use of word-endings which rhyme is such a help in guessing unknown words(as with "gate" and "plate"). Of course, rhyming "phonics" is useless with Pascal sounding-and-blending phonics. But the "experts" preferred, particularly at first grade, to use only PARTS of known sight words to guess an unknown word from context, preferably initial consonants (guessing "g-ate" from the context because it begins like "g-un," if "gun" is a sight word a child already knows.) Today's basal readers, despite their mountains of accompanying workbook pages with phony phonics exercises, are not too different from the 1930 and 1931 Gates and Gray books. Their most harmful aspect, just as with Gates' and Gray's readers, is their rigidly controlled reading vocabulary.

When a child is constantly guessing from the context of a carefully controlled vocabulary as in today's sight-word basal readers, he will increase his stock of sight words, if he has a good visual memory, just as a deaf child can. He may still be totally unable to read new words, however, but only to guess from remembered sight words which are similar to the unknown one, or to guess from the sounds of some of the letters plus the context. I have had adult, intelligent Americans tell me that they skip all the "hard" words when they are reading. By adulthood, of course, most people who have been trained to read like the deaf can nevertheless finally sound out a whole new word if they are forced to, but their habits are formed and they find it difficult to change them.

CHAPTER 2

WHY WOULD ANYONE IN HIS RIGHT MIND WANT TO TEACH SIGHT WORDS, ANYWAY?

Sight-word trained children have obviously been made almost deaf to print if they are unable to sound out a new printed word like "gate" or "frog" by the beginning of second grade. They are almost as deaf to the sounds of printed words as a stone-deaf person is to the sound of spoken words. THAT IS NO ACCIDENT, because the reading experts of the period from 1910 to 1930 carefully arranged it that way by teaching normal children to read as the deaf were taught, with no reference, or almost none, to sounds. Their dim-witted psychology made them think that this was necessary to protect so-called "reading comprehension."

A simplistic little diagram in the 1913 *Cyclopedia of Education* clearly shows why. The article containing the diagram was written by Henry Suzzallo, who was then a professor of education at Columbia Teachers College. He had been E. L. Thorndike's graduate student at Columbia Teachers College about 1902. Suzzallo's little diagram shown below is, appropriately, just like a stimulus-response printed circuit, and it is surprisingly easy to understand.

Meaning

Oral   Visual

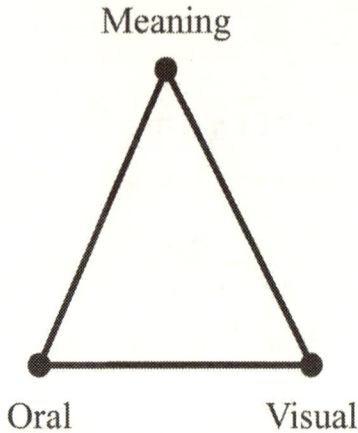

In his article published in the *Cyclopedia* in 1913 (but obviously written somewhat earlier), Suzzallo wrote that, in listening to language, we travel clockwise on his triangle, on the leg from Oral (the sound of the word) directly to Meaning (the meaning of the word). However, in reading, as opposed to listening, if children have been taught by phonics, they must go clockwise first from Visual, which is the sight of the printed word, next to Oral, the phonic sound of the word, and only then can reach the last leg, the Meaning of the word. Obviously, while "listening" has only one step in getting to word Meaning, (Oral directly to Meaning), phonic "reading" inserts that additional step in getting to Meaning (first Visual - the printed word, secondly Oral - the phonic sound of the word, and only then the Meaning of the word).

But even the early experts in those days before 1913 wanted to use straight sight words, instead of phonics, so the children could go counterclockwise from Visual, the sight of the word, straight to Meaning, skipping sound completely. They thought the phonics method made children get hung up on sounds, at the Oral stop, so that they sometimes never finished the second leg of the trip, to the

Meaning of the word. But, since sight words were so difficult to memorize, the experts were forced, against their will in those early days, to use "supplemental" phonics, not long after the beginning of the first grade, and so to use the disliked phonics clockwise route on the reading triangle, as well as the preferred sight-word counterclockwise route.

Something else was worrying them. Educated people actually know at least two languages. One is the vocabulary of the spoken language, and the other, as Dr. Charles C. Walcutt pointed out, is the vocabulary of the written language, the language of books, which Dr. Walcutt called Reading 3 to distinguish it from the beginning stages of reading. We all know many words and sentence constructions from our reading which we have never actually spoken aloud. We got their meaning from understanding what we were reading, just as we got the vocabulary of our spoken language from understanding what we were hearing. But if children in their reading were stopped at the Oral "phonic" point of the triangle, if they were often just making sounds and not thinking about the meaning of what they were reading, they would hardly be able to increase their vocabulary! Their education would be ruined!

Actually, the experts WERE getting wildly fluctuating silent reading comprehension scores, like those reported by H. A. Brown in the June, 1914, *Elementary School Journal* of the University of Chicago. Brown was Deputy State Superintendent in New Hampshire at the time, and had received his master's degree from Columbia Teachers College on June 13, 1912. It is interesting that the oft-quoted pro-sight-word classroom experiment reported by Currier and Duguid in the *Elementary School Journal* in 1916 was done in New Hampshire about the time that Brown was Deputy State Superintendent.

But the most interesting individual silent reading comprehension scores were from Miss Middleton's third and fourth grade class, reported by Karl Douglas Waldo, a graduate student at the University of Chicago, in the *Elementary School Journal* of January, 1915. Some of Miss Middleton's children who scored very high in the fall scored very low in the spring, and some who scored very low in the fall scored very high in the spring. Almost none scored the same, but either went up or down, often WAY up or WAY down.

Any reasonable person might conclude that those high-scoring children in Miss Middleton's class who later scored very low were simply not paying attention, as we can sometimes read the newspaper vacantly and not know what we read.

But you have to believe in consciousness before you can believe in attention, because it is consciousness that PAYS attention. You have to believe in a free human will before you decide that anyone can voluntarily CHOOSE to pay attention. But neither consciousness nor free will existed for most of those "enlightened" turn-of-the- century psychologists.

William James, who had been E. L. Thorndike's professor about 1896 at Harvard, wrote a famous essay in 1904 titled, "Does Consciousness Exist?" According to the *Encyclopedia Brittanica*, in this essay James traded in his earlier ideas for a belief in "monism," which means he thought the only thing that exists is the material universe. He said, "The word consciousness is just a loose way of indicating that certain sensory occurrences form part of my life history."

In the spring of 1908, James went to Columbia University to give lectures on pragmatism, his philosophy, on which John Dewey is presumed to have based his own. The *Encyclopedia Brittanica* said that it was as though a new prophet had arrived. His lectures were crowded from first to last, with people overflowing outside the room. Photographs were taken of James and parties were given. In his own words, James talked of the visit as the "high tide of my existence."

So it seems probable that there were those at Columbia in 1908 who agreed with James that there can be no consciousness, but only matter.

Concerning free will: for a 1908 book, *Essays Philosophical and Psychological in Honor of William James*, Edward L. Thorndike, who had been James' student about 12 years before at Harvard, wrote a chapter with this interesting title, "A Pragmatic Substitute for Free Will". Thorndike said he had managed to discuss the subject "without any need of our going against, or even beyond, the scientific, matter-of-fact point of view and habit of interpreting the universe" and within the bounds of instinctive responses and the habits built on them.

Edward L. Thorndike was an enormously influential man. This was acknowledged in the 1948 book, *Theories of Learning* by Ernest R. Hilgard, in which Hilgard said that Thorndike's theory of learning had been the dominant one in America for 50 years.

In a stimulus-response psychology like Thorndike's, the entire mind is seen as a printed circuit, neither more nor less, just like the circuits on the infamous little triangle on reading. Such a theory makes no distinction between consciousness and the automatic levels in the human mind.

It is interesting to see how this printed-circuit psychology looks when discussed by another "expert," this time Dr. Frank N. Freeman, then of the University of Chicago, who reviewed in the *Elementary School Journal* of June, 1922, Thorndike's 1922 book, *The Psychology of Arithmetic*. Freeman wrote:

"This book is the author's definition of arithmetic in terms of the "new psychology". Among these psychological principles, the most general and prominent is the "bond" conception. In the author's view, learning consists of the formation of bonds or connections between situations and responses. These bonds can be analyzed into groups of very minute and simple connections, and a complex activity is simply a collection of a large number of elementary bonds.... The higher mental processes are reducible to exactly the same kind of bonds as the simplest motor responses and "habit rules in the realm of thought as truly and fully as in the realm of action." There is therefore no fundamental distinction between reasoning, analysis, abstraction, etc., and acts of skill.... The theory provides no cement by which the bonds may be united to explain the process of organization of thought...."

So "organization of thought" bothered Freeman, which, of course, is just a roundabout way of talking about consciousness. One of the psychologists of the general period, the Englishman Charles Spearman, had proposed in 1904 that there WAS such a thing as a General Factor, or G factor in intelligence, so that intelligence was not just a lot of splintered potential abilities. But, in Thorndike's March, 1921, article, "On the Organization of Intellect," he doubted Spearman's theory.

When these people came up with an explanation for scores like Miss Middleton's wildly gyrating "silent reading comprehension scores" reported in 1915, they DID agree with Binet that reading comprehension was potentially controlled by native intelligence, but native intelligence itself was just a bunch of splintered potential abilities, each of which had to be developed independently. There was, after all, according to Thorndike, no such thing as "transfer of training."

Wavering attention could not be the cause of the fluctuating comprehension scores in classes like Miss Middleton's because, if there were no such thing as consciousness or will, then there could be no such thing as voluntary attention. The experts had a BETTER, a REALLY SCIENTIFIC explanation: The little kids in Miss Middleton's third and fourth grade class were, after all, just a bunch of robots like R2D2, so it was obvious that their printed circuits were not operating efficiently in the little computers they had tucked between their ears - their brains. It was because of that awful stuff called phonics, which kept stopping the kids at Oral on the reading triangle printed circuit, so that they frequently did not complete the trip to Meaning. Phonics HAD to go!

By then they had found out, by actual experimental proof, that there WERE two kinds of readers in people with normal hearing: whole word readers who went counterclockwise on the triangle right to meaning, guessing from the context in the process and sometimes making errors, and highly accurate, syllable readers, who went clockwise straight to sound on the triangle, where the experts were afraid they frequently were stopped. So the experts had determined to try to develop whole-word, counterclockwise readers, to use ONLY what Francesco Valles in the 17th century had called the OPPOSITE way, the path of deaf-mutes (wrongly taught deaf-mutes, that is).

The thing that apparently really sparked the change in reading methods and brought about those awful 1930 and 1931 readers of Gray and Gates was "A Study of the Reading Vocabulary of Children," reported by Myrtle Sholty in February,1912, in the *Elementary School Journal*. Sholty's study really must have been a bombshell, which is why I am convinced that it was so effectively buried that no one today has heard of it. W. S. Gray "forgot" to mention it in the body of his famed 1925 summary of reading research to that date, just listing it in the index, with the wrong description.

Myrtle Sholty had worked with three little girls half-way through second grade (most probably in 1911), flashing at high speed the 1,588 words they had been taught by then in their sight-word readers, which readers had been supplemented with diluted phonics in the University of Chicago laboratory school which the girls attended. Against their will at that time, the laboratory schools HAD to teach supplemental phonics or children could not remember enough sight words. Of the words the little girls could not read, Sholty found that two of the three girls were at least able to get the beginning sounds of a large percentage correctly. Yet the third little girl was unable to read words in parts but could read ONLY whole words. Nevertheless, she had managed to read correctly 977 of the total 1,588 words, about the same as the other two girls.

So the experts obviously concluded that she had managed to do WITHOUT supplementary phonics (the clockwise route on the triangle that they so hated which stopped first at "Oral" or sound before going on to "Meaning"). But they ALSO knew that it is impossible for most children to remember more than a limited number of sight words without SOME kind of analysis, so they assumed the third little girl must have been using a different method, comparing a whole meaning-bearing sight word in her memory to another meaning-bearing sight word in order to tell them apart. Yet that was ALSO the same as the visual analysis of meaning-bearing sight-words taught to deaf-mutes in Gallaudet's approach! So "intrinsic phonics" was invented which goes ONLY the counterclockwise route and compares whole meaning-bearing sight words to each other in order to see like parts. Since "intrinsic phonics" always has to go through Meaning first, the meaning of the sight words, before it can get to the sound stop, "Oral", (if, indeed, it ever gets to the "Oral" sound stop) they believed "intrinsic phonics" protected "reading comprehension."

Sholty was also impressed by the fact that all *three* girls, not just the whole-word reader, knew far more words in context than out of context. This showed that even those laboratory school girls who could use supplementary phonics did not use it all the time (clockwise) but sometimes went counterclockwise through Meaning (the context of the selection) for word identification.

With the triangle plus Sholty's study, the mystifying remarks about "intrinsic phonics" and the necessity to read for meaning which were made continually by William S. Gray and Arthur I. suddenly make sense. The triangle plus Sholty's study provide what Charles C. Fries in *Linguistics and Reading* (1962) said is missing in reading research, a thread of continuity of basic assumptions.

However, the triangle and Sholty's study ALSO provide an explanation for WHY they were buried for seventy years. If children, going clockwise with phonics, are stopped on Oral, and do not go on to Meaning, then other children, going counterclockwise to Meaning, may get stopped there and not go on to Oral, the sounds of the words . They may, in other words, read inaccurately and spell badly, just as the phonics-trained children (or so they thought!) might not understand what they read but would read accurately. After all, Sholty DID say, "The children who depended most upon phonics read with fewer errors than the one who read by word wholes." The triangle plus Sholty's study presented a distinct public relations problem to the early "experts," which they apparently handled by burying BOTH the triangle AND Sholty's study, as the public might NOT like the price to be paid for "reading with meaning:" which price is stumbling, inaccurate oral reading and bad spelling.

The three little girls that Sholty worked with had been recommended to her by their classroom teacher. The girl who could read only whole words, called "A," was described as the best reader, and the other two as an average reader and a poor reader. The fact that the "whole word" reader was described as the "best" reader must have impressed those early experts, so they probably overlooked the fact that the teacher ALSO said that Girl A was

27

much below the average in all her OTHER school work besides reading, "had no initiative", and "could never be depended upon to do a piece of work." Obviously, the poor little child could not READ but could only guess from sight words! She certainly would not be able to spell, so how COULD she "do a piece of work"? Equally obviously, since ALL THREE GIRLS had to guess from context, that means that NONE of these University of Chicago laboratory-school girls back in 1911 or so could really read! In reading through their school readers used since first grade, Sholty found that Girl A scored 87.6%, Girl B 90.5% and Girl C 82.4%. So only Girl B, the girl who most used phonics, managed to score above the frustration level for oral reading of 90% (set after this study was done). Of course, that means she just squeaked through. After all, since these girls were only being asked to read the same reading books they had studied in school from first grade to midway in second, they SHOULD have been able to read them above frustration level!

It was obvious to Myrtle Sholty that these little girls represented two different kinds of readers: those who could see words in parts, and those who could only read whole words. Sholty immediately referred to a 1903 study by Oskar Messmer in Germany, discussed on page 92 of Edmund Burke Huey's famous and widely read 1908 book, *The Psychology and Pedagogy of Reading*. Sholty's reference to Messmer's 1903 work on the two different kinds of readers, which had been discussed in Huey's famous 1908 book, certainly suggests that the existence of two different kinds of readers was almost common knowledge at that time. That is because Myrtle Sholty apparently knew right away what her study meant and that her study had only confirmed what Oskar Messmer had already found, the existence of two different kinds of readers.

Arguing with Cattell after 1885 about whether people did or did not immediately see "whole words" when reading, the German experimenters had kept on with their high-speed flashing of words when Cattell returned home to America, after having first spent some time studying in England with the famous scientist, Sir Francis Galton. Disproving Cattell's results, a man in Germany named Julius Zeitler found in 1900 that the people he tested had FIRST read dominating letter complexes (which I suggest are syllables) and only AFTERWARDS read words. Zeitler wrote:

"The word-form is indeed apparently assimilated as a whole, secondarily, but primarily it is apperceived only in its dominating constituent parts."

Zeitler also said that, when reading:

"...we arrange the dominating complexes successively one after another...."

Another German, Oskar Messmer, tried it again and turned up something really new in 1903. It was the very thing which I had considered the great discovery of my 1977-1978 sabbatical research, in which I had individually tested the oral reading of approximately 900 second graders in this country and Europe in their own languages, after having observed the teaching methods used in the first grades in their schools. I had been absolutely dumbfounded to find, by stumbling across Messmer's results in December, 1980, that my "great discovery" of 1978 had already been announced 75 years earlier!

Messmer had announced in 1903 that there are TWO DIFFERENT KINDS OF READERS, which was exactly what I had found in 1978! Messmer found that one kind reads Zeitler's dominant complexes off the page with great accuracy. He found that

29

the other kind reads whole words off the page instantly but, in doing so, guesses, and in that guessing, makes errors. Messmer called the readers of dominant complexes (which I suggest are syllables) "objective" readers, and he called the whole-word, consciously "guessing" readers the "subjective" readers.

Germany had been teaching the analytic-synthetic method for years, teaching phonics from words, but, in crowded classes, the probability is that it sometimes degenerated into a straight sight-word method, which might account for Messmer's "subjective" whole-word readers.

Zeitler can be said to have confirmed the existence of Level 1, the syllable, in reading, followed by Level 2, words-in-syntax. However, very interestingly, Messmer confirmed the use of Level 3, consciousness, in reading, but ONLY for the subjective readers, since they obviously have to use consciousness in order to guess at sight words. Messmer's subjectives, therefore, by definition, can NEVER read automatically because they must use consciousness to decide on words. By contrast, Messmer's objectives have the potential to read either WITH conscious attention on the reading act itself or to read automatically, which means WITHOUT conscious attention on the reading act itself. That leaves their consciousness totally free to concentrate, if they freely choose to, on the meaning of the text. Unlike Messmer's subjectives, Messmer objectives do not have to read with a flickering, divided attention, the strained attention of the hard of hearing, who must divide their attention, one moment trying to figure out what words must be, and the next moment trying to use those words to figure out the content of the conversation. Therefore, the objectives, who can have UNDIVIDED attention, have the potential to read with greater understanding, when they do not permit their (totally free) attention to wander.

So Myrtle Sholty turned up the same accurate little dominant-complex objective readers that Messmer had turned up nine years before, which are the clockwise kind on Suzzallo's triangle, and she also turned up the inaccurate, context-guessing whole-word subjective readers, who are the counterclockwise kind on Suzzallo's triangle. But Myrtle Sholty did not think of it in the way just discussed, that it is the subjective readers who are the disabled readers because of their divided attention, just as the hard of hearing are disabled listeners because of their divided attention. Instead, she concluded exactly what anyone would have concluded in the University of Chicago climate of the time. Phonics may train children to read words in parts, and that might interfere with concentrating on the meaning of the words. They might not complete the circuit to meaning on the *Cyclopedia* 1913 triangle (to which she did not refer and of which she may not have known). Concentrating on word parts (phonics), might therefore interfere with "reading comprehension."

CHAPTER 3

THE RETOOLING OF AMERICA'S SCHOOLS SO THAT ALL CHILDREN COULD BE TAUGHT TO READ LIKE BADLY TAUGHT DEAF-MUTES

Myrtle Sholty's study was published in February, 1912, in the *Elementary School Journal* of the University of Chicago. That academic year of 1911-1912 was the first time that Edward L. Thorndike of Columbia Teachers College gave his course, "Psychology of the Elementary School Subjects". According to both Arthur I. Gates' and E. L. Thorndike's own statements, that was the very year in which Thorndike began his approximately ten-year-job of searching out the 10,000 commonest words in English. To do this, Thorndike, himself, counted three and a half million running words in selected literature.

So there is a very likely cause-effect relationship between Sholty's conclusion published in 1912 and Thorndike's initiating also about 1912 the word count to identify the commonest (highest-frequency) words. Identifying those commonest words was necessary before children could be taught to read without ANY supplemental phonics at all since children would need the very large context bed that would be provided by those commonest words in order to guess unknown words. Teaching the same number of commonest words as the number of basic characters in Chinese (wrongly identified at about 1,400 by E. B. Huey, the well-known reading authority at that time), should have made context guessing exceedingly accurate on words outside of the 1,400 or 2,000 commonest words (or so they thought).

Their basic error was in equating sight words with Chinese characters. Chinese characters, unlike sight words, are highly distinctive and far easier to remember, but sight words all look dismally alike.

Most people do not realize that only about 250 common words of the highest frequency compose more than half of anything written in English (as determined by J . McNally and W. Murray in *Key Words to Literacy*, London, who said that 100 of the very-highest-frequency words make up just about half of the words used in juvenile reading, and a total of 300 would cover three-quarters). With the knowledge of about 250 of the highest-frequency sight words, with the sound of the first letter or so of unknown words, and with the use of the MEANING of the context of a written selection, it is possible for a child to guess his way through "reading comprehension" tests up to about the fourth grade level, even if the child cannot read in the true sense at all, which means to HEAR print. That ability to guess the meaning of a selection, even when many of its words are unknown, is what accounted for Simon's remarks about stumbling, inaccurate readers in France being able to pass reading comprehension IQ tests. By 1924, the "global" method had infected Europe (the global method being the sight- word method), and they were turning up reading failures in Europe, too. As a primary-grades school teacher for 18 years, I have found many children who know all these 250 common sight words and who pass reading comprehension tests nicely but who cannot read "hard" unknown words like "frog" or "splash" if they are in library books without the controlled vocabulary of the school readers, which readers are carefully written to assure correct guesses.

But if children are taught by beginning fourth grade NOT just the 250 commonest words, but about the 1,500 or 2,000 commonest, this provides a matrix from which it is possible for a reader, for the rest of his life, very successfully and fairly accurately to guess his way through almost ANYTHING that is written, using only "intrinsic" whole-sight-word phonics, and NEVER using real Pascal sounding-and-blending phonics. Such guessing readers can get the GENERAL meaning, the way a partially deaf person does, but DON'T ask them to read aloud!

W. S. Gray and A. I. Gates would never have been able to write their sight-word readers up to the fourth grade level, which fourth grade readers were totally dependent on about 2,000 of the commonest words, if E. L. Thorndike had not spent ten years of exquisitely boring work counting and tallying millions of words all by himself, so as to identify the 2,000 (and up to the 10,000) commonest words. Thorndike must have been highly motivated to spend the 10 years from 1912 and afterwards doing something so agonizingly tedious.

Yet Thorndike stood scrupulously apart from the discussion of beginning reading. His point of view on beginning reading, however, can be easily known from the opening paragraph of his 1934 article in the *Teachers College Record*, when he spoke of a beginning FOURTH grade student as someone who should know 2,000 or more words as "totals" and who should come close enough to judge the sounds of unknown words beyond those 2,000 to say them, if he had heard those unknown words already as spoken words. With present-day American phonic reading books (and with the Russian present-day program), children know about 2,000 words, not by the beginning of fourth grade, BUT BY THE END OF FIRST GRADE!

An American study by Gregory in 1923 showed that the

34

required reading vocabulary of THIRD grade students in Oregon was, then, conservatively, 6,000 words. Oregon was not doing anything very different from almost anyone else in America in 1923. So, it is VERY striking to read Thorndike's requirement in 1934 of only 2,000 words taught by the beginning of fourth grade.

It is also very striking that Thorndike said that beginning fourth graders should know this pathetic store of 2,000 words as "totals." J. McKeen Cattell had been Thorndike's professor at Columbia before 1900 and was his neighbor at home and personal and professional friend at least as late as 1925. (Cattell had been fired from Columbia, however, in 1917, reportedly for his support of conscientious objectors in World War I.) In the February, 1926, *Columbia Teachers College Record* issue which honored Thorndike on his 25th anniversary as a professor, Cattell said that he had been closer to Thorndike than to any other student or colleague except Boas and Woodworth, and that Thorndike's and his views and interests had coincided to an uncommon degree. In the 1971 *Current Encyclopedia of Education*, Thorndike is reported as having devoted his energies almost exclusively after 1921 to the Institute of Educational Research at Teachers College (funded by Carnegie Corporation, the General Education Board and the Commonwealth Fund). The "studies" Arthur Gates referred to in his *New York Times* article of March 27, 1932, announcing Gates' glorious new readers, were done at this Institute, and the inspiration for Gates' materials were earlier materials which has been successfully used to teach deaf-mute five-year-olds.[2]

So, that means if Thorndike devoted his energies almost exclusively after 1921 to the Institute, it must have been his office there which Henry Suzzallo mentioned visiting in Suzzallo's article on Thorndike for the February, 1926, honorary issue.

─────────────────────

2 [See Gates' 1930 Interest and Ability in Reading, pages 17 to 37.]

Suzzallo spoke of the accidental eavesdropper, waiting his turn outside Thorndike's office, who might be annoyed or amused by the conversations he overheard. He said Thorndike was always patient with such callers, whether it was the silly questions of a beginning student or the twisted convictions of a rigid mind. Suzzallo spoke of the sick nature of set ideas saturated with emotion. But he said Thorndike was always sympathetic with all men, as they were "respected embodiments of experience." That anyone could speak of other human beings, with a straight face, as "respected embodiments of experience," makes me doubt who it was who had the twisted convictions.

In a biography on Thorndike in *Current Biography*, H. W. Wilson Co., 1941, the statement is made:

"A colleague at Teachers College remarked that Thorndike has always been a center of controversy."

Nor was the controversy always outside Columbia. I. L. Kandel, Professor of Education at Teachers College, Columbia, made these remarks in the *Teachers College Record* of February, 1933, obviously in violent opposition to both Thorndike AND John Dewey:

"It was not the progressives but their critics who preached against the philosophy of hedonism, the pain-pleasure or annoyance-satisfaction theory of education which has dominated educational thought for the past twenty years. And it was the critics and not the progressives who saw the weakness of an intellectual training built... wholly on S -R bond principles.... Discarding the experience of the past, each individual must try out each situation for himself to see how it works, and what works is true, good and beautiful; there may be room for authority but only the authority of individually tested knowledge - whether in arithmetic or morals, in spelling or literary taste.... the consequences (Van Wyck Brooks) ascribes to a rootless people threaten a rootless education. 'A rootless people,' he says, 'cannot endure forever, and we shall pay in the end for our superficiality in ways more terrible than we can yet conceive.'"

That is pretty strong language from a colleague INSIDE Columbia. The heated conversation which Suzzallo overheard may have taken place between Thorndike and a fellow faculty member.

But Cattell's anecdotes in his article for the Thorndike honorary issue establish the fact that there was a VERY close tie between Cattell, who decided in 1885 that people read words as "totals" and not letters, and Thorndike, who in 1934 spoke of beginning fourth graders reading as little as 2,000 words as "totals."

In Interest Ability in Reading in 1930, Arthur I. Gates quoted directly from lecture notes he had taken during his class with Thorndike in approximately 1916 or 1917. Since he puts the excerpt in quotation marks, it is apparent these are Thorndike's own words.

"The association of seen words with their sounds will come without special effort on the part of the teacher if the words are associated with their appropriate realities and if the spoken names of these realities are clearly and accurately pronounced.... The association of single letters and letter combinations with the sounds will also be obtained to a considerable degree if the children learn to see words as composites of letters and letter combinations. For the child who sees a word, say plate as made up of pl-ate, while he is saying plate will inevitably be forming to

37

some degree correct sound associations with pl- and -ate."

This, of course, is the kind of whole-word, intrinsic rhyming phonics which was handled in the Gallaudet reader, a spin-off from the visual analysis of the deaf.

In Thorndike's article from the September, 1921, *Teachers College Record*, "Word Knowledge in Elementary School," which reported on Thorndike's new book, the *Teachers' Word Book*, which had his list of the 10,000 commonest words, he included a section, "Material for Phonic Drills." Thorndike wrote:

"It is interesting to note those words which are suitable to develop phonic insights and habits and are among the thousand most important words according to our count. I have, therefore, taken out seventy of the most useful phonograms...."

This list of "phonograms" is the basis for most of the "phonics" which has been taught in basal readers ever since. For example, the common beginning, "pl," was followed by the common words he listed with that beginning: place, plain, plan, plant, play, pleasant, pleasure. The common ending, "ine," he showed with the following common words: line, mine, nine, shine.

The Grand Canyon could probably be filled by the basal reader workbook pages that American children have done since that 1921 article, dealing with the very "word parts" listed by Thorndike in that article (almost always "intrinsic" phonics, dealing with words that had been seen first in context). But Thorndike did not invent that kind of "phonics," himself. It came from Gallaudet's reader and had entered into American reading instruction ever afterward, as a review of readers after Gallaudet will show. (See the comments in the bibliography under Spaulding and Bryce, for an example.)

In the June, 1917, edition of the *Journal of Educational Psychology*, E. L. Thorndike wrote:

"The vice of the poor reader is to say the words to himself without actively making judgments concerning what they reveal."

Such a reader was obviously going clockwise on the *Cyclopedia* reading triangle, but not so far as Meaning, stopping at Oral. The dictionary defines a vice as a bad habit, so poor readers had this "bad habit," according to Thorndike.

It was because of the "vice" of the "poor reader" that silent reading replaced oral reading in American schools about 1920, with much uproar at the time about its excellence. But there was no mention of the reading triangle printed circuit, and the fact that they wanted children to use a route of the deaf.

Thorndike wrote an article for the November, 1916, *Teachers College Record*, "Education for Initiative and Originality," in which he asked for the development of experts in the field of education, who would have control of educational policy. In the April, 1920, issue of *Harpers Magazine*, Thorndike wrote an article, "The Psychology of the Half Educated Man," asking that experts be allowed to do our thinking for us, in areas where we lack sufficient information. So he obviously approved of experts and personally developed the two leading "experts" in American reading instruction for about forty years: Arthur Irving Gates and William Scott Gray.

Arthur I. Gates had been E. L. Thorndike's graduate Ph. D. student in 1916, and William S. Gray had been Thorndike's master's degree graduate student in 1913-1914. Gray wrote his original oral reading test as his master's thesis directly under Thorndike's supervision, as Thorndike himself mentioned in a 1914 *Teachers*

College Record article. The year previously, Gray had been at the University of Chicago, where C. H. Judd was head of the department of education. Judd had been Thorndike's undergraduate classmate at Wesleyan in the early 1890's. Gray returned to the University of Chicago after working with Thorndike to get his Ph. D. there in 1916 on more elaborate work on his oral reading tests.

It was these ex-students of Thorndike's, the experts Gates and Gray, who wrote the first deaf-mute -method readers for normal children which were officially published in 1930 and 1931, though, as with an earthquake or a volcano, there had been warning rumbles of their coming for many years.

Those reading books were constructed with the greatest care so that sight-word-taught children who were unable to read by sounds could nevertheless guess their way through them. The deaf-mute method used in the books limited "new" sight words to only a few on a page to be guessed from the context of the known sight-words in the story and from the sentence construction, aided by the use of picture clues. The only kind of phonics to be used was so-called "intrinsic" phonics (a term invented by Gates), by which a child checks a sight-word guess by using the sounds (or appearance) of only SOME of the letters in an already known sight word. The preference was to use as few letters as possible in making the guess, so "intrinsic" phonics usually used either the initial consonant of an unknown word, comparing it to the beginning of known sight words, or the ending of an unknown word, using it in a rhyming analysis with a known sight word (pl - ate, g - ate). Such "phonics" is really only a jig-saw puzzle operation, pulling sight words apart and putting the parts together again in different combinations. Deaf-mute students had to use the jig-saw comparison operation, of course, in order to commit new words to memory, but they obviously had to do so without the use of any sound.

Gates and Gray practically shrieked that their "intrinsic"

phonics should NEVER be taught in isolation but always as a part of meaningful, connected reading, as in whole sentences, and that any phonic drill in such connected reading had to be on words which the children had already met in their text. That would obviously protect the "bonds" to word meaning and avoid the use of meaningless, pure sound. But they were very careful NOT to explain why they insisted so intensely on meaningful reading and were so adamantly opposed to the use of isolated sound. The explanation which they were so studiously avoiding to give is provided by that article written by Suzzallo in the *Cyclopedia of Education* in 1913. Suzzallo's printed-circuit triangle can demonstrate the "soundless" counter-clockwise route of the deaf in learning to read, the route Gates and Gray were promoting. To introduce any pure "sound" would switch the route used in reading from counter-clockwise to clockwise. Gray and Gates obviously thought the clockwise route would short-circuit the trip to "meaning."

A letter of August 4, 1931, to the New York Times published on August 7, by William V. Saunders, New York, responded to a letter by Frank Vizetelly. In his letter, Saunders said he had spent five years (apparently as a graduate student) under the guidance of such men as Kilpatrick, Thorndike, Bagley, and Snedden, and had "primary acquaintance" with the ideas of Butler, Dewey, Strayer and Cubberly. In taking Vizetelly to task for his views, Saunders referred to the:

"...propaganda which our leading (sometimes misleading, too, I must admit) educators must get published continually to force change which is essential to growth."

Concerning "propaganda" which "misleading" reading experts decided was "essential" to bring about change, it is very interesting to read Gates' article in the *New York Times* in 1932 announcing his new readers. Gates did NOT use the following expression that Henry Suzzallo did in Suzzallo's 1913 article with the triangle:

"The most active battleground in the reform of school teaching is found in the primary grades, particularly in the first school year where beginners are taught to read."

Gates did not say ANYTHING about the triangle. He did not say his books were based on a method almost two centuries old that had been used to teach the deaf. Gates DID just casually mention that the method had worked with deaf children which just showed how GOOD it was. Gates had said in his June, 1925, article in the *Elementary School Journal*, "The Supplementary Device Versus the Intrinsic Method of Teaching Reading":

"Incidentally, study of the deaf should throw light on the values of phonetic training, since they cannot, of course, utilize this device."

Gates said his materials were:

"...divested of the older types of formal and artificial group drills like phonetics and formal oral recitation, which are distasteful to all save the academically minded child" [and they were] "self teaching" [and] "adaptable to individual differences."

Gates' article on the new readers was entitled, "The Child's Reading Steps Made Easier, "in the March 27, 1932, issue of the *New York Times*. But Gates did not mention in the article the child he had told about in his June, 1925 article on supplementary vs.

42

intrinsic methods. He had said, in that article, when teaching sight words to children from three and a half to six years:

"Failure on the first attempt was usually followed by other failures, which invariably killed the initial interest in the 'game.' After several such days, the child was 'busy' when called, or hid behind the piano, or blurted out, 'I hate that old game.'"

Gates was not any more disturbed by the child who hid behind the piano than Josephine Bowden had been by the children who did not care whether they were asked to read sight words right side up or upside down. Instead, Gates told of using other "approaches," which succeeded with the poor little kid hiding behind the piano - who, so far as I know, may STILL not be reading today! That really is no joke: Nelson Rockefeller was reported as a "dyslexic" and he learned in the "best" schools of the progressive educators of the day, the kind of school that Gates was talking about in his article. Nelson Rockefeller came within a hair's breadth of being President of the United States! DO reading methods matter, then?

But, in any event, in Gates' *New York Times* announcement of his new readers, there was, to put it mildly, no mention of what they REALLY were: deaf-mute-method readers.

But Gates and Gray were NOT the first of Thorndike's students to use his list of the commonest words, although it had apparently taken them about ten years to produce the final product. (In March, 1926, Gates said in the *Teachers College Record* that a reading course already had been written and was being tried out, using all the first 200 words on Gates' own list, made up of Thorndike's and three other special lists, and Nila Banton Smith gives a puzzling 1927 date for the first Scott, Foresman of Gray's, even though Scott, Foresman themselves listed it as 1930 in a recent advertisement. Gates' readers were advertised in the Macmillan catalog of 1929, but the whole series was not published until 1931, when the First Reader cost 56 cents and the workbook 32 cents.

The first to use Thorndike's word list was ANOTHER student of his, S. A. Courtis, Thorndike's 46-year-old undergraduate student in 1919 and his graduate student in 1920. With Courtis's assistant, Nila Banton Smith, Courtis wrote experience chart lessons for teachers in 1920 but obviously could not control the vocabulary of such chart lessons as Gates and Gray could to provide for the deadening repetition of sight words, over and over, which is necessary when deaf children learn sight words. But Gray and Gates could do that in 1930 and 1931 with their high-frequency, controlled vocabulary, context-guessing, "intrinsic" phonics readers, the first such materials ever written anywhere on earth for NORMAL children instead of deaf-mute children. Gallaudet's *Mother's Primer* was only a faint suggestion of what was to come 100 years later.

Courtis' and Smith's 1920 material was called *Picture Story Reading Lessons*. It used 265 words "having the highest frequency in the Thorndike list together with... ten common primers." It is interesting that Gallaudet's earlier book, before his *Mother's Primer* was entitled, *The Child's Picture and Defining Book*, and it was written for BOTH normal and deaf children,

Both Courtis' and Gates' mention of about 250 words, however, is meaningful, since more than half of anything written in English is composed of less than these same 250 words . When children begin to read only with these high-frequency sight words and the "guessing" technique, I believe they generally become confirmed deaf-mute readers, or Messmer subjectives, for the rest of their lives, always going counter-clockwise on the triangle, to use the experts' explanation, or always laboriously using Level 3, consciousness, my explanation.

In addition to being Thorndike's graduate student in middle age, Courtis had been associated with Cattell earlier in 1913 when both were officers of the American Association for the Advancement of Science (whose magazine, *Science*, Cattell personally owned). Thorndike was also a member and sometime officer. Courtis, who had attended the Massachusetts Institute of Technology for two years and who was head of the department of science and mathematics at the Liggett School in Detroit (1898-1914) made his first entry on the public scene about the time he was a member of the Hanus Committee on a School Inquiry of New York City (1911). Born in Wyandotte, Michigan, in 1874, and a student at Detroit Central High School and Detroit Business University in Detroit, he was living in Detroit at the time that John Dewey was at the University of Michigan (1884-88, 1889-94). So the possibility exists that Courtis as a young man knew Dewey. If so, he was acquainted with *all* three men: Dewey, Cattell and Thorndike, but Dewey perhaps first. If not, it would at least appear probable that he knew Cattell *before* he knew Thorndike.

CHAPTER 4

THE GREAT COVER-UP BEGINS BECAUSE THEY KNEW THEY HAD SOMETHING TO HIDE AS THEY WENT ABOUT CHANGING THINGS.

B ut it was not very long after 1912 that the experts knew the cost of going counterclockwise around their circuit, and they probably interpreted it nicely with their "bond" psychology. They had found that children who learn to read "with meaning" were FAR less accurate oral readers and FAR less accurate spellers. Presumably, they explained this by saying that THEIR kinds of readers were getting stopped at Meaning, just as they believed the phonics-trained children had been stopped at Oral. Their sight-word children were not continuing on to what was, for them, the second leg, Oral, but the experts did not think Oral was important, anyway. They were protecting that most sacred thing of all, MEANING, or "reading comprehension," with THEIR method.

However, the experts knew very well that parents would never stand for having their children read inaccurately and spell badly, just because some psychologists somewhere thought it would protect their "reading comprehension," of which "skill" no one on earth had ever heard before 1912. Almost all those parents out there in America before 1930, from Coast to Coast, BELIEVED in consciousness and free will, which were obviously sufficient explanations for the kinds of scores in classes like Miss Middleton's. Parents would never accept having their normal children taught by a reading method used specifically to teach deaf-mutes language for almost two hundred years (and an inferior method at that for teaching the deaf, in contrast to the lip-reading method promoted by Alexander Graham Bell and his father, Alexander Melville Bell.) So the experts knew they were going to have a big sales job on their hands, if they were going to save America from itself. But these pragmatists had a definition for "truth" that unhappily was NOT like our old-fashioned definitions. "Truth" for them was whatever worked! And their counter-clockwise route on the triangle worked (or so they thought.) Besides that, they all just KNEW that "science" (but their kind of science, of course) was going to save the world! So they went underground.

These 1914 (NOT 1984) Orwellian Big Brothers began to engage in Unthink on a very large scale, and their followers have never stopped. The Big Brothers, however, took their secrets with them when they died, so it has taken a lot of research into surviving records to find what they were hiding. Mae Cardin, who trained at Columbia in the early 1930's, who left there in horror without taking her Ph. D., and who then produced one of the best known phonics systems, apparently never knew the background I have given . Neither did Dr. Samuel Orton, who opposed the experts so unsuccessfully in the early 1930's. So, when the waters of time finally closed over the early experts, they closed over their secrets, too.

What keeps our newer reading experts engaging in Unthink is something less palatable than a desire to save the world from itself. It is instead money-making and position-protecting vested interests. Today's reading experts are at colleges all over America where they were seeded by the early experts from Columbia Teachers College in New York and the University of Chicago, which schools no longer are the central location of the reading authorities. Today's reading experts all over America wear their reading professor hats when they praise the basal readers they write and their basal author hats when they go to the bank with the money they earn writing the things.

The sums of money involved appear to be considerable. In 1973, Samuel Blumenfeld quoted Hillel Black in *The American Schoolbook*. Blumenfeld reported that Black said that the *Alice and Jerry* readers, at that time published by Row, Peterson and Company of Evanston, Illinois, and written by Miss Mabel O'Donnell, had earned her $2,700,000 in royalties since 1936. The Row Peterson series was out of print when Blumenfeld quoted this in his own book, *The New Illiterates* in 1973, and O'Donnell's new series had been copyrighted in 1966 by Harper & Row.

But, just as Unthink operated with the old experts who are now gone, it still operates today with many of the newer ones, who manage to overlook and discount the terrible reading failures that result from the high-frequency sight-word basal readers.

Unthink operated VERY effectively while some of the early experts were still around. Neither in Nila Bantan Smith's "history" of reading, *American Reading Instruction*, originally written in 1934 but updated in 1956, nor in W. S. Gray's *The Teaching of Reading and Writing*, published in 1956, a year after Rudolf Flesch's block-busting and best-selling 1955 book, could I find any mention of Flesch's publication or its thesis. So Smith and Gray actually had the gall to leave out Rudolf Flesch and his 1955 best-selling book from reading "history, "even though his book had made such an impact in 1955 that *Time* magazine called it the outstanding educational event of that year when they reviewed events in January, 1956. *Time* suggested that Flesch represented, I believe, "the devil in the Flesch" to the reading community. But Gates and Smith (and most of the OTHER experts since then) made

Flesch an Unperson, a la Orwell.

In at least one teacher's college, to my own personal knowledge, Flesch's 1955 world-shaking book is not only NOT on the shelves, it is not even in the card catalog! (Strangely, they have his OTHER books that do not deal with reading!) So it is a rare American teacher who was trained after 1955 who ever heard of the uproar in 1955. Their "reading instruction texts" in college, written by reading experts, carefully shield them from Flesch's "errors" by their censorship, and imply that the ONLY right way to teach reading is to teach it "meaningfully" with children's basal readers which often produce profits for the SAME professors who write the "reading instruction texts" for student teachers. It is an exceedingly unpalatable mess, but, unfortunately, it is legal, SO FAR, at least. Isn't it about time we found a way to change things?

But, back in 1912 and 1914, the reading experts knew it would be a long, long time before controlled vocabulary basal readers could be written, based on the 2,000 or so commonly used words, because first these words would have to be identified. After that, it would take years to write and publish such nit-picking sight-word readers, in which, after a tiny sight-word vocabulary was built up, new words would have to be introduced slowly in a context of those known sight words so that the new words could be guessed. Then those new words would have to be repeated, over and over again in "stories" just the right number of times, so that the children could form the necessary "bonds" on them.

In the meantime, the reading experts had their selling job to do, and they would write what ordinary sight-word readers they could, forced to use, of course, the hated "supplementary phonics." Supplementary phonics would continue to be a necessary evil until the great day dawned that the controlled vocabulary deaf-mute readers had finally been written and had finally reached the market, which readers could use "meaningful" "intrinsic phonics" instead of the hated supplementary but real phonics. The dawning of that great day turned out to be in 1930, when the lethal Scott, Foresman Dick and Jane readers by Gray were published. Gates' Macmillan series came out in 1931, and it was every bit as bad as Gray's.

So, although the true deaf-mute-method readers did not arrive until 1930, various reading experts' names associated with the Thorndike, et al, group, begin to turn up on sight-word reading series after 1920. But it is hard to get copies of these books. For example, I was unable to get a copy of the Bobbs-Merrill primer written in the early 1920's by George Herbert Betts (M. Ph. University of Chicago, 1904, and Ph. D. 1909 from Columbia University.) In Betts' 1906 psychology book, *The Mind and Its Education*, he gave a standard treatment of consciousness, fully accepting it. I also suspect, from its tone (he appeared to be a genuinely religious man) that he never changed his ideas on consciousness to accept instead the printed circuit of the stimulus-response psychologists in all its "glory." Betts' tie to the sight-word community appears to have originated BEFORE the ideas of Thorndike and his followers had been set, and to have come from John Dewey.

In a preface to his psychology book, Betts referred to a particular comment made by Professor John Dewey, when Betts was Dewey's graduate student at the University of Chicago in 1904, the year Dewey changed over to Columbia, so Betts obviously was influenced to some extent by Dewey. Betts later graduated with a Ph. D. from Columbia University in 1909, three years after writing his psychology book, but before the ideas on the controlled high-frequency vocabulary primers had been conceived, which was 1912, in all probability, as a result of Sholty's study.

In the *Teachers College Record* of January and September, 1906, Edith C. Barnum wrote about the beginning reading program then being taught in the Horace Mann School first grade, attached to

Columbia Teachers College. She said:

"...There are many different methods of teaching reading - the best being still a subject of much discussion. It would undoubtedly be admitted by all, however, that the end in view is to give the child the power to get thought from printed symbols. Professor Dewey's idea, 'The child should have a personal interest in what is read; a personal hunger for it, a personal power of - satisfying the appetite,' although a high one, does not seem too difficult to be attained.... for it is only when he desires to learn to read that he becomes self-active.... phonetics are of little value in reading until the child has gained some proficiency in getting separate words rapidly."

Once the children learned the sounds of the letters at Horace Mann School, they were "encouraged to use the initial sound together with the content of the sentence in getting new words." This use of context plus initial consonants, of course, was similar to the "intrinsic phonics" of the 1930 and 1931 basal readers.

Although the children at Horace Mann were also taught to read one-syllable words with long and short vowel sounds by the end of first grade, indicating some use of real phonics, a great part of the Horace Mann School program in 1906, according to Barnum, was straight sight-word teaching. So Betts probably got sight word ideas through exposure to Dewey and the practices of both the University of Chicago laboratory school in 1904 and Columbia Teachers College laboratory school up to 1909. The record also suggests he may be the man who exported sight words to lucky Iowa.

G. H. Betts was professor of Psychology at Cornell College in Mount Vernon, Iowa, from 1901 to 1918. (Most of the rest of his career afterwards was at Northwestern University in Evanston,

Illinois, till his death in 1934. Mabel O'Donnell's *Alice and Jerry* readers were published by a company in Evanston, Row, Peterson and Company, in 1936, indicating a possible influence from G. H. Betts. Whether G. H. Betts is related to E. A. Betts, also from Iowa, one of the major experts in reading after 1934, I do not know. While in Iowa, G. H. Betts is reported to have been in great demand as a speaker and was involved in Iowa teacher associations. In 1915, he wrote a book, *Outlines for Schools in Iowa*, so he would appear to have had considerable influence on curriculum there.

It is amazing how very little influence REAL facts have had generally on the public schools' acceptance of sight words. In a study by J. H. Harris and H. W. Anderson, *Measuring Primary Reading in the Dubuque Schools*, (Dubuque, Iowa), run by Harris who was Superintendent of Schools there, the Beacon phonic method, published by Ginn, outscored the "sentence" sight word methods of Aldine and Horace Mann in ALL tests. Although this Superintendent of Schools, Harris, went to the trouble to prove that phonics was best, it apparently had little influence elsewhere in Iowa, even though it was a very carefully run, scientific study. The Harris and Anderson study, printed in book form by Ginn and Company who published the Beacon phonic readers used in the study, was reported in the *Elementary School Journal* in 1916, but has totally dropped from reading "history." Yet that same year, the *Elementary School Journal* reported on a ludicrous study, without ANY data, by Currier and Duguid in New Hampshire, and THAT study which concluded sight words were best has survived, to be quoted as part of the "research" as late as 1967 in Chall's *Learning to Read: The Great Debate*.

Iowa was the very first large sight-word outpost in America in the 20th century outside Teachers College, Columbia and the University of Chicago. It seems highly possible that Betts was the one to bring the sight-word method there, to protect so-called reading "comprehension," and "to give the child the power to get thought from printed symbols," as Edith C. Barnum of the Horace Mann School put it in 1906.

But, by the early 1920's, the Iowa neurologist, Dr. Samuel T. Orton, was finding galloping dyslexia or reading failure in schools all over Iowa, which he attributed almost solely to the sight-word method. Orton went on to become nationally famous for his treatment of dyslexic children, because galloping dyslexia took over ALL the schools in America after 1930, after the introduction of the Gray and Gates deaf-mute-method readers.

So, G. H. Betts was recorded as one of the authors on a Bobbs-Merrill reading series in the early 1920's. Wishing to see what was almost certainly an early sight-word approach, I tried to get the primer at the 42nd Street Library in New York. Despite several of my repeated written requests sent back to the stacks, they could not send me down the primer of the series, which would have shown this beginning reading approach, but only Book 2 or 3 or 4. The primer, it would appear, was missing.

It reminded me of Samuel Blumenfeld's fruitless efforts to locate the Gallaudet primer before Blumenfeld published his superb 1973 book, *The New Illiterates,* in which he identified the Gallaudet primer as the source for the 1930 sight-word deaf-mute method. It reminded me of Blumenfeld's quotation from Charles F. Heartman's third edition (1934) of the *Bibliographical Check-list of the New England Primer.* Heartman had commented on the "most curious fact" that it was impossible to locate some of the *New England Primers* mentioned in the first and second edition, which had disappeared from libraries and elsewhere:

"...probably due to the crime wave which spread, a few years ago, over all the libraries in the country."

Whether I would be able to locate primers by other "experts" before 1930, I do not know. Here are the names of some of them, by other "experts" besides G. H. Betts. For most, I omitted the names of their co-authors, listing only the well-known "experts".

Guy T. Buswell of the University of Chicago, *The Silent Reading Hour*, Wheeler Publishing Company, 1923.

Ernest Horn and Grace Shields, University of Iowa, *The Learn to Study Readers*, Book 1, Ginn and Company, Boston, 1924.

Frank N. Freeman, University of Chicago, *Child Story Readers*, Lyons and Carnahan, 1927-1928.

Henry Suzzallo, *Fact and Story Readers*, American Book Company, 1930. Henry Suzzallo when at Columbia Teachers College was the author of the 1913 *Cyclopedia* article with the triangle on reading, in which he made the statement, "The most active battleground in the reform of school teaching is found in the primary grades, particularly in the first school year where beginners are taught to read." Suzzallo had been Thorndike's graduate student about 1902. He was Professor of the Philosophy of Education at Teachers College, Columbia University, from 1909 to 1915. He was then President of the University of Washington, until he was fired, reportedly for too aggressive fund-raising activities, by the Governor of Washington in 1926. After that, he was with the Carnegie Foundation until his death in 1933.

Stuart A. Courtis and Nila Banton Smith, *Picture Story Reading Lessons*,.1920, World Book Co., 1926. Stuart A. Courtis received degrees from Columbia in 1919 and 1921, and his Ph. D. from the University of Michigan in 1925. Nila Banton. Smith received a Ph. B. degree from University of Chicago in 1928 and M. A. in 1929, and a Ph. D. in 1932 from Columbia. She was Director of Reading Instruction at New York University from 1949 to 1963.

Ashley H. Thorndike (brother of E. L. Thorndike), Professor of English, Columbia; Fannie W. Dunn, Asst. Professor of Education,

Teachers College, Columbia; and Franklin T. Baker: *Everyday Classics*, Macmillan, 1923. In Arthur Gates' 1925 *Teachers College Record* article, "Problems in Beginning Reading," he said the vocabulary in this primer had been compared to E. L. Thorndike's word list, and this primer gave a rough correlation between the two. Nila Banton Smith said this primer used the sentence method. Gates' own readers were published by Macmillan in 1931.

Of course, there were the Horace Mann Readers, published by Longmans, Green and Company, about 1912, which Nila Banton Smith said used Farnham's sentence method, as did the Aldine readers, both of which were outscored by the Beacon phonic method in Superintendent of Schools Harris's study in Dubuque in 1916.

But the two REALLY important ones were the grand finale: the Gray and Gates deaf-mute-method readers of 1930 and 1931!

CHAPTER 5

WHAT IS LAUGHABLY CALLED READING RESEARCH

It is amazing to find that, except for eye movement studies, there is exceedingly little experimental reading research prior to about 1914. In that year, E. L. Thorndike published his first materials on reading comprehension in the *Teachers College Record* of September, 1914, and included W. S. Gray's oral reading paragraphs from Gray's master's thesis prepared under Thorndike's direction. About the same time, in 1914, H. A. Brown, Deputy State Superintendent of New Hampshire and a Columbia Teachers College master's degree graduate student of June 13, 1912, published his report on silent reading comprehension tests in New Hampshire. This was his conclusion:

> "The data which have grown out of these tests suggests emphatically that the prevailing pedagogy of primary reading is in need of thoroughgoing reconsideration in important particulars.... A new and more correct pedagogy of primary reading must be constructed, based upon the known laws of the learning process."

On the opposite page in this June, 1914, issue of the *Elementary*

School Journal of the University of Chicago was C. H. Judd's review of Thorndike's *Educational Psychology* of 1913, which was, of course, full of "known" laws about the learning process. (Judd of the University of Chicago had been Thorndike's classmate at Wesleyan before 1895.)

Brown's remark was like that of Henry A. Suzzallo in 1913, when he published the diagram of the reading triangle with the remark:

"The most active battleground in the reform of school teaching is found in the primary grades, particularly in the first school year where beginners are taught to read.... A discussion of the problem of teaching beginners to read is, therefore, crucial."

In the same year, 1914, that Thorndike published his and Gray's studies, and that Brown published his study, almost the only other "studies" published were Oberholtzer's, a graduate student at the University of Chicago; Waldo's, another graduate student there ; and Judd's , Thorndike's classmate at Wesleyan. In 1914, Judd was head of education at the University of Chicago. There were also two seeming outsiders: Daniel Starch of Wisconsin on silent reading tests, and Clara Schmitt of the Chicago schools, who had tested the oral reading of normal and subnormal children. Clara Schmitt found that the thing which most characterized the mentally defective child was that HE USED CONTEXT TO GUESS WORDS!! So, obviously, Clara Schmitt did not stay long in the reading instruction "club" but was gently guided to the door. (I ran across only one other article by her on "Developmental Alexia" in the May, 1918, *Elementary School Journal*, which had a footnote on the need for phonics.)

But, in 1914, except for Clara Schmitt and Daniel Starch, there

WAS virtually no experimental reading research community at all, outside that seedling with its one root in Teachers College, Columbia, where E. L. Thorndike was located, and its other root at the University of Chicago, where Thorndike's ex-classmate, Judd, was located. If someone had snipped that seedling at its base in 1914, America would not have either a reading research community or a reading problem today. (Other countries generally have NEITHER, such as Russia, for instance.) But the experts' sales job worked, and they exported their graduate students to universities all over America, where they eventually trained more graduate students, and the trickle of what is laughably called "reading research" soon became a flood, so that by now about a thousand "studies" are completed each year. By 1925, the trickle had already become a small flood. That was the year William Scott Gray wrote what is considered the classic summary of experimental reading research to that date.

Dr. Charles C. Fries, who wrote *Linguistics and Reading* in 1962, said that we are in debt to W. S. Gray for his "patient" recording of previous research, which Gray continued to do after 1925. But Fries also marveled at the fact that, by 1962, it was IMPOSSIBLE to find any thread of continuity of basic assumptions to connect the development of the mountains of reading research done since 1914, which was NOT true in any other field of experimental research but reading.

Fries did not realize that it was precisely BECAUSE of his "debt" to W. S. Gray that he could NOT find that continuity. Actually, one of the most fundamental axioms in scholarly work is to go back to original sources, so it really is inexcusable for any researcher to have accepted W. S. Gray's "patient" recording of previous research and not to have examined primary sources carefully himself.

Yet, one of the best sources is Gray himself, before his 1925 summary of research. On his 1917 publication, *Studies of Elementary School Reading through Standardized Tests*, which was really his Ph. D. thesis, he had to show, as is normal, a summary of previous research. It is this 1917 summary that yields the important information. Gray had arranged his 48 entries in alphabetical order. When I arranged them in chronological instead of alphabetical order, the clear pattern emerged: There was virtually no "classroom" or "related" research (his terms) before 1914, when it suddenly exploded. Something had happened BEFORE that date to make this occur, and the "lead time" was probably about two years, which put the "Thing," whatever it was, back in 1912, or possibly 1911. So I looked up those studies, through 1915, and found it did happen in 1912. The "Thing" was Sholty's 1911 (or so) study, not reported till February, 1912, but in Gray's description of it in his 1917 summary, its real finding was omitted. That real finding was that there are two KINDS of readers. I had to get a copy of her study to find out what it really said.

But people fundamentally are lazy, so Gray got away with it when he covered up the really critical studies, that of Sholty, and, of course, of Messmer and Zéitler, as well as another reported in the *Elementary School Journal* in 1911 by Josephine Bowden which is the apparent explanation for the fact that the pre-primer vocabulary is so ludicrously low in the 1930-1931 readers. But, thanks to Gray's "patient" work, no one in the reading instruction community to my knowledge has heard of either Sholty's or Messmer's conclusions for almost 70 years. (Jean Chall lists Sholty's study in her long bibliography to *Learning to Read: The Great Debate* but it must have been picked up by something like a computer check of the *Elementary School Journal* index or the Gray 1925 summary, where it is only described in the bibliography, under a totally misleading description. It is not mentioned in the body of Gray's book reporting on all previous research. Chall's only reference to

Sholty's study is in Chall's bibliography, and she does not mention Messmer, Bowden, or Zéitler at all. If she had known of the significance of any of these studies, I believe she certainly would have referred to them.)

It should be apparent that the early experts of 1914 did not WANT people to know there are two different kinds of readers, and the kind you get depends on how you teach them in first grade. Buswell at the University of Chicago, doing research on eye movements in 1922, made some vague comments about different paths with different methods, but he did not imply that they were permanent. Gray referred to different emphases with different methods, in his U. N. book, *The Teaching of Reading and Writing*, but he also did not clearly state there are two totally different kinds of readers, depending on the method used to teach them initially.

All these early experts are dead and gone and took this secret with them. Now the newer experts are discovering to their surprise that there IS a difference in the kinds of oral reading errors that phonics-trained children make compared to sight-word- trained children. The new experts are gleefully announcing that sight-word-trained children more often make errors which do not change the meaning, but phonics children make mistakes which more often come close to sound, not realizing they are saying that today's sight-word trained children are reading exactly like Clara Schmitt's mentally defective children in Chicago in 1914, and like the deaf. Actually, these studies that reading experts have been shoving into ERIC, the Government's computer file on education research, are the most damning evidence against the sight-word method.

It is really flatly impossible to credit the reading community, taken as a whole, with good faith. (Obviously, some of the people in the "reading community" are exceptions and sincerely dedicated to excellence, and some are also doing worthwhile research). I discovered, in doing my sabbatical research, that there are only about ten oral reading accuracy studies comparing sight-word approaches to phonics since 1912, yet there are now about one thousand reading "research" studies done each year. Since the one SURE way to prove the weakness of the sight-word method is to HEAR THE CHILDREN READ, this alone is enough to convict the reading research community, again taken as a whole, with bad faith: only TEN comparative oral reading accuracy studies, but MANY TENS OF THOUSANDS of other "studies", many of which were funded with Government money! It seems apparent that there are still some experts today who know very well the kinds of results they are going to get if they compare the oral reading accuracy of phonics-trained children to sight-word-trained children. Therefore, experts have managed to convince even died-in-the-wool phonics supporters like the Reading Reform Foundation and Rudolf Flesch that it MEANS something to quote "silent reading comprehension test" results instead of oral accuracy tests, but it DOES NOT!

Dr. Guy L. Bond and Dr. Robert Dykstra coordinated the data from *The Cooperative Research Program in First Grade Reading Instruction*, that massive U. S. Office of Education study which was reported in 1967. Dr. Guy L. Bond had worked with Arthur I. Gates in reading research back in the 1930's, doing graduate work at Columbia. Bond was the author of texts for teachers on reading, and also the senior author of *The Developmental Reading Series* for grades one to eight. Dr. Dykstra, a Professor of Education at the University of Minnesota, had taught in elementary schools and, unlike Bond, is an outspoken supporter of phonics. Dr. Dykstra wrote a summary of existing research, which concluded that it shows the superiority of phonics, and his summary forms a part of Walcutt, Lamport and McCracken's pro-phonics teacher's text on the teaching of reading. Dr. Dykstra also was a speaker at the Reading Reform Foundation Convention in 1977. But Dr. Dykstra, like the Reading Reform Foundation itself, and Dr. Flesch, unfortunately seems to believe that silent reading comprehension tests MEAN something, so, when he gave his talk, he mentioned that the first grade oral tests, given in March of first grade, had shown the superiority of phonics, and so did the silent reading comprehension tests. But the silent reading comprehension test scores, unlike the oral test data, showed great variation between school systems. He suggested that the cause for these differences lay in the differences in the quality of instruction in the different school systems. Instead, I believe that the differences reveal only relative degrees of attention on the "silent reading comprehension" tests. (Scores had been adjusted in the USOE studies to allow for differences in IQ, based on pretests.) School systems which scored higher were probably encouraging attention to this kind of test by giving relatively greater amounts of practice on things like SRA cards, which have the same kind of make-up as "reading comprehension tests."

Actually, the USOE studies got the same effect on "silent reading comprehension tests" that Arthur I. Gates did when he tested "silent reading comprehension" in 1926. In six fourth-grade classes in six different New York schools (which IQ tests had shown to be equal in intelligence) he found silent reading comprehension test scores on Test C, "Reading to Understand Precise Directions," and Test D, "Reading to Note Details," going all over the scale, from bad to good. By 1926, many schools were stressing "reading comprehension," so he assumed the higher scoring classes were being taught better.

E. L. Thorndike's graduate student, William A. McCall, published his "Standard Test Lessons in Reading" in the *Teachers College Record* of November, 1925. He reported on previous efforts to teach "reading comprehension" elsewhere which involved real teaching in actual class lessons and said they had been very disappointing. However, his materials (in essence, like the present

SRA Kits - which are reading matter followed by questions) were producing great results. The pupils were computing their own scores after each test session. The children therefore had feedback on their performance. As they received this feedback, their scores rose on subsequent tests. McCall seems to have been convinced these higher scores meant his materials were "teaching" reading comprehension. I think it should be pretty obvious that, when the children saw they had failed on the first tests, they concentrated better on the later tests. The only thing at issue was simple attention. I suggest the same thing was true on the silent reading comprehension test differences on the USOE studies and on the results Arthur I. Gates got back in 1926.

CHAPTER 6

WHAT IS LAUGHABLY CALLED READING HISTORY

Then there is the misrepresentation of American reading history by Nila Banton Smith, Courtis' 1920's assistant, after she had examined 2,500 separate pieces of historical material. In examining far, far fewer, I came up with a completely different history from Nila Banton Smith's! She was a reputed scholar, and it is inexcusable that she bungled the job so badly.

Because Nila Banton Smith DID rewrite history in 1934, and she has been the semi-official "historian" of the reading research community ever since, just as W. S. Gray was officially in charge of summarizing its "research." Smith's Ph. D. from Columbia Teachers College was on reading history, and her thesis was published in book form in 1934 under the title, *American Reading Instruction*. Her revised edition came out in 1965.

For some reason, the reading history written by Harold Boyne Lamport as a Ph. D. dissertation in 1935 is almost completely unknown. It is entitled, *A History of the Teaching of Beginning Reading*. Yet W. S. Gray said in a footnote on page 76 of his 1956 book, *The Teaching of Reading and Writing*, that Lamport's dissertation "was prepared under the writer's supervision."

In Mitford Mathews' excellent book, *Teaching to Read,*

Historically Considered, Mathews referred to his frequent "sidewalk seminars" with Dean William S. Gray of the University of Chicago. Mathews own interest in beginning reading could not have come from his own professional background since he was a professor of English at the University of Chicago and he also taught linguistics and was a lexicographer. Mathews' interest in the teaching of beginning reading therefore very possibly came from his "sidewalk" discussions with Dean Gray and Mathews DID refer to Lamport's material.

Mathews said that Lamport had called an April 15, 1843, lecture by the Reverend Cyrus Peirce "epoch making." In that lecture, Peirce had mightily praised the sight-word method. Experts would have found no fault with that, of course, but, in that same lecture, Peirce had praised Gallaudet's 1835 *Mother's Primer*, unmentioned in the experts' literature since the 1911 *Cyclopedia* article on Gallaudet. Gallaudet's *Mother's Primer* used the deaf-mute method, though Gallaudet had made no reference to the fact that he was using in the *Mother's Primer* the same deaf-mute method that he had used in his school for deaf-mutes. Besides resurrecting the deaf-mute-method *Mother's Primer*, Lamport's mention of Peirce's lecture opened the Pandora's box on the history of the terrible battles back in Massachusetts in the 1840's on the subject of sight words, in which battles Gallaudet's primer had played a large part. Those facts would appear to be sufficient reasons to overlook Lamport's history, even though it was a pro-sight-word one in which Lamport had called Peirce's 1843 lecture "epoch making."

But Nila Banton Smith had apparently never HEARD of Gallaudet! Not only that, she had never heard of Cyrus Peirce or the American Institute of Instruction that Peirce had addressed in 1843 (even though that Institute had published bound volumes of its lectures from 1830 to 1882). Smith's apparently not having heard of either Peirce or the American Institute of Instruction was a VERY good thing, because the year after Peirce's "epoch making" lecture, Samuel R. Green gave a withering response. Mann had called the alphabet skeletal-shaped ghosts which would repulse children. Greene's response was that it was an odd thing to "relieve children from such painful emotions" by asking them to deal with "whole clusters of deformity" - sight words! But the annals of the American Institute of Instruction, addressed by Peirce and Green and Mann and others, gave a clear history on the use of Gallaudet's primer, so it really was ideal that Nila Banton Smith had never heard of any of them. She was a "natural" for the semi-official historian of the "reading instruction community."

When the experts of 1914 deliberately set about to develop Messmer's and Myrtle Sholty's subjective kind of readers by preparing materials that had originally been tailored for deaf-mutes, they worked to cover up the roots of the deaf-mute method, because they knew that children taught to read by that method would read inaccurately and spell badly. The public just MIGHT not think that giving up accurate reading and good spelling would be a good trade-in for presumed improvements in the experts' so-called "reading comprehension," that brand new "skill" that the "experts" only began promoting publicly in 1914 with their brand-new "reading comprehension tests." So, no one corrected Nila Banton Smith when she published her "history" of reading in 1934, *American Reading Instruction*, and totally omitted Gallaudet, even though his primer had been well know.

Yet Smith's ex-boss, Stuart A. Courtis, had worked with Otis W. Caldwell in 1924, writing *Then and Now in Education*, comparing students' scores obtained in various tests in Massachusetts in the 1840's with those about 1919. That testing in the 1840's in Massachusetts was the direct outgrowth of the conflicts Horace Mann had in Massachusetts over educational methods, including the introduction and terrible results from the Gallaudet reader in 1835. Therefore, it is virtually unthinkable that Courtis could not have known about Gallaudet's primer and could have overlooked mentioning it to Smith when she was preparing her history, or that Smith would not have known about Courtis's 1924 study, which most probably was highly publicized.

Smith wrote that it had been commonly said that the alphabet method was abandoned in America about 1840, but, pronounced she, that saying was NOT true. But that "common" saying, meaning it was common knowledge at the time, which her Unthink altered, was ABSOLUTELY true! It is only a play on words. What the common saying meant was that Noah Webster's phonics had been dropped. It did not mean that the oral spelling of new words had been dropped when the sight word primers arrived to displace Webster's phonic speller. What was not dropped, with the switch to sight-words, was that oral spelling of new words.[3]

All that is necessary is to compare Noah Webster's highly phonic syllable spelling book, first written in 1783, with McGuffey's dismal sight-word-plus-spelling primer of 1846, to realize that the two methods were TOTALLY different, even though both happened to include oral spelling (see-aye-tee, cat). [Editor's 2006 note: The original McGuffey materials appeared from 1835 to 1838, and they were sight-word materials. McGuffey's original materials were changed in various editions over the years. However, a truly phonic McGuffey's edition did not appear until 1879, although there had been a version of an earlier edition published in Leigh phonetic print in 1868.]

Gallaudet's book included oral spelling, which means reciting the names of the letters as a sight word is read. What was at issue,

_____

3 Editor's 2006 Note: The dropping of Webster's speller for beginners took place after 1826, not 1840.

of course, was not whether a child orally named the letters in new words, but whether the child was, or was not, taught to sound out those new words, a la Pascal, with real phonics. Webster (and those like him) taught children how to sound out words by themselves, but Gallaudet and the McGuffey primer in 1846 and others like them did NOT do that. Instead, teachers had to read the "new" words aloud to the children because the children could not read them by themselves!

But, since both approaches (the Webster phonic one and the Gallaudet sight-word one) happened to include oral spelling, Smith pronounced they were the same, calling them both the ABC method. She reserved the term, word method, only for the few extreme sight-word followers of Gallaudet who dispensed with oral spelling altogether.

Despite the mystifying references to huge sales for Webster's speller, authorities of the day (such as James Pyle Wickersham, Principal of the Pennsylvania State Normal School at Millersville, Pennsylvania, in his *Methods of Instruction* in 1865) make it very clear that Webster's approach had been out of use for many, many years by that date, and that the dominant method at the time was instead the word method, which just happened to include oral spelling (reciting the letters after naming the sight word).

Smith spoke of the word method coming in to some degree about 1880. Here, again, it is a play on words. All it means is that the actual spelling of the sight words, usually present in 1865, was finally dropped about 1870, which, of course, left the sight words standing all alone.

The reason for the sight-word primer's displacement of Webster's phonic speller - and those like it - was a much-publicized interest by the activists of the time in promoting reading for "meaning." Despite familiarity today with that "reading for meaning" phrase, "reading comprehension tests" were unknown, though primers sometimes had questions following stories.

The Boston schoolmasters who fought Horace Mann have been assumed to have won the sight-word fight, and to have held off the sight-word method for 50 years or more, which Nila Banton Smith's history would seem to confirm. But her history is wrong, and they really lost. They lost because Horace Mann and his followers founded the very first normal schools, which were staffed with their adherents. Cyrus Peirce, for instance, had been Principal of the Normal School at Lexington, and he taught the sight-word method in his school, as an article in Barnard's *American Journal of Education* in 1857 makes very clear.

These normal schools were raising up the next generation. After the heat of the battle with the schoolmasters and others was forgotten, these "well-trained" people moved into the schools and did what they had been taught to do: they taught sight words. And they DID it to protect reading for meaning, or what we today call "reading comprehension," the topic that sent Horace Mann into his temper tantrums, and the cause for the dropping of the Webster-type primers. They had apparently found out that sight-word trained children, who MUST pay attention or cannot read at all, may remember more of what they read than phonics- trained children who, being able to read automatically, may or may not pay attention and remember.

The same thing had been discovered in Europe by the 1920's. By then, teaching reading "for meaning" was the big thing on both sides of the Atlantic. However, the true sight-word method was generally discredited in Europe by the 1970's. Change was brought about by such things as those reported in a 1950 *Enfance* article. In France, 2% of dyslexic children were discovered in schools that used the phonics approach, but 20% of dyslexic children were discovered in schools that used the global approach. In the 1960's, according to Franz Biglmaier in John Downing's 1973 *Comparative*

Reading, German newspapers were critical of the global (sight-word) method , with headlines like, "Stupid Children or Stupid Methods?" and "The Thalidomide Case of Education." I found when I was in Hamburg in 1977 that of eight teachers with whom I spoke, seven used a very heavy phonic method for beginning reading, and expressed great contempt for the global method. (They apparently had the option to use it if they chose, because one DID use a very heavy global program.)

But the global method had wide use in the world after 1920, being used in Russia until 1932. (Celestin Freinet of France undoubtedly discussed it in his 1925 visit with Krupskaya, Lenin's widow, then in charge of education, who received Freinet and the rest of the first small delegation of educators from Europe who came to see the schools after the Russian Revolution.) Berta Perelstein de Braslavsky of Argentina wrote in Downing's *Comparative Reading*:

> "When the "ideovisual," or "natural" method was at its zenith in Europe in the 1930's, one of the most orthodox variations of its "pure" form was elaborated in Argentina. It is contained in *The Teaching of the Written Language* by Dezeo and Munoz."

She said, concerning the method's results:

> "An increasing number of children showed signs of difficulty in reading, writing, and spelling, both in primary school and, even worse, in alarming numbers in secondary school."

Even though the International Conference of Public Education held by UNESCO in July, 1948, in Geneva, recommended the global method, it was not long before it was very badly discredited in many parts of the world. But one of the main arguments for its use in the first place was that it protected "reading comprehension."

Au Seuil de la Culture (1965), by Robert Dottrens of Switzerland, is an imaginary conversation with an imaginary parent (a composite of many such conversations he had while Director of the experimental school at Mail, Geneva). Dottrens mentions that the global method was prohibited in Geneva in 1955. He explains to this initially outraged parent why his school used the global method. (The "maman" had begun by saying, "Her teacher uses this global method that all the world knows is worthless.") While praising sight words, Dottrens cautioned against context guessing, calling it a "danger" fraught with "the menace of veritable catastrophes." Dottrens did not seem to know that context guessing is the inevitable result of the sight word method (and is exactly what Messmer saw with his 1903 "subjective" readers). But, concerning the effects of straight phonics, which he considered awful, Dottrens said:

> "To have learned to read by the letters and the combinations of syllables is to have acquired a mechanism in which comprehension [has no part] and it is probably the most grave reproach that one can address to the synthetic method. A child can learn to read rapidly without understanding."

Dottrens obviously had discovered phonics-trained children, unlike sight-word trained children, had the freedom NOT to pay attention (and also confirmed, like W. S. Gray himself in a Bloomfield method classroom about 1940, that phonics-trained children learn to read quickly and accurately). So the effect of forced (but harmfully divided) attention noted by Dottrens, was

71

obviously also noted by Horace Mann and Peirce and the normal schools back in the 1840's, and it provides the REAL selling point for the take-over of sight words from Noah Webster's wonderful old phonic method. The use of "meaningful" sight-words was to protect "meaning," or what is now called "reading comprehension."

An 1858 issue of Barnard's *American Journal* had the following to say concerning the trouble that Horace Mann had in Massachusetts because of the ideas contained in his 1843 report, which also included Mann's ideas on sight words:

"The personal animosities which this controversy engendered, we trust, are allayed or forgotten, and we have no disposition to revive or perpetuate them by any further notice."

But the *American Journal* article DID say that Mann's controversial 1843 report led "to the adoption, very widely, of the methods described," which would, obviously, include reading methods.

Can you see the parallel? Ignore the opposition, staff the teachers' colleges, and win in the long run! Sounds just like 1930, doesn't it?

But sight words after the 1840's brought with them, as necessary baggage, massive reading failures. No one knows now of the massive reading failures rampant in America in the 1870's which resulted in the swing back to phonics in the 1880's with books like Rebecca Pollard's or the huge revision of the McGuffey readers in 1879, which used straight phonics to replace their sight-word earlier editions. (To protect itself with all users, though, the preface to the first reader read that it could be used with "the Phonic Method., the Word Method, the Alphabet Method, or any combination of these methods."

By 1879, the Alphabet Method meant sight words plus spelling, but by then that added spelling was "nasty" with the experts of the day. In 1882, at a Teachers' Institute at Columbia, South Carolina,

Professor M. A. Newell said:

"Oral spelling, (so-called; there is no such thing outside of a schoolhouse or a lunatic asylum as oral spelling; all true spelling is by writing or printing).... When we recognize the fact that our language is not and cannot be made, except in a very slight degree, phonetic, and adapt our method of teaching to this undesirable but unalterable condition, by excluding the ear and the mouth from the process of spelling, and using the eye and the hand alone, we shall stand in but little need of further 'reform.'"

Obviously, the 1879 McGuffey's had to be careful what was said in the preface to their new phonic first reader, so as not to lose that large part of the textbook market which believed, along with Professor Newell, that our language "is not and cannot be made" phonetic.

Concerning the failures from the sight-word method, Nila Banton Smith herself quoted Rebecca Pollard in 1889, who had said:

"There is quite a general complaint among teachers, principals, and superintendents that pupils in the higher grades... have so little mastery over words that an exercise in reading becomes a laborious effort at word calling.... We are inclined to think the inability of pupils in the higher grades to call words is the legitimate outgrowth of the teaching of the word method."

Experts like Smith after September, 1911, when the *Elementary School Journal* published Josephine Bowden's article, 'Learning to Read," were willing to allow for the necessity of SOME kind of phonics: supplementary phonics until 1930 when the deaf-mute readers arrived, and after that "intrinsic" phonics. Bowden had demonstrated by working with little beginning readers that the number of words they could remember without ANY analysis was severely limited. Working with one little girl individually a half hour a day five days a week for two months in the spring before the little girl started first grade, she found the child had learned 88 sight words out of context and 130 words in context . Bowden wrote:

"The material, which was home-made, i.e., made primarily by the child, had as its subject-matter incidents of home-life, dolls, etc. The story, made one day, was typewritten for the next day's lesson with each new word on a separate card."

Neither the little girl nor the four other first graders who worked with the little girl and Bowden the following fall were disturbed by interesting little variations Bowden introduced into the lessons. For instance, when words were presented upside down, only 2 of 5 children tested even noticed the difference, and most as happily read the spelling "nettims" for the word "mittens" as the correct spelling itself, not noticing such trivial little differences in spelling as Bowden introduced. Bowden DID conclude:

"But that a word method can be used very long without some detailed analysis of the structure and parts of the word is altogether too common a notion in the theory if not in the practice of teaching."

So today's pre-primer vocabulary limit of about 65 words, after which "intrinsic phonics" is introduced, was apparently set by this little six-year-old girl, working for two months in her own home in the spring of 1910, some place near Chicago, and later with four other first graders. After Bowden's study, the necessity for "supplementary" and later "intrinsic" phonics was admitted by experts such as Nila Banton Smith.

We adults who can read cannot appreciate the difficulty sight words give to little six year olds. Remember: the normal six year old child has less than half the mental horsepower of an adult. And sight words would be exceedingly difficult for adults to learn!

It IS possible to demonstrate how hard sight words are to learn even for adults by translating our alphabet into another alphabet, and setting down normal English sentences in that other alphabet. The Russian alphabet differs from ours, since it has more letters, and gives different values to some letters than we do. For instance, p in the Russian alphabet is R!

The "Sentence" method discussed by Nila Banton Smith sometimes had children memorize sentences before reading their printed form. Now, here is a sentence we all know, in its normal printed English form:

Mary had a little lamb,
its fleece was white as snow.
But everywhere Mary went,
the lamb was sure to go.

Now, to spell the SAME English words, but to use the Russian letters, here is what you get:

Мэри хэд эй литль лэм. Ыц флийс уоз фуайт эз сноу. Бат эвэрихвэр Мэри уент, за лэм уоз шур ту гоу.

How easy is it for you to pick out which word spells the sound "white," and which one spells the sound, "lamb"? Can you do it instantly, and with assurance? Can you copy even ONE of them from memory?

So maybe you have a good visual memory, and find that not too difficult. Let's try an "experience chart story," now, the kind of thing that has been done ever since foreign visitors arrived to exclaim with pleasure over the practices in Colonel Parker's Chicago school, later the Chicago Institute. Miss Flora J. Cooke, who Mitford Matthews said was one of Parker's best teachers, made a record of such an experience chart, and it is recorded in E. B. Huey's book, on page 298:

> "October 2, 1897, we went to visit a farm. It was a beautiful day. There was a deep blue sky above us, with not a cloud in it, and cool fresh air around us. We had bright sunshine all day long. 'The nicest day of all the year!' said Fritz.
>
> "The farm we visited is 15 miles from our school. It is on Halsted Street. We might have gone all the way in wagons, but that was too slow for us. It only took us 42 minutes to go on the train...." (etc.)

Aren't experience stories sweet? Now let's try a grown-up experience story. Let's go on a trip with Mark Twain, as he describes it in *Life on the Mississippi* (page 69):

> "I went to work now to learn the shape of the river, and of all the eluding and ungraspable objects that ever I tried to get mind or hands on, that was the chief. I would fasten my eyes upon a sharp, wooded point that projected far into the river some miles ahead of me, and go to laboriously

photographing its shape upon my brain; and just as I was beginning to succeed to my satisfaction, we would draw up toward it and the exasperating thing would begin to melt away and fold back into the bank!"

Now, can you read that experience story when it is printed in Russian, instead of our own, letters? Can you pick out ANY of the words? Which one is "miles" or "bank" or "beginning"?

Ай уэнт то уорк нау ту лерн за шэйп оф за рывэр; энд оф олл зи элюдинг энд ангреспабл обджэктс зат эвэр Ай трайд то гет майнд ор хэндс ан, зат уоз за чиф. Ай ууд фастен май айс апон эй шарп уудэд пойнт зат проджэктэт фаар инту за рывэр сам майльс ахед оф ми, энд гоу ту лабориосли фотографинг ыц шэйп апон май брэйн; энд джаст эз Ай уоз бэгиннинг ту саксийд ту май сатысфэкшон, уи ууд дро ап тууард ыт энд зи эгзаспэрэйтинг цсинг ууд бэгин то мэлт ауэй энд фоульд бэк инту за бэнк!

Do you find it easy to pick out the words? I know I do not! So, if you do not find it easy to read English when it is just transliterated into a different alphabet, then do you think it is fair to ask little six-year-olds to read "sight words" when they are beginning school? Because, that is ALL these Russian transliterations are: PURE SIGHT WORDS! No wonder Bowden's little first graders could not care less whether the sight words were shown to them right side up or upside down!

So Nila Banton Smith wrote of the sight word method in use in 1889, and also admitted it failed because it did not have wonderful "intrinsic" phonics, but she in no way indicated that the word method had been in almost exclusive use in American schools from

77

1840 to 1880 (except for slight advances made by the Leigh phonetic print readers, and a few others). Yet this is what the facts ARE. In Wickersham's 1865 book, *Methods of Instruction*, he said that the word method plus spelling "is the method generally practiced in our schools" and said that with it, children were unable to pronounce new words, but had to be told new words by their teachers, as:

> "...the name of a word [is not a synthesis of] the names of the letters composing it.... The child is not guided to the pronunciation of a word by naming its letters.... he learns to associate the name of the word which the teacher gives him with its form.... Every teacher who has used this method will testify that after pupils had named the letters composing a word, he has to give them its pronunciation, and sometimes to repeat it again and again, before it became fixed in their minds."

Obviously the Alphabet Method was a sight word method, and according to James Pyle Wickersham, Principal of the State Normal School at Millersville, Pennsylvania, who was a major authority in 1865, the word method was the dominant method in the schools.

In William Russell's article, "Cultivation of the Reflective Faculties," in Barnard's 1857 American Journal, Russell made the same point when he spoke of children learning to read:

> "...perhaps without ever acquiring knowledge of the power, or actual sound of any one of the whole group [of letters]. But he is not allowed the satisfaction of recognizing the fact, that these troublesome and perplexing marks before his eye, are little graphic characters to suggest, phonetically to eye and ear, the very words which

he is constantly uttering...."

Nila Banton Smith quoted Rebecca Pollard in the 1880's, who said:

"Pupils read usually very well through the first three readers, according to our present standard of reading in these grades. But the trouble begins in the fourth, and by the time the class is in the fifth, the reading recitation is torture to the teacher and a hateful task to the pupils."

But children "read usually very well through the first three readers" ONLY because they had learned the sight words in those readers, whose vocabularies were controlled, like Gallaudet's, but obviously they were not using high frequency words as they had not yet been adequately identified. They DID make a stab at doing that, though. The children read these reading books out loud in class, in chorus, over and over again, and memorized them, and read them again, singly, over and over again.

The idea of a controlled vocabulary was so engrained by that time that even the 1879 phonic McGuffey's first reader had a controlled vocabulary. But, being able to read a handful of sight words in a few school readers is OBVIOUSLY not reading, particularly since they were not all the high-frequency words, and so the reading problem was FAR from limited to the higher grades, as Pollard said.

How massive it was is reported by a French visitor to the 1876 Philadelphia Exposition, Ferdinand Buisson. Buisson was a remarkable man, and the editor of the incredible *Dictionnaire de Pedagogie et d'Instruction Primaire* of 1887, which is an absolutely monumental and unparalleled work. Buisson also visited the Vienna Exhibition of 1873 and reported, concerning American exhibits, that the majority of the school readers there were sight word readers.

When Buisson visited the Philadelphia Exposition in 1876, he also made extensive visits to American schools in the months of August and September, and in his report he said that the dominant method of teaching was the sight-word method, although phonics was beginning to come back as with the use of Leigh phonetic type. Buisson's most illuminating remarks in his account came from the American school superintendents' reports that he saw. Those remarks appeared in connection with Buisson's praise of the Leigh method, which was a special type of phonetic print in the United States on which Pascal's sounding- and-blending phonics could be used, but primers in Leigh print were sometimes taught by the sight-word method, anyway!

Buisson's report on the 1876 Philadelphia Exposition was published in Paris in French, and an abbreviated report in English was printed in America, but the English version is most unsatisfactory. It is only his report in French which contains such comments as the following, which he provided in a footnote:

"Numerous reports of St. Louis, Washington, New York, Boston, Fall River, Massachusetts, and Burlington (Iowa), attest to the advantages of the Leigh method. They attribute to it 1) a great economy of time (a year or more.) 2) a better pronunciation. 3) a better spelling. Mr. Philbrick, after five years experience in the schools of Boston writes in view of his striking results: 'The word method should fall before the phonetic.'"

Obviously, this confirms the word method had been used in Boston before the partial adoption of the Leigh method about 1867. But, Buisson went on:

"With the old method, in the schools opened in New York in 1872, for the little sellers of newspapers (news-boys lodging houses) 20 children out of 100 said they were unable to learn to read, although many had attended school two years or more, a large number of others (perhaps again 20 of 100) claiming they knew how to read, were discovered incapable of fluent reading of print.

"Things are about the same for the 20,000 children who annually leave the public schools of New York. They have not learned well enough to read to be intelligent readers. The reports of Mr. Kiddie, Superintendent of New York, agree with those of Cleveland, of Chicago, of Cincinnati, of St. Louis and of Milwaukee. 'A half or a third of our children stay in school only three years or less, and during this time, most learn to read only imperfectly. In this situation, the economy of a year is of capital importance. This gained time can be employed with profit to read books appropriate to their age and to their needs.'"

These reports of school superintendents, presumably among other school reports that march along the shelves of the stacks in the Library of Congress, which reports Mr. Buisson very obviously saw with his very own eyes, tell of the existence of an absolutely massive reading problem in the America of the early 1870's.

To appreciate the size of it, I can cite for comparison the results of my oral reading research in 1977-1978. 1 used a 144-word portion of a silent speed test copyrighted by the International Education Association, IEA, Sweden, and was given permission to do so provided I indicate in my writing that it was their copyrighted material (sending them a copy where possible) . The material has a grade level of approximately November of second grade. I had it translated into native languages and personally gave individual oral tests to approximately 900 second graders in this country and in Sweden, Germany, Luxembourg, Austria, Holland and France in the fall and winter of 1977-78. The test consists almost exclusively of high-frequency words, 40 of the 64 different words being among the 250 commonest words in English, according to the *Key Words to Literacy* count of McNally and Murray in England. Only 11 of the 64 are above the 500 commonest, according to E. L. Thorndike's count. It was therefore completely suitable to use with sight-word trained classes in this country who are taught with high frequency words, and who should have been able to guess the 11 words above the 500 frequency, out of the total 144 words, from the context plus "letter clues." Even if they did not guess those 11 words, they still should not fail the test, but would score above 90% or "passing" if they made no errors on words below 500 frequency. Obviously, however, this test did not even begin to test the potential of phonics-trained classes.

I found that 96% of European children from heavy phonics programs could read this simple material above the frustration level of 90% accuracy by November of second grade, after only 13 months in school, and European children from moderate sight word programs which still had a heavy phonics emphasis scored with 86.5% passing. American children from phonics programs (Open Court, Lippincott, and Alpha One) had 92% read above the frustration level in January of second grade, after only about 15 months in school, and despite the irregular spellings in English which make it more difficult to learn than the European languages tested.

But, although sight-word trained American children are drilled on such high-frequency words as in this test, only 75% of those in Houghton Mifflin and Scott Foresman Systems classes passed, meaning one out of four failed this easy, easy, easy test! Obviously, even those who did pass had not been taught to read with systematic, total Pascal sounding-and-blending phonics skills. Instead, they had been taught with only partial phonics, such as beginning and ending letters, and with dependence on sight words that had been taught to them as "wholes," and with the use of context to help in guessing unknown words. To demonstrate the paralyzing weakness that results from such "teaching," one little Houghton Mifflin girl who scored 99% on word accuracy and 80% on comprehension of the five questions on the test (which high scores might suggest to the uninformed that she was a very competent reader) was wearing a shirt which had the word "outrageous" printed all over it as a design. I asked her what that word printed all over her very own shirt said. She answered, "Australia." Of course, her shirt had no context to serve as a clue, and, as a Houghton Mifflin student, she had been drilled on using context to help in guessing words. So she floundered helplessly when faced with a "new" word which had to be read by sounding-and-blending phonics.

However, concerning the percentages of successful readers from properly taught children, in the fall and early winter term of 1977-1978, 96% of European phonics-trained children after 13 months in school and 92% of American phonics-trained children after 15 months in school were able to read simple second grade materials successfully. Furthermore, since they had been taught systematic Pascal sounding-and-blending phonics, they had the potential, given time, to read anything printed in their own languages. Compare these scores from properly taught classes to the scores reported by school superintendents in America in the early 1870's, when only 60% of pupils were able to read successfully, 20% more were able to read only stumblingly, and 20% were not able to read at all! Yet these horrible scores came after 20 or MORE months in school!

Those terrible failures brought about the 1881 revision of

McGuffey's to a phonic method, and the 1880's Pollard phonic materials, and eventually the 1894 Ward method and others. Yet, by the time Dr. Joseph M. Rice made his extensive tour of American schools in 1892, reported in his book, *The Public School System of the United States*, he found that HALF were still using sight words! Rice considered the Word Method (sight-words) and the Alphabet Method (the spelling of sight words) abject wastes of time. Rice supported phonics (and progressive education).

Rice complained mightily of what he called the daily spelling "grind," but this is apparently how reading was REALLY taught after about 1889 in those schools which did not finally adopt phonics. Also, some apparently bought phonics reader like McGuffey's new 1879 one and tried to teach them with the sight-word method. But, since the new books were systematically graded in introducing phonic sounds, they were effectively teaching a kind of analytic phonics even when they taught these books with the sight word method.

It was in the late 1880's that phonic spelling books began to be used, and children learned words by phonics from those books for written spelling tests. By the time Rice gave his written spelling tests in the year 1896, his high spelling scores made it clear that American children by that year HAD finally learned to read, unlike the children Pollard had complained about in the 1880's. That is because, since spelling is, to a large extent, only the opposite of reading, Rice's excellent spelling scores meant that the children he tested had learned to read very well, too.

But the phonics reform in the teaching of reading itself, obviously desperately needed in the 1870's and 1880's from what I have quoted, had apparently run into an enormous snag. It was the emotional rejection of phonics by school personnel who, themselves, had been raised to read by sight words and so were Messmer's subjective readers. As Messmer showed, there are TWO kinds of readers: syllable readers, the accurate kind, who read the printed syllables of their language with ease, automatically, and MAY or MAY NOT pay attention, and whole word readers, who make errors as they guess their way along but who have to pay attention or they cannot read at all.

Actually, my sabbatical research data shows a gradual increase from Messmer's pure "subjectives" to Messmer's pure "objectives". I had ranked programs from Code 1 for pure "meaning" up to Code 10 for pure "sound", with mixtures falling from Code 2 to Code 9. When I compared the scores from classes with higher codes to scores from classes from lower codes on oral accuracy, speed, reversals and reading comprehension, a consistent profile of differences appeared. The consistent profile of scores showed the presence of a force acting to produce that profile.

When I compared groups with greater phonic emphasis to groups with lesser phonic emphasis, the accuracy and speed were higher for the groups with more phonics, and the reversals were fewer. The "comprehension" scores for the phonic groups were sometimes much lower than for the sight word groups but sometimes much higher. That wide spread of scores indicated, obviously, the presence of more free attention in the phonic groups. But the comprehension scores for the sight-word groups were very consistent and fell in a narrow band, higher than the worst phonic scores but lower than the best. That indicated that the sight-word scores had been controlled by the sight-word "guessing" method and that the attention was not free, but forced, and that it was a function of the sight-word method's lower word accuracy and speed and greater numbers of reversals.

I turned up this profile, this relationship, whether I compared American phonics to American sight words, American phonics to European sight words, American sight words to European phonics, or any possible combination. It even showed up when I compared the slightly more phonic Houghton Mifflin Code 3 to the less phonic Scott Foresman Code 2!

So readers are not normally "pure" Messmer subjectives or "pure" Messmer objectives, but a mixture of each. That is why I propose the use of a reading scale with Code 1 indicating a mythically pure sight word reader, comparable to someone who can read Chinese characters and therefore has no need to context-guess because he knows all the words (or characters). Code 10 on the scale is the pure "objective" type who can instantly read syllables off the page accurately, having learned to do so with Pascal sounding-and-blending phonics. In between the two extremes, context guessing is necessary, to a greater or lesser extent. I suggest that Code 5 might be a good point at which to locate or our modern "linguistic" readers. Today's sight word basals fall at about Code 2 or 3.

Therefore, the phonics reform of the late 1870's and 1880's was initiated in a school population where it is likely that the school personnel themselves were close to pure Messmer subjectives, having been taught as children by sight words . They really did not understand what phonics is, and that it is something meant to help little children to learn the printed syllables of their own language during the first part of first grade.

One of these people was Colonel Francis W. Parker, who had gone to school as a little six-year-old probably only about 50 miles from Boston, where Gallaudet's primer had been introduced only a few years before. Francis W. Parker wrote widely and emotionally on the subject of progressive education (which in a proper and reasonable form I totally support for primary school children , as did Rice , by the way), and on the subject of sight words (which I personally totally reject). But Parker's writings, in the late 1870's and early 1880's, were considered to be the BEST to be had in the educational climate of America at the time.

A young man graduated from the University of Vermont in 1879 and spent the next two years or so teaching high school. Being an intelligent young man, and dedicated to the "best," he found and adopted Parker's point of view, including teaching reading "meaningfully" with "whole words." As late as 1930, he said that Parker, more than any other man, was the founder of the progressive education movement in America.

Parker had brought his matured ideas back from a trip to Europe where he saw in operation schools which grew out of Basedow's and Pestalozzi's approaches, which were both, of course, ultimately based on Locke's idea that the mind grows from sense impressions.

Who was that young school teacher from 1879 to about 1881 who so idolized Colonel Parker? It was John Dewey. John Dewey had been a school teacher at the time of the onslaught of the new phonics movement. Taught by sight words himself in all probability as a six-year-old in 1865, he would have been a Messmer subjective, with no understanding of the ease of reading printed syllables automatically off the page, like a Messmer objective. He would totally have agreed with Colonel Francis W. Parker's statement in his *Tracts Teachers No .1, Spelling* of 1882:

> "Words should always be closely associated with the thought they express in writing as in reading; that is, the thought they express should be in the mind of the writer, for the stimulus of the thought enables us by association to recall the word-forms. This leads to the conclusion that with few exceptions - and those merely preparatory - spelling should be in *sentences*, the forms of written thought expression."[4]

4 [Editor's note from 2006: A very complicated history lay behind Parker's 1882 statement, which, in

Then John Dewey left teaching, and enrolled in the new, endowed Johns Hopkins University for graduate work, and eventually began his world- shaking career in philosophy and psychology.

Twenty-three year old Dewey, from rural Vermont, the young school teacher from a humble background, made friends at the new Johns Hopkins School with a twenty-two- year-old from a far more glamorous background. He was the son of the President of Lafayette College and was to go the following year to study psychology with the famed Wilhelm Wundt in Germany, and then go on to England to work with the famous Sir Francis Galton, cousin of Charles Darwin. What would these two friends talk about, from such divergent backgrounds, the young, small-town man whose only experience was teaching high school, and the glamorous student who would go to the laboratories of one of Europe's most advanced scientists?

Each would talk of what he knew best: Dewey, the current controversies in teaching, and the young son of the Lafayette College president, who happened to be named J. McKeen Cattell, what most interested him - experiments in psychology in Germany. Besides this, they both had as a teacher at Johns Hopkins another former student of Wilhelm Wundt, named G. Stanley Hall, who might have understood such discussions. Hall went on to become

---

different words, only repeats the thesis of G. L. Farnham's 1881 *Sentence Method of Teaching Reading*, which reported on Farnham's 1870 experiment with the sentence method in the Binghamton, New York, schools. The rationale for Farnham's sentence method was that sentences are totally unbreakable (though Farnham did not claim to have originated that idea), so reading should always be taught in whole sentences. In William James' 1890 *The Principles of Psychology*, with no reference to anyone else, James made it clear that he thought that the idea that a sentence is totally unbreakable was original with him. My 1998 book, *The Hidden Story*, discusses this in depth.]

president of Clark University, where E. B. Huey later did his work, after Huey graduated from Lafayette in 1895, at the age of 25, the same school Cattell had attended and where Cattell's father had been president. (This would appear to place a possible tie between Cattell and Huey, heretofore not suggested.) [5]

It is not unreasonable to speculate that the reason Cattell went to Germany and in a little more than a year published his famous experiment, purporting to show that people read whole words and not letters, was to settle a discussion begun back at Johns Hopkins in 1883 with John Dewey (and possibly G. Stanley Hall in his classroom) which was sparked by the great rebellion of the phonics advocates against the sight-word methods of Colonel Parker and his supporters. [6]

It is obvious that the relationship between Cattell and Dewey was not an impersonal and casual one. It is in the book, *John*

---

5 [Editor's note from 2006: The Cattell manuscript files at the Library of Congress contain a letter from Huey to Cattell, while Huey was still a school teacher, asking for Cattell to help Huey enroll to study psychology. Huey late enrolled in Hall's Clark University.]

6 [Editor's note in 2006: As recorded in Michael M. Sokal's incredibly good 1981 book, *An Education in Psychology, James McKeen Cattell's Journal and Letters from Germany and England, 1881-1888*, Cattell first tried his sight-word experiments with a revolving drum at Johns Hopkins on the night of March 17, 1883, and his subjects included his classmate, John Dewey, and instructor, G. Stanley Hall. Hall had been a student of William James at Harvard and had returned to Germany to study with Wundt, apparently at James' suggestion, before receiving his Ph. D. at Harvard under James in 1878. The record suggests that Cattell's idea for his reading experiments grew from two roots: (1) hearing of Hall's experiences with German laboratory equipment and methods, and (2) hearing Hall talk of James' ideas on the nature of words and sentences. William James later published his ideas on the nature of words and sentences in his 1890 book, *The Principles of Psychology*. In 1878, James had contracted with Henry Holt and Company, Inc., to write that book, and it took him 12 years to do so. The year after studying at Johns Hopkins, Cattell studied with Wundt in Germany, where Cattell continued his sight-word experiments that were begun at Johns Hopkins.]

Dewey, His Thought and Influence, edited by John Blewett, S. J., that an article by Blewett mentions that Dewey and Cattell were both graduate students at Johns Hopkins in 1882-1883. Blewett said:

> "The friendly association with teachers and fellow students, which Dewey enjoyed in his graduate education at Johns Hopkins from 1882 to 1884, must have deepened his belief in the power of cooperation to achieve what the independent action of an individual could only begin. (It was a friend from those days, James McKeen Cattell, who in 1904 came to Dewey's rescue by smoothing his way to a professorship at Columbia after his resignation from Chicago.)

This is doubly interesting for two reasons, not only because it shows a close relationship between Cattell and Dewey, but because it seems to imply that Dewey at the University of Chicago in 1904, like Cattell himself at Columbia in 1917, and Suzzallo at the University of Washington in 1926, had run into some trouble with university superiors.

In 1899, John Dewey published his famous book, *School and Society*, and that is the precise title Cattell chose for the magazine he founded in 1915 as a journal for American education. By that time, of course, Dewey, Cattell and Thorndike were ALL teaching at Columbia or Columbia Teachers College in New York City. All three were there between the years of 1904, when Dewey arrived (Cattell coming in 1891 and Thorndike in 1899) until 1917 when Cattell was fired.

Cattell had a curious penchant for publishing and for acquiring magazines. For instance, take the famous article quoted by E. B. Huey in his 1908 book, The Psychology and Pedagogy of Reading, which article was written by G. T. W. Patrick. Patrick's article was published in what became Cattell's magazine after 1900, Popular Science Monthly in January, 1899, and asked, "Should Children under Ten Learn to Read and Write?" (Of course, Patrick's answer was a resounding NO!)

Among Cattell's other magazine activities besides *Popular Science Monthly*, he acquired *Scientific Monthly* in 1900 and *American Naturalist* in 1908. But it was in 1895 that Cattell bought *Science* from Alexander Graham Bell, which became the official publication of the American Association for the Advancement of Science in 1900, being willed at Cattell's death in 1944 to the organization (which, curiously means he probably controlled it in the meantime to a large extent since he owned it). At the time he bought Bell's magazine in 1895, Cattell had already been at Columbia four years, having begun there in 1891.

Alexander Graham Bell's life-long enthusiasm was NOT his telephone, but the teaching of the deaf, continuing the interest in speech education of his renowned Scottish father, Alexander Melville Bell. Alexander Graham Bell supported the oral method for teaching the deaf, which meant to teach the deaf FIRST to make the sounds of speech and THEN to learn meanings (obviously the clockwise route on the triangle, the same as that followed by people with normal hearing). But there was an opposite school, the school which supported the teaching of sign language and sight words to the deaf, before the teaching of speech (the counterclockwise route on the triangle). It was a very old controversy, as Samuel Blumenfeld pointed out, originating in the violent war of words about 1780 between the French Abbe de l'Epee who supported signs and written language (counterclockwise on the triangle) and Samuel Heinecke of Germany who supported the teaching of phonics to the deaf, and oral speech (clockwise). Not surprisingly, Heinecke later wrote a phonics primer for normal German children, just as Gallaudet, who trained in 1816 in the school founded by the Abbe de l'Epee, wrote a sight-word primer for normal American children. (It is conceivable that Heinecke might have been influenced by the early writings of Basedow, in choosing to use Pascal's phonics, but Heinecke's earlier book was published in 1773 and Basedow's final *Elementary Work* in 1774.)

So the connection in 1895 between Cattell, who already was intensely interested in the subject of "words," clearly demonstrated by his 1880's experiments, and Alexander Graham Bell, who supported "phonics" for the deaf, and NOT whole words, is exceedingly curious. It seems unlikely that after 1895 Cattell could be unfamiliar with the controversies then very current in the world of the education of the deaf, the oral method vs. the sign method. Is THIS where the triangle originated, with some unknown contestant in that ancient war doodling it in some article he wrote to make his point, and Cattell's running across it?[7]

In Edmund B. Huey's 1908 book, *The Psychology and Pedagogy of Reading*, he referred to the Horace Mann School for the Deaf in recommending for normal children as ideal the *Illustrated Primer* of 1898 by Sarah Fuller which was used there. This primer by Sarah Fuller, who was the principal of the Boston Horace Mann School for the Deaf since 1869, gave:

> "...large numbers of pictures of familiar objects, with the names just below each. These familiarize with words, and other pictures show the meaning of sentences placed

---

7 [Editor's note from 2006: As discussed in my book, The Hidden Story, it seems far more likely that the reading triangle originated with William James, since such psychological association diagrams appear in his 1890 book. Thorndike had been James' student at Harvard in the 1890's, and Suzzallo, who was Thorndike's student, used the reading triangle in his article in the 1913 *Cyclopedia of Education*.]

below each."

This, of course, might also have inspired Courtis and Smith in their 1920 book, *Picture Story Reading Lessons*.

Those at Teachers College Columbia by 1908, apart from Cattell's personal contact with Alexander Graham Bell, were probably acquainted with the methods used in the teaching of the deaf which Huey described in this quote from his popular book.

Concerning the prime movers among these early reading experts, the searchlight shines most sharply on Dewey, Cattell and Thorndike. My book, *The Case for the Prosecution*, which you are now reading, was completed in draft form when on July 20, 1981, I finally received a copy of *The Leipzig Connection*, 1980, Heron Books, Portland, Oregon, mailed to me on June 17 from Willamina, Oregon. (Although it had been sent fourth class mail, that is quite a commentary on our present mail service!) I was surprised but pleased to see that Lance J. Klass and Paolo Lionni, the authors, suggested these same names, Dewey, Cattell and Thorndike, as the prime movers in American educational change, confirming my own research. *The Leipzig Connection* is a highly important but frightening book, concerning the whole of education, and should be read by anyone who cares about America's schools.

In Thorndike's writings, it is startling to find phrases which occurred originally in Colonel Parker's. Parker died about the time that Thorndike began his teaching career, and there is no direct connection between them. Dewey did not come to Columbia until eight years AFTER Thorndike received his Ph. D. It seems apparent that Parker's ideas filtered first through Dewey, then through Cattell, and finally to Thorndike, for the parallels in the writings of Parker and Thorndike are striking.

Take this excerpt from *Method of Teaching Reading in the Primary Schools*, published by the Board of Supervisors for the

Public Schools of Boston, which Mitford Mathews feels was written either by Parker or by someone under his influence:

> "A written or printed word is used to recall an idea; it has no other use. A word which has been associated with a particular idea in the mind will, when seen, recall that idea, faintly if the association is weak, vividly, if the association is strong. An association grows ... stronger by repetition of those acts which first produced it. A word is learned only when this bond of association has grown so strong that the word instantly at sight recalls its appropriate idea. It follows that the teaching of reading consists essentially in acts of association between written or printed words and their appropriate ideas. That teaching which assists these acts of association assists the child in learning to read, that which does not assist these acts is useless. If this be so, the best method of teaching reading will include all those devices, and only those, which aid efficiently in causing associative acts between ideas and written or printed words." (Board of Supervisors for the Public Schools of Boston, *Method of Teaching Reading in the Primary Schools* (Boston, n.d.) pp. 3-4.

Not only the, "this bond of association, "but the entire selection is eery. Written, according to Mathews, in the period when Parker was in charge of the schools, it could have come from the pen of Thorndike himself. Rudolf Flesch, in his new book, *Johnny STILL Can't Read: A New Look at the Scandal of Our Schools*, quotes an excerpt from Parker's *Talks on Pedagogics*:

> "...the child's mind, his whole being, is brought face to face with the truth, intrinsic knowledge, and consequently

with intrinsic thought...."

So Parker not only used phrases like "bond of association" but liked using the word, "intrinsic"![8]

The developments in reading in America after the early 1880's very possibly went from John Dewey to J. McKeen Cattell to E. L. Thorndike, judging from the historical background (from Tinker to Evers to Chance, so to speak). Dewey was obviously close to Cattell, and Cattell by his own words was close to Thorndike, and ALL had a personal interest in teaching reading, which can be shown by their own writings. Yet, to see their biographies in

---

8 [Editor's note from 2006: At the time I wrote this, I had little contact with materials written by Parker. Having had the misfortune to have read more of his material, I now think that Colonel Parker's writing demonstrates that he was barely literate and not very bright. His use of the word, "intrinsic," is of interest because it was used later by Gates, and so may show continuity in associations (from Parker to Dewey to Thorndike to Gates). Nevertheless, the above quotation from Parker is largely meaningless, intense, and pompous, and that is characteristic of almost anything of Parker's that I have read. If clever Mitford Mathews had read much of what Parker wrote, he could NEVER have attributed to bumbling Parker the quotation before the one above, from the Boston supervisors about 1883, because that quotation was beautifully and sparsely written and contained clearly expressed ideas (even though they were wrong). Obviously, it was recommending teaching reading by "meaning," and not by "sound," the counter-clockwise route on the triangle. It seems readily apparent that the material was written by a psychologist. Having read a considerable portion of James' 1890 psychology text, I have reached the conclusion that the Boston supervisors' quotation given previously was written by William James, who was living in Cambridge, across the Charles River from Boston, because the material sounds like his prose. Furthermore, James was almost the only psychologist in America at that time except for G. Stanley Hall, who wrote painfully muddy prose and was incapable of producing such a text. I now think, contrary to what follows, that James passed his interest in reading to his friend, Cattell, and to his student, Thorndike, before James' death in 1910, and that John Dewey's influence on reading instruction was not very great, although Dewey was very influential in promoting Colonel Parker's ideas on progressive education.]

encyclopedias and elsewhere, not only would you find this interest in teaching reading usually totally omitted, but you usually would find NO indication that these men even knew each other! This is POSITIVELY ASTOUNDING since these three world-famous men were simultaneously employed at Columbia from 1904 to 1917! So no one today seems to know it went, probably, in the history of reading, from Dewey to Cattell to Thorndike (from Tinker to Evers to Chance).

For their national selling job to push sight words after 1912, the early experts and their followers wrote articles, served on committees, ran school surveys, wrote books, trained graduate students, and in general were enormously active. The amount of "reading instruction" literature that began to be ground out after 1912 is really impressive. But, on examining these early reports, articles, committee memberships and so on, a reader is reminded of the consummate English actors, David Niven and Alec Guinness, who star in comic movies and manage to play all by themselves about EIGHT of the TEN roles. Because the same names keep recurring on this early material before about 1920 - that same small clique from Columbia and the University of Chicago or from Iowa or their graduate students.

They blithely ignored or discounted bad results, like that from the Harris and Anderson study, OR the 1917 survey of the Indianapolis schools, on which Gray himself reported in the *Elementary School Journal* of March, 1919. In this report, he said the aim of first grade reading:

"...is twofold, namely, to train pupils to attach meanings to printed symbols and to develop independence in the recognition of simple unfamiliar words."

But it must have pained him to have to go on to say:

"...the low record of Indianapolis in accuracy of pronunciation is due to the fact that pupils do not have adequate training in word analysis. Phonetic training which was recommended for the first grade should be continued in the second and third grades to the end that pupils may recognize quickly and accurately simple, unfamiliar words."

Of course, this would have to be "supplementary" phonics because his intrinsic phonics readers had not been started yet. But he makes it clear that Indianapolis, which taught reading by sight words and "meaning, "produced disastrous scores on oral reading. In future years, he would never refer to the Indianapolis results on sight words, but only to the studies like the 1917 Cleveland one, where methods like Aldine scored comparably (meaning that the Aldine sight-word program used the supplementary phonics that Gray recommended for Indianapolis!)

In Gates' 1924 article in the *Teachers College Record*, "A Test of Ability in the Pronunciation of Words," he reported results of tests given to 1800 pupils in Grades 1 to 6 in schools in or near New York. He had lists of words running from groups of two letter words to groups of 12 letter words. He said:

"Since many of the words were pronounced by 100 per cent of the pupils in Grades 5 and 6, the final computation of the relative difficulty of the words was based only on the data for Grades 1 to 4 inclusive (approximately 1500 pupils.)"

Even at fourth grade, 99% of the pupils could read words like only, play, here and fine. OBVIOUSLY New York had no reading problem then. But Gates and Gray thought it did, with "reading comprehension," so they worked hard and produced the "deaf-mute readers" to set things right!

The record after 1912 shows that the experts spent their time pushing silent reading and silent reading comprehension tests, and insisting that "large" vocabularies were inappropriate for little first graders, thus paving the way for the pitifully small vocabularies of the proposed new deaf-mute readers then in the works.

CHAPTER 7

THE PRO-PHONICS COMMUNITY WALKS ITSELF OVER A CLIFF, BY ACCEPTING THE VALIDITY OF "SILENT READING COMPREHENSION TESTS"

As the only respectable kind of phonics, experts accepted in 1912 what was known as "supplemental" phonics, to be covered APART from the actual teaching of reading for meaning, because they knew that without it children would hardly be able to read at all. This was until the date of the publication of the new deaf-mute-method readers approached. Then Gates wrote about how terrible "supplemental" phonics and flash-card sight-word drill was, and about how wonderful the new, soon-to-be-delivered "intrinsic" phonics would be in its place, making the nasty supplementary phonics unnecessary. Gates' talk, "The Supplementary Device Versus the Intrinsic Method of Teaching Reading," was reprinted in the *Elementary School Journal* of 1925.

That is why it was more than disturbing to read in D. H. Russell's book, *Children Learn to Read* (1949) on page 210, a statement that a reaction that was natural developed in the late 1920's against systematic phonics systems, that it may have been hurried along by Gates' study on the value of the intrinsic rather than the supplementary phonics method, which study had been contained in Gates' book, *New Methods in Primary Reading* (1928).

After all the hard work these people had put in for 16 years to get their points across, it is a little difficult to accept anyone's calling that affair a natural one. It is particularly so in this case, since David H. Russell might be expected to have had SOME acquaintance with the history, since he had personally worked with Arthur I. Gates in 1938 on a study comparing look-say and phonic methods, and he had worked with both Gates and Bond in 1939 comparing beginning readers' letter knowledge to school achievement. (That was the same Guy L. Bond who headed the USOE first-grade program with Dr. Dykstra in 1967).

But, as Dr. Rudolf Flesch reported in his 1955 book, *Why Johnny Can't Read*, and as Dr. Jeanne S. Chall clearly noted in a table in her book, *Learning to Read: The Great Debate* (1967), it was Russell who found in 1943 that phonics-trained children did better on all the tests he gave, INCLUDING ON READING COMPREHENSION.

Flesch commented back in 1955 on Russell's "astonishing reversal," Russell's going back to write a sight-word reader after having himself given tests which proved phonics to be superior. (Russell was the senior author on the 1948 to 1963 Ginn readers, and also wrote the pro-sight-word text, *Children Learn to Read* 1949.)

Russell, obviously, was a firm believer in teaching "for meaning," and probably considered that his study was only a temporary set-back, a freak statistical result. As it turned out, his study (and the others like it) have served to keep sight words in permanent use. That is because the silent reading comprehension study of his which proved the superiority of phonics, and the others like it, have led phonics supporters to try to win the phonics/sight-word battle with the unreal weapon of the silent reading comprehension tests.

But silent reading comprehension tests do NOT test the ability to read texts accurately, for those who know, out of the half million or so words in English, at least the thousand commonest words that compose 90 per cent of almost any text. Those highest-frequency thousand words are drilled on constantly in the first three years of elementary school in sight-word readers. Anyone who can read 90 per cent of a selection (which means those thousand highest-frequency words) is automatically reading above the "frustration" level set by most reading experts. That means he will not be too badly "frustrated" in making context guesses on the meanings of unknown words in the selection (depending, obviously, on the degree of his mental horsepower). Instead of testing reading accuracy, what is being tested with "reading comprehension" tests is how well test-takers can context guess, and whether or not they paid sufficient attention to the content of the selection. Therefore, for most test-takers, reading comprehension tests REALLY test only IQ plus varying degrees of attention!

Sight-word trained children will ALWAYS score at least fairly well on simple "reading comprehension" questions (like Simon's and Binet's little stumblers in France about 1908), because they cannot decode the print at all, UNLESS they pay attention to the print's "meaning". However, like the partially deaf listening to a conversation, sight-word trained children must read with a divided attention, giving part one moment to word identification and switching another moment to the ultimate meaning of the selection. Therefore, they can never focus totally on the selection's meaning, and this must lower their degree of "comprehension." In contrast, since phonics- trained children can read automatically, which leaves their attention potentially totally free to concentrate on the meaning of a selection, sight-word trained children are therefore outscored by phonic children who choose to pay attention to the meaning of what they are reading. That was obviously the case with the phonically-trained children that Russell tested.

As S. J. Samuels of the University of Minnesota has stated, research has shown the brain to be what is called a single-channel processor. As he pointed out, attention can be on only one thing at a time. However, attention is not needed for the performance of automatic operations, which can operate perfectly well while conscious attention is focused elsewhere. When we are performing such automatic operations (like dancing, or typing - and, as he said, reading, once it is thoroughly mastered), we can do them while our conscious attention is on something else. Here is where Thorndike's stimulus-response ideas are absolutely true, at the automatic (not the conscious) level in the brain. We DO carry computers in our heads, as we can hold them in our hands, which process all our automatic behaviors. It has been shown that the lower levels of speech are automatic - the forming of syllable sounds, and the generation of syntax. Strokes sometimes wipe out these sectors in the brain and poor stroke victims painfully try to communicate the meaning they are holding consciously in their heads, WITHOUT the avenue of speech.

In summary, children who have learned to read by the "meaning" of sight words can never read automatically because they have forced attention to "meaning". Syllables and syntax-generating-words can be handled automatically, but meaning, which takes place at the level of consciousness, can never be handled automatically. Unlike phonically trained students, sight-word "meaning" trained students MUST use consciousness in decoding. While that raises their "reading comprehension" far above that of a phonics-trained child who may be paying NO conscious attention to the text that he is reading automatically, the "reading comprehension" of the sight-word-trained child has to suffer because his attention is divided - part to decoding words - and only what is left over for the ultimate meaning of the selection. In contrast, the phonics child is not reading with the divided attention of the sight-word context guesser, who is "hard of hearing" when faced with print. But, since the phonics-trained child has the freedom to pay conscious attention or NOT to pay conscious attention to "meaning", like the phonic-trained children in Miss Middleton's class before 1915, the phonic child might score EITHER higher OR lower than the sight-word-trained child on "reading comprehension" tests.

Therefore, it should be obvious that, if phonics proponents try to win the battle against sight words with the "weapon" of reading comprehension scores, they are going to lose the battle in the long run. Reading comprehension tests really test only IQ plus attention. (Of course, they also test that thousand-words highest-frequency vocabulary necessary in order to read above the "frustration level," and that obviously means the person must be able to speak the language being tested. Also obviously, the test-taker must already know any necessary background information used in the selection.) Given a class or school system where teachers and students are feeling at the moment that the reading comprehension test is very important, (as perhaps in formal testing projects), phonics-trained children pay close attention and do superbly well. But, given routine performances in the classroom, as when children have to take the Iowa or California standardized tests twice a year, which they find exceedingly boring and which they dislike, phonics classes run the risk of doing poorly.

On my sabbatical research, I tested two second-grade classes which had been taught to read by the Open Court phonic program in two first-grade classes. When the first-grade classes had been promoted, they had been shuffled, so that each second-grade class had about the same number of children from each of the two first-grade rooms. Half of the children in each room had Teacher A in first grade, and the other half Teacher B. There was therefore no meaningful variable apparent between these two second-grade classes. Yet I found that one second-grade class had 82% of the children pass the comprehension part of my oral test, but the other had only 44% passing. Obviously, it could not have been the Open Court phonics program that produced the striking difference. Neither could it have been the first-grade teacher's competence in teaching, since the children from the first-grade classes had been equally divided in making up the second grade classes. Neither was it economic background, again equally divided.

Something had happened in those second-grade rooms. As a teacher, I think I know what it was. One of the second-grade teachers must have been giving reading exercises very like my test, and the other second-grade teacher must not have been doing so. So, in one class, children must have been encouraged to pay attention to the particular kind of exercise used on my test, which was to read a short selection, and then to choose, from three possible choices, a "correct" answer for each of the five questions on the selection. It is obvious, however, that both phonically-taught classes could read the material (the oral reading accuracy of both classes was very high) and both classes WOULD pay attention, if they were interested or encouraged to do so.

There is a reason that Dr. Rudolf Flesch came up with a depressing statistic in his new 1981 book *Why Johnny Still Can't Read, A New Look at the Scandal of Our Schools*. Flesch said that 85% of American schools are still using the dismal sight-word readers, over a quarter century after he published his landmark 1955 book, *Why Johnny Can't Read*. The reason that schools are still using these sight-word readers is because of these utterly fallacious reading comprehension tests! I found, when I graphed my class scores, particularly from Europe, that I frequently got what suggested a double bell curve, something IMPOSSIBLE if only one variable is being measured. But TWO things are being measured in reading comprehension tests: IQ plus attention! Yet when I graphed sight- classes in America, I got a single, flawless, bell curve, because attention in these classes is involuntarily controlled by the context-guessing reading methods, so the TWO variables become tied together, like Siamese twins.

The phonics curves I got in Europe, where "reading comprehension" is happily not so much stressed, were sometimes very amusing. I like the ones which started out with a peak at the score of zero, fell into a huge crater in the middle (where the high point of the curve is SUPPOSED to be), and then rose to triumphant peaks at 100%! Obviously, two things were being measured: relative attention (totally missing with the children who scored zero) and relative comprehension (total with the children who scored 100%). But when I averaged such phonic class scores, of course, they fell somewhat below the sight-word class scores which had controlled but divided attention. Of course, it is only meaningless "averages" that reading experts use, but it should be apparent from the background I have given that the averages on reading comprehension on my tests were useless!

Experts found out about "averages" which can hide what is really going on just about the time they printed Miss Middleton's scores. The flat, table-shaped so-called "curves" from Miss Middleton's class, with little hiccup-raised spots in them, were the result of measuring two things, reading comprehension and attention, but the experts, of course, did not believe in attention. They undoubtedly explained Miss Middleton's scores, and others like them, by frayed connections on the reading triangle. But they were getting BETTER averaged silent reading comprehension scores with their methods, undoubtedly, because attention was involuntarily controlled. They stopped getting the wildly fluctuating scores like the ski-slide curves I got from some European schools, or the off-again, on-again scores from classes like Miss Middleton's before 1915. They stopped getting what really were TWO bell curves, one on top of the other, one measuring relative attention and the other measuring relative comprehension. Instead, they got the nice, regular, statistical single bell-shaped curve you are supposed to get when you graph ANYTHING in a population that is inborn. But they were getting those higher "comprehension" scores from children who would have read orally like Simon's little stumbler in France, who could pass the IQ test when the people listening to him "read" could not understand what he was saying. Obviously, he "passed" the comprehension test the way a hard-of-hearing person "listens," with great strain and a loss of part of the message.

My reading comprehension scores on whole phonics classes went from terrible class scores to marvelous class scores, proving, obviously, that the teaching of phonics did not affect reading comprehension either positively or negatively. In those phonics classes with a very high average, virtually ALL the children passed the "comprehension" test. So the teaching of phonics had not controlled children's scores, but left them free potentially to score very high.

Arthur I. Gates found the same thing when he tested six fourth-grade classes in six New York City schools on reading comprehension, which he reported in "Measurement of Reading Ability", September, 1926, in the *Teachers College Record*. About twelve years after Miss Middleton's class scores, "reading comprehension" had become a big thing, and many teachers were stressing it by then. (In a letter Gates wrote to Chall, quoted in *Learning to Read: The Great Debate*, Gates said that virtually all American schools before 1930 had heavy phonics programs - obviously supplementary phonics, in many, so the New York schools can be assumed to be phonics schools.) These New York classes, he said, were of comparable quality, yet the class scores went all over the scale, just like my phonics class scores, from terrible to marvelous. Gates said some teachers were doing a better job teaching comprehension, but I think it is evident they were encouraging attention.

When I averaged my class scores, here in the United States, I found that some of the phonics-trained classes outscored all the sight-word trained classes on reading comprehension and had absolutely marvelous scores. Phonics programs therefore produced the very best readers. But the phonic classes, considered as a whole, scored anywhere on the reading comprehension scale, from terrible to marvelous. Yet the sight-word trained class scores did not have that absolutely wild variation but instead fell into a very narrow band, lower than the best phonics scores, but much higher than the worst. Since the phonics scores went all over the scale, from terrible to marvelous, that proved they were showing they were not a function of the teaching method. However, since the sight-word scores fell into a very narrow band that indicated they had been a function the teaching method.

The problem with "reading comprehension test" scores turns up with those phonics classes which have NOT been encouraged to pay attention. Such classes still can read, beautifully, but may not show their ability on silent reading comprehension tests because their attention is not involuntarily forced. They have the FREEDOM to read inattentively, as we have the freedom to listen inattentively, and so may score lower on the Iowas or Californias than the stumbling, forced sight word readers.

A school administrator who has phonics-trained classes may get, if he is unlucky, lower - sometimes far lower - averaged reading comprehension scores, but a school administrator who has sight-word-trained classes which use a sight word basal reading series will get consistent, fairly high reading comprehension scores , though not so good as the best phonics scores. However, if he visited the classrooms and LISTENED to his children read orally, instead of just looking in his office at standardized print-out sheets on "reading comprehension" tests and reading them like the Dow scale on stocks, he would find many children who cannot really read, just as Simon reported in France about 1908!

What is at issue is NOT how well children read, and NOT whether they are getting an education, and NOT whether they can really read their school texts or library books, but SOLELY what numbers the computers will spit out when the standardized reading comprehension tests are fed into them each year. It is precisely like the old idol, Baal, into whose fiery furnace "mouth" each year the practical minded ancients used to throw live babies, because they thought it was "necessary" so that they could get prosperity back as a product.

Then, is it the school administrators with whom we should be angry, 85% of whom order sight-word readers that will produce these higher reading comprehension scores? Hardly. In the first place, just like Rudolf Flesch and the Reading Reform Foundation and Dr. Dykstra, they BELIEVE in reading comprehension tests. Further, they have actually been brain-washed into buying these sight-word basal readers by the advertising jargon with which they are sold, which makes much of phony phonics, so the school administrators THINK they are buying phonics texts. The inexperienced person, seeing such materials, could easily be misled by their appearance, but they are still all "intrinsic" phonics, the same aid to context guessing that was dreamed up before 1930. They only SEEM like the real thing. What is even more astonishing is that even the authors of these series sometimes think they teach real phonics. Dr. William Durr, an author on the Houghton Mifflin reading series, actually asked Mrs. Raymond Rubicam why the series was not included on the Reading Reform Foundation list of approved systems. Mrs. Rubicam reported that Dr. Durr, said, "We teach phonics."

In plain language, school administrators are forced to buy readers which produce higher "reading comprehension" scores by the system which judges the administrators' job performances by the scores achieved, and this sick system is ALSO just about as old as the sick sight-word basals themselves.

As long ago as 1913, when J. M. Rice (a pure phonics man, himself, by the way) wrote *Scientific Management in Education,* the mess we have today was well under way. Rice complained that it was common practice in 1913 that the judgment of a superintendent of schools was sufficient as to the best way to run a school system or to get results, and wasn't that terrible? Who was watching the superintendent?

That is a little bit like someone complaining that there HAS to be something to hold the world up, so someone else studies the matter and comes back and announces he has the answer: the thing that is holding up the earth is a TURTLE!

Rice and all the rest of them found a turtle on which all of our superintendents of schools could sit, and that turtle is the standardized silent reading comprehension test.

But, it wouldn't have been very long, in the ancient, less naive world, before someone ELSE asked, "Well, what is the turtle sitting on?"

So, isn't it astounding that no one has ever, REALLY, asked the same question about these standardized reading comprehension tests? What are THEY sitting on? Or, to go Rice one better, instead of asking who is watching the superintendents of schools, shouldn't we be asking, "Who is watching the test makers?"

The judgment on how our schools should be run was once split among thousands of superintendents of schools, each intimately acquainted with his own school system and its problems, and each of whom had been hired specifically because of his competence in education.

Then the day of the standardized test arrived, with much self-congratulation among the psychologists (such as E. L. Thorndike). I will limit my remarks for the purpose of this discussion to the silent reading comprehension tests, although there are now hosts of other standardized tests and massive tomes are published just to list such tests. I have had to give this trash to my classes for 18 years and wish to go on record that it is an outrage that taxpayers' money is spent on such drivel. These tests are dreamed up in some office far removed from real schools and real children by faceless drudges and do NOT test real reading ability.

What is WRONG with the judgment of individual superintendents of schools about how to run, and to devise tests for, their own systems? They were selected because they were superior men. Should they have to knuckle under to these idiot marks that come out of the computer each year, and to run school systems so they will produce the right ones, according to the "judgment" of a handful of profit-making commercial testing companies that NEVER taught ANYONE anything?

THE REASON 85% OF AMERICAN SCHOOL SYSTEMS ARE TEACHING SIGHT WORD BASAL READERS IS BECAUSE THEY HAVE TO IN ORDER TO PRODUCE HIGHER AVERAGED STANDARDIZED SILENT READING COMPREHENSION SCORES! SO WHAT ARE WE GOING TO DO ABOUT THOSE WORTHLESS TESTS?

CHAPTER 8

NOW LET'S GIVE REAL, NOT FAKE, READING TESTS, FOR THE FIRST TIME IN SEVENTY YEARS!

I know what to suggest about those standardized silent reading comprehension tests. Throw them out, and go back to testing reading the way it USED to be tested before 1914, by having someone (sometimes the superintendent of schools, himself!) sit down and listen to the children read orally. Also, by giving DICTATED spelling tests (not recognition spelling tests, on which all a child has to do is to check whether a word is spelled right or wrong).

We may be in for a big, bad surprise, though, because there are NORMS for how children used to read and spell back in 1914 and 1916! W. S. Gray, himself, in his Ph. D. dissertation, gave norms for children in sixth grade reading orally in 1916, and Leonard P. Ayres gave norms for spelling of thousands upon thousands of American children in 1914. When we test today's children with these SAME tests, we are going to be in for a very unpleasant surprise!

The truth is that NO ONE today has the SLIGHTEST idea how well students in America read, despite the millions of dollars spent on standardized silent reading comprehension tests every year.

If New York City, or Dubuque, Iowa, or Dallas, Texas really want to know how their children are reading today, they are going to have to give them these oral reading tests and DICTATED spelling tests.

Jean Chall wrote that William Scott Gray was the principal interpreter and summarizer of research in reading for 40 years. Gray was the author for about 40 years of the best selling basal reader series in America, the Scott, Foresman. Therefore, it is very appropriate that Gray, himself, has provided us with the best material for those oral reading tests, in his very earliest oral reading tests and very earliest test results. However, his final oral tests, which he carefully treated to yield "standard" scores, are an absolutely worthless indication of how the thousands upon thousands of American children who were tested with them before 1920 actually read. That is because the experts did find out, very early, that the BEST way to hide what is really going on is to report "average" scores, and then to throw in, perhaps, high and low scores. But the only kinds of test results that mean anything are RANKED test results, where a failing level is established, and the test then reports the percentage of children performing ABOVE that failing level. That simple method is the method Gray used originally on his oral reading tests, from 1913 to 1917.

It is no accident that the test programs being carried out by our states on competency are reporting their scores in precisely the fashion that Gray did before 1917, instead of by "averages." With the ranking method, we can tell at a glance how many children performed satisfactorily ("passed") and how many did not ("failed"). But, of course, in the reading comprehension part of any such tests, since all that is usually being tested is only IQ combined with varying degrees of attention, the reading comprehension tests are worthless.

The very first report on W. S. Gray's oral test paragraphs

appeared in the September, 1914, article, "The Measurement of Ability in Reading", by Edward L. Thorndike in *Teachers College Record*, Columbia Teachers College, which article included Thorndike's first report on his own silent reading comprehension tests. Gray had prepared his oral test paragraphs under Thorndike's personal direction while Gray was working for his master's degree at Columbia Teachers College, before returning to the University of Chicago to study for his 1917 doctorate under Thorndike's college classmate, Judd. In Gray's 1914 material, his statistics were reported in PRECISELY the same form as are used in our current state competency tests, by ranking. Gray simply established a failing level, and then just reported how many children succeeded in reading above it!

It is W. S. Gray's final report, his 1917 Ph. D. dissertation, which provides the most useful material for an oral test comparison today. In this, of course, Gray had to explain the convoluted thinking which supported his 1917 treated standard scores. It was such convoluted "standard scores" which managed to hide the real results from the tens of thousands of children orally tested in official school surveys all over the country in the next two years or so. But, to produce Gray's 1917 "treated" scores, Gray still had to start originally with actual firm test results (how many passed above the frustration level of 90%) just as Thorndike showed in his1914 article that included Gray's oral test data, and just as Gray had used in 1914, 1915 and 1916.

In 1914, Gray had prepared a series of original paragraphs, progressing from easy to difficult, and made minor revisions in the original list of paragraphs until 1917. Children failed a paragraph when they could not read it with four or fewer errors, which meant when they could not read it at 90% accuracy or better since the paragraphs were about 50 words in length. Meaningfully, four or fewer words per 50 running words was also just about the

AVERAGE for the new words introduced by Gallaudet in his 1835 *Mother's Primer*.

Very interestingly, 32 years after Gray's initial 1914 work, 90% accuracy was set as the "passing" level, above the "frustrational" level, by the very famous "reading expert," E. A. Betts, on page 448 of his 1946 book, *Foundations of Reading Instruction*, published by American Book Company. Below 90% word accuracy on a connected text, a child was considered to be reading at the "frustrational" level, which apparently meant the child would be unable to guess the meaning of unknown word in the selection. However, oral reading tests for groups of children were non-existent in 1946, and still are today. Using a "frustrational" level in testing a child was to be done only on an individual basis, just about the time a reading disabled child was ready to "graduate" into reading remediation.

So the idea of an easily recognizable passing standard of oral reading accuracy (90%) went out the back door when Gray carefully treated his oral reading paragraph tests to produce standard scores so that they really did not tell anything about the children's oral reading accuracy. He did this at a time when American children could read VERY accurately, indeed, in 1917. But the 90% passing level came back in through the front door in E .A. Bett's 1946 book, after America had swung over wholesale to the deaf-mute-method readers. Teachers by then NEEDED to know what was the failing oral accuracy level so that they could see how well their children were doing, relatively, with the awful deaf-mute readers. By 1946, it was well established that children had terrible trouble reading, and many different reading groups were needed in classrooms to provide for the enormous differences in reading levels. Teachers needed a reliable passing oral reading grade on materials from simple to difficult, so that they could put children in the right groups.

In the old days in America, and as I saw all over Europe in 1977, it was possible to teach a first grade as a unit, and ALL the children had the teacher's attention ALL day, unless she chose, for their benefit, to work with some individually. But once the deaf-mute-method readers came into our schools, children spread out in their achievement, to match their IQ and visual memory and language background and a million other things. There were only a few at the top of the class, most dribbling through the middle, and a few at the bottom. This was the origin of our three happy little reading groups in classrooms all over America today, the Eagles group, the Bluebirds group, and the poor little Vultures group.

So it is no accident that Emmet A. Betts, a sight-word man, was an apostle of grouping in schools, with his outraged writings against that terrible practice in America, called "lockstep" instruction. "Lockstep" instruction was once very workable in American first grades, as it is today all over Europe, but it became a total impossibility once the great day had dawned that the Gates and Gray readers hit the schools.

Betts, most naturally, went on to write his OWN sight word basal reader in 1948. By then a lot of people had apparently made a lot of money, when the schools went from phonics to sight words. Coincidentally, it just happened to be during the Great Depression, when most people could not make any money at all. It is vested interests now which keep the practice in our schools, with experts writing books for teachers' colleges explaining how necessary the sight-word, context- "guessing" method is, and then writing the basal readers for the children themselves. As vested interests, obviously, they are incapable of seeing straight, but, as vested interests, equally obviously, they should NOT be in control of our reading instruction.

This is how Gray described his early oral tests in his 1917 Ph. D. dissertation:

"The test was given to 565 pupils from the third to the eighth grade inclusive. These pupils represented four schools, three in the city of New York and one in a small city in Central Illinois. Two of the schools in New York are located in foreign districts of the city. The third New York school represents a more truly American population, economically independent. The Illinois school represents an American population of average economic rank. The pupils were about equally divided between Native American and foreign-born children, and represent practically every economic level."

So here is Paragraph 7 from his paragraph scale, which paragraph he gave in 1916 to 212 children at sixth grade in four schools, two schools of which were in foreign districts, and a third in which half the children were foreign born. No child could pass if he made more than four errors.

"It was a glad summer morning. Little birds teetered on the twigs of the trees. They opened their throats and sang as loud as they could. Flowers nodded to each other in the gardens and along the wayside. Butterflies went flitting about gaily [sic], the morning air was fresh and sweet, and all was gladness."

Of the 212 sixth-grade children who were tested on their oral reading accuracy with this paragraph, about half of whom were from foreign backgrounds, NINETY-EIGHT PER CENT PASSED! Why don't we try that same paragraph to test oral reading accuracy NOW in New York or Chicago or Upper Montclair, New Jersey? Can you see WHY we have had only ten oral reading comparisons between phonics and sight-word trained children since 1912?

You can forget about left-backs or repeaters having being omitted, to be used as an excuse to deflate these extraordinarily high 1916 sixth-grade scores. That is because Leonard P. Ayres wrote a famous book, *Laggards in Our Schools*. In it, he published a graph comparing Binet's IQ scores to a graph comparing the promotions of 14,762 children in 28 cities in the United States about 1909. The vast majority of the children, the graph showed, were in the right grade or only a year lower or higher. Very few had been left back more than one year, and virtually none more than two years. So Gray's sixth-grade scores represented children who either belonged in sixth grade or were a year too young or too old, with very few exceptions, since Gray's 1916 class make-up should have been very much like Ayres 1909 classes.

I was in a camera store a couple of years ago, and mentioned to the young man clerk, about 25 or 30 years old, that I was researching reading instruction. He said he had always thought he was a good reader until he reached ninth grade and a teacher put him in the remedial reading class. He said he guessed he always thought he was good because he was "so much better than the other kids!"

I told him that 115 individual Dutch and Swedish sixth graders had read to me orally from Verses 10 to 18 of the 104th Psalm in the Protestant Dutch and Swedish Bibles in the fall of 1977. They read almost like the wind, and more than half made no errors. None had read below the 90% "frustrational" level. He replied that in HIS sixth grade, when children tried to read aloud, some missed so many words that the others had to call them out to them, and the "readers" broke right down and cried out loud in class.

Cried out loud in class! But no one had tested their oral reading, as Gray tested sixth graders back in 1916, when 98.1% could read beautifully (and HALF from foreign backgrounds!) But you can be absolutely certain that the children in that young man's

117

American sixth-grade room about 1963 or so had their "reading comprehension" tested, and they probably passed, just like Simon's little French stumbler.

Where are the spokesmen for these sixth-graders only a few years ago who "cried out loud in class" and the others like them? What does charity require: that we ignore the errors of this vested interest group, or that we do everything in our power to remove them from control over the reading curriculum? But W. S. Gray knew ALL about the wonderful reading accuracy of phonics- trained children. In a Bloomfield linguistic (essentially phonic) method classroom about 1940, as reported by Mitford Mathews in his 1966 book, *Teaching to Read, Historically Considered*, Gray heard first-graders read with remarkable ease and accuracy. Instead of being impressed, Gray said that experts had LONG known it was easy to teach children to read accurately and quickly, but they were heading for real trouble in "reading comprehension." What ELSE could Gray have meant except the terrible triangle, when he made this remark? Yet it is impossible not to feel sympathy for Gray, who invested his life's work in the errors of Dewey, Cattell and Thorndike.

As the final footnote to "reading with comprehension" by going the non-oral route of the deaf, here is what Dr. R. Orin Cornett, Research Professor at Gallaudet College, Washington, had to say at the Reading Reform Foundation Conference at Princeton in 1979.

Dr. Cornett had been Assistant U. S. Commissioner of Education and Director of the Division of Higher Education, which meant that he saw college reports from Gallaudet College. Cornett said, as reported in *The Reading Informer* of October, 1979:

"Because I had to approve these reports, I read them carefully. In one such report I read the following statements, back to back:

"The average IQ of students at Gallaudet College (the world's only separate college specifically for deaf persons) is probably higher than that in any other institution of higher education in the world."

"The point, of course, is that deaf students have to be brilliant in order to reach college level.

"Eighty percent of the students at Gallaudet College never read for pleasure, and three fourths of the 20% who do were not born deaf."

"It was the second statement that aroused my interest in deafness. I was horrified. If any one of you lost your hearing, the amount of time you spend reading would increase greatly.... Reading is the only hope of the deaf for learning about the world and what is happening in it.

"The average reading level of 19-year-olds in schools and programs for the deaf in the United States is about that of a nine-year-old hearing child. We fail the deaf in their area of greatest need. It was this shocking fact that caused me to begin learning about the problems of deaf persons and in 1965 to accept a position at Gallaudet College. I came to Gallaudet with the avowed intention of doing something about this problem."

He DID do something, and it was something remarkable. He developed cued speech, by which people use eight handshapes in four places near the face to make lip reading absolutely clear, turning it into something with the clarity of heard language. In other words, it is a visual form of phonics. The method has been extraordinarily successful, particularly with little deaf preschoolers, who can then learn to read WITH PHONICS!

So, if phonics has been found indispensable to teaching deaf children to read, isn't it time we started to use it for children with NORMAL hearing? Isn't it time we got rid of the 50-year old method we have been using in our schools, the Gates, Gray and subsequent readers, based on the OUTMODED manner of teaching the deaf?

But, after this oral reading test is given to our sixth-graders to see how they compare to the 1916 sixth-graders that Gray tested, it would be a very good idea to give a DICTATED, not recognition, spelling test. Obviously, a recognition spelling test, when a child checks whether or not a word in print is or is not spelled correctly, is just another form of sight-word recognition. Such printed recognition spelling tests first came into use, most meaningfully, just about 1930, after "experts" wrote articles claiming they were equivalent to dictated spelling tests. (The logic from *Alice in Wonderland*, again....)

In 1915, Leonard P. Ayres, who had been engaged in various school surveys on a large scale for years, published as the result of much research his 1915 *A Measuring Scale for Ability in Spelling*, which was a standardized spelling scale. According to Dr. William Henry Gray (not Dr. William Scott Gray), who was an Associate Professor of Psychology at Kansas State Teachers College of Emporia, and who wrote *Psychology of Elementary School Subjects* in 1938, Ayres tested 1,000 of the highest-frequency words used in writing (not reading), which list had been compiled by Ayres himself and also from studies by various authors. Ayres divided those 1,000 words into 50 lists of 20 words each. Ayres then obtained a total of 1,400,000 spellings from 70,000 children in 84 cities on those words, and, from their scores, designed norms for spelling ability at each grade. Ayres' spelling scale was subsequently used for years in testing all over the United States.

Obviously, Ayres' scale would be an irrefutable source for spelling ability in the United States schools in 1915, since it was based on testing 70,000 children in 84 American cities.

I called the Russell Sage Foundation in New York., who had published Ayres' scale. They said they no longer had copies of it, having dropped their educational section perhaps some thirty years ago. The last copy of the scale had been given away long before. The education library that they once had, I was told, had been divided between the New York Public Library and Columbia University, but the bulk of it went to Columbia University.

So, since I was doing research at the Library of Congress in early July, 1981, I tried to get a copy of *A Measuring Scale for Ability in Spelling* by Leonard P. Ayres, New York: Russell Sage Foundation, 1915. What was sent down to me from the stacks was the COVER of his 1915 spelling scale, but inside was his earlier handwriting, not spelling, scale. I could see when I opened the cover where the original contents had been ripped out of the sewn binder that had originally been stitched in three places.

I reported this, and the gracious librarian brought me back to the stacks to see what we could find. We DID find on the shelves (under its proper number, different from the spelling scale) MANY copies of the Ayres handwriting scale, but when we went to the numbered section for the Ayres spelling scale, there was nary another one on the shelf, just the empty folder I had been sent down, with its ripped binding, and with the wrong contents inside. Curious?

But I did find at the Library of Congress Leonard P. Ayres' 1914 report for the Russell Sage Foundation on a school survey he did, *The Public Schools of Springfield, Illinois*. In those pre-deaf-mute-method reader days, they did not have to spend so much time worrying about teaching children to read and write, so a lot of Ayres' report is about such things as lighting, drinking water and janitor work. But on pages 71 to 7 Ayres mentions, casually, the work done in Springfield on spelling:

"Spelling tests of 10 dictated words were given through the

system in all the grades from the second to the eighth inclusive. The words used in the tests were chosen from lists used by the Division of Education of the Russell Sage Foundation in an investigation that it is now conducting of the spelling ability of children in elementary schools. The Division has conducted studies to discover the 1,000 words most commonly used in writing and it has made these words into spelling lists with which children in nearly 100 American cities have been tested. From among these words, 10 were chosen which this investigation has shown are on the average spelled correctly by 70 per cent of the children in the second grades of other cities. Similarly 10 words were chosen which children in the third grades of other cities spell on the average 70 per cent correctly. In the same way, 10 words were chosen for each of the other elementary grades and in each case they were of such difficulty that on the average seven out of 10 children spell them correctly while three misspell them. These lists of 10 words for each grade are shown in Table 18.

"Results of these tests showed that in general the children of this city can spell as well as the children in other cities. Their spelling ability is neither greater nor less; it is precisely the average. In all, 3,612 children were tested with words that children in other cities on the average spell 70 per cent correctly, and the result was that the final average for the Springfield children was also 70 per cent. It was found, however, that there was variation in the results for the different grades and schools."

The content from Ayres' Table 18 is shown on the following page. Ayres showed in another table that the variations in Springfield ran no lower than 65% right in Grade 3, and no higher than 75% right in Grade 8. When he compared the 18 different schools in Springfield, not the grades, the scores ran from an average at the very weakest, Palmer, of 58%, to 64% at the next three weakest, Douglas, McClernan, and Iles, up to the best at Hay of 86% correct on the average for the whole school.

In the 1918 *Elementary School Journal*, Joseph P. O'Hern, Assistant Superintendent of Schools of Rochester, New York, quoted the Ayres average of 70% for Springfield and reported that Rochester averaged 82%; Butte, Montana, 80%; Oakland, California, 77%; and Salt Lake City, 86%. Children could spell all OVER the United States in those days!

"Table 18" From Ayres 1914 Work
The Public Schools of Springfield, Illinois

2nd Grade	3rd Grade	4th Grade	5th Grade
foot	fill	forty	several
get	point	rate	leaving
for	state	children	publish
horse	ready	prison	o'clock
cut	almost	title	running
well	high	getting	known
name	event	need	secure
room	done	throw	wait
left	pass	feel	matter
with	Tuesday	speak	flight

6th Grade	7th Grade	8th Grade
decide	district	petrified
general	consideration	tariff
manner	athletic	emergency
too	distinguish	corporation
automobile	evidence	convenience
victim	conference	receipt
hospital	amendment	cordially
neither	liquor	discussion
toward	experience	appreciate
business	receive	decision

Even in this preliminary form (though the 1915 final norms should be available from the Columbia library since they received the bulk of the Russell Sage library, and available from other libraries, as well) is a firm standard by which to compare today's students to those before 1920. I suggest the test be given in New York and elsewhere on the first school day in September, 1981.

To make it very fair, give grade 2 at beginning grade 3, and so on up the grades. But we already have a very clear idea of what kinds of results to expect.

In 1954, before Rudolf Flesch's book made the basal authors, in self-defense, begin to introduce a little more phonics, thousands of children at second grade were tested for the Iowa spelling survey. Five of the words on the second-grade Iowa list (*The Spelling Scale*, State University of Iowa, Iowa City, 1954) are also on the second-grade 1914 Ayres list. Without the 1915 scale, I can not determine at what point in second grade the Ayres test was given (though the report by O'Hern indicates it is probable that it is an average of the class that entered in September and. the class that came in February, half-year classes being normal then). The Iowa scores, however, were for beginning second grade, which obviously might lower scores to some degree compared to Ayres.

On the five words on both the 1914 Ayres second-grade list and the 1954 Iowa second-grade list, the 1914 Ayres second-grade children, probably at about mid-term, scored SEVENTY PER CENT correct on EACH of the second grade words. On the 1954 Iowa second-grade scores on those same five words, at the beginning of second grade, the average score for the thousands of second graders tested was LESS THAN THIRTY PER CENT on each of those words! The time that the test was given in second grade cannot explain away the difference between 70% accuracy and less than 30% accuracy!

All through the 1920's, experts stated in the literature that one of the signs of weak reading was the use of regressions in eye movements. As children read, a machine was available to record their eye movements. Good readers were presumed to make very few regressions, but instead to have a uniform sweep of the eyes across the page. E. A. Taylor reported in "The Spans: Perception, Apprehension, and Recognition," in the *American Journal of Opthalmology*, 1954, that tests on 5,000 U. S. readers from Grade 1 to college showed that first graders made 23% regressions in all eye movements and college students made 15%.

Yet in Huey's 1898 work with American adults, reported on pages 27-29 of his 1908 book, *The Psychology and Pedagogy of Reading*, Huey cited "retrocals," presumably regressions, which work out to only 3% when analyzed. The German experimenters of the time made NO mention of regressions, but just a uniform sweep of the eyes across the page and back. An increase in regressions - from none, apparently in Germany, and 3% in America, to 15% for college students in 1954 is a clear indication of a reading problem. People ONLY go back to look at what they thought they read if they are not certain about what it said! If such tests as reported in the *American Journal of Opthalmology* in 1954 could be done on students today from phonics programs in comparison to students from sight word programs, some very interesting data might emerge!

But Unthink operates to cover data on eye movement and perception research, just as on everything else. We have heard unendingly of Cattell and his 1885 experiment proving (so he thought) the value of sight words, but no one in America ever heard of H. von Grashey in Germany, who stated the same year, 1885, that he "maintained on his authority as a psychiatrist concerned with aphasia that the letters successively pass the macula lutea, or yellow spot of the eye, and successively provoke relevant sounds," as was also reported by Franz Biglmaier of Germany in Downing's

Comparative Reading in 1973. (Biglmaier's article in Downing's book is the only place I have heard Messmer's objective and subjective readers mentioned outside Huey's 1908 book, but Biglmaier only mentioned them in passing.)

In most other countries, reading is properly taught in first grade, so they have the time to teach SUBJECTS from second grade up. The Russians do not waste any time teaching reading "for meaning" in the first grade. D. B. Elkonin of the Institute Academy of Educational Science states flatly what they consider reading to be, reported in his article reprinted in Brian and Joan Simon's *Educational Psychology in the USSR*, 1963:

> "In the present paper we start from the proposition that reading is a reconstitution of the sound forms of a word on the basis of its graphic representation. Understanding, which is often considered as the basic content of the process of reading arises as a result of correct recreation of the sound forms of words. He who, independently of the level of understanding of words, can correctly recreate their sound forms is able to read."

Clear as a bell!

In the December, 1959, *The Reading Teacher* article by Gertrude Hildreth, "How Russian Children Learn to Read," she wrote that Russian children did NOT use high frequency words and did NOT repeat words to fix them in memory. Words were only used to demonstrate the sounds being learned. Hildreth found that a Russian 1930 primer divided the syllables in words. The article, "Primer," in Volume 4 of the *Great Soviet Encyclopedia*, reported that Russian primers dropped the use of sight words in 1932 and went back to using analytic-synthetic phonics in 1932, the same as Tolstoy had used in the primer he wrote in 1872. However, since

Hildreth saw a 1930 primer in which words were divided (and the only reason for dividing words is to indicate pronunciation), it appears that the Russian use of phonics preceded 1932 by at least two years.

Nor are the Chinese wasting time teaching their little ones to read "meaningfully." Since they have the ORIGINAL sight-word printed language, but one that has been highly successful for thousands of years, it would be expected that they would at least concentrate on sight words. But the Chinese are now using, besides the sight-word characters, an alphabet called Pinyin. First graders begin with Pinyin and phonics as soon as they enter school, later learning characters, but Pinyin continues in use all through school.

The American Frank Laubach is famous for the magnificent work he has done in teaching reading all over the world in undeveloped areas, and in hosts of languages. It would be assumed, then, that when UNESCO prepared a functional literacy guide it would be modeled on Laubach's phonic approach or on the Russian or Chinese phonics approach. It is more than disturbing to find that UNESCO's 1973 *Guide to Functional Literacy* is a sight-word global approach and that it cites William Scott Gray as an authority, in a footnote on page 104, for instance. I consider this a tragic betrayal of the trust of innocent illiterates the world over. It is mystifying that UNESCO chose to write a basal-reader-guide approach, complete with all the jargon of our American basal-reader series, instead of a straight-forward phonics primer approach.

So the Chinese are using both a sound-bearing-alphabet and meaning-bearing characters, but the Japanese have been doing that for centuries, with their Kana and Kanji characters. Kana are sound-bearing syllable characters which children usually learn before they come to school, and Kanji are picture characters like the Chinese ones, and are learned over a period of years after starting school. Japanese children rarely have reading disabilities, according to

127

Kiyoshi Makita in the 1968 *American Journal of Orthopsychiatry*. Reading Japanese would be like watching a movie with part of the information coming from the picture and part from the sound.

S. Sasanuma and O. Fujimura reported in 1971 that Japanese patients with brain damage (presumably stroke victims) sometimes are able to read only one part of Japanese script: EITHER the Kana OR the Kanji. This shows clearly that Kana and Kanji are processed in different parts of the brain, one part of the brain handling the visual stimuli, and another part the auditory stimuli. (Their article, "Selective Impairment of Phonetic and Non-phonetic Transcription of Words in Japanese Aphasic Patients, Kana vs. Kanji in Visual Recognition and Writing," *Cortex*, 7 (1971), 1-18, was cited in C. K. Leong's article, "Learning to Read in English and Chinese: Some Psycholinguistic and Cognitive Considerations," in Dina Feitelson's *Cross Cultural Perspectives on Reading and Reading Research*, International Reading Association, Newark, Delaware, 1978.)

In Stella S. F. Liu's article entitled "Decoding and Comprehension in Reading Chinese," a part of Dina Feitelson's book, *Cross-Cultural Perspectives on Reading and Reading Research*, Stella Liu printed a diagram on page 154 she called "Figure 1." It is a drawing of a rectangle. On the left side of the rectangle are two circles, one on the top left-hand corner and one on the bottom left-hand corner. The right side of the rectangle is covered with only one large circle. The drawing does not look like it, but from the labeling of the two circles on the left (Aural - acoustic image on the top circle and Visual - graphic input on the bottom circle) , and from the label on the large circle on the right (Meaning), the figure is in essence the triangle from the 1913 *Cyclopedia* article of Suzzallo! It even has arrows on the connecting lines. What I personally find most amazing is the reference Liu gave on page 153 for the concepts shown by the diagram, "mediated (indirect) and immediate (direct) meaning identification". After using these last terms, she cites this reference in her bibliography: (15:206), which turns out to be "Smith, Frank. *Understanding Reading*, New York: Holt, Rinehart and Winston, 1971." The triangle may not have been showing up in reading instruction texts, but it has stayed alive someplace since 1913.

Sasanuma's and Fujimura's study, plus the triangle, show what is really wrong with sight words. With sight words today, children are asked to use BOTH the auditory path AND the visual path on the SAME stimulus at the SAME time. By contrast, Japanese children reserve the auditory path only for the Kana characters and the visual path only for the Kanji characters, and so have almost no reading disabilities. But our reading methods, which try to use BOTH paths on the same stimulus at the same time, set up the conflict that results in habitual context guessing . We have learned that it is impossible to remember as many pure sight words as can be remembered with distinctive Chinese characters. In alphabetic print, therefore, it is impossible for children to go ONLY the visual route as can be done when reading Chinese. So the only alternative we have is to teach words by phonics, alone, so that children can go ONLY the auditory route, thereby avoiding the conflict that arises from trying to use two sensory paths at the SAME time on the SAME stimulus, something that apparently occurs no where else in nature except in the reading of sight words. Perhaps if we finally go only the auditory route, or phonics, American schools, too, will end up with few reading disabilities in children, just like the lucky Japanese.

But today, we are not free after first grade, as so many other countries are, to teach subjects instead of reading. So most of our primary school day is spent in "reading groups" which are really teaching only context guessing and "reading comprehension." Page 187 of Level 2 of Scott, Foresman's *Systems*, on which Kenneth

Goodman of the University of Arizona was a coauthor, shows the kind of phonics used in the first half of first grade in many basal reader programs, only the use of initial consonants and context guessing. Vowels are not covered in *Systems* until about Level 3, about January of first grade.

When doing my sabbatical oral reading research, I tested one little second grader in January of second grade who had been taught with the *Systems* program in first grade. Instead of reading, "The dog has learned to do...." she said, "The dog has lemon to do...." I asked her to read it again, and she repeated the same nonsense. So much for reading meaningfully! Oh, yes, she DID pass my comprehension test. She scored 100%! Yet she failed accuracy at a terrible 85%, saying, "...it was a shell puppy" instead of "...it was a small puppy," and "the name of times," instead of "the number of times. Her pathetic mis-readings (lemon for learned, shell for small, and name for number) came from having been forced by Goodman's vicious *Systems* series into becoming a Messmer subjective reader. She was incapable of reading words in parts by their sound, and could only come up with whole-word guesses, guessing whole words that began with the same letter. Yet her intense but pathetic concentration on ultimate "meaning" showed up with her 100% score on the five simple reading comprehension questions on the oral test. It is obvious, however, her terrible reading disability would make it impossible for her to handle textbooks with any degree of success.

Of course, there was also the child who read the word, "catch," easily. I asked him how he knew it, as first he had read the word "cat," paused, and then added the "ch" sound to say "catch." He said, "My mom taught me, not school. That's how I got it."

As mentioned, a coauthor on the Scott, Foresman Systems was Kenneth Goodman of the University of Arizona. He was also one of the authors, with DeWayne Triplett and Frank Greene, of a book,

The Disabled Reader: The Right Not to Read, reviewed in the National Council of Teachers of English *Catalog* for 1978-79. The *Catalog* said:

> "We've been inflicting unreadable textbooks on college students for generations; only recently have we begun to do something about it. Goodman says this leaves the impression that we suddenly have a "reading problem" in colleges. There is indeed a problem with text readability. Goodman says the answer lies in having teachers trained in the reading process and using multiple materials, but with reading no longer the crucial means in learning."

So the little girl who had been taught only initial consonants and context guessing before January of first grade with the Scott Foresman *Systems* (plus sight words, of course), on which Goodman was an author, and who then read "The dog has lemon to do," in January of second grade, instead of "The dog has learned to do..." will at least have the right NOT to read when she grows up, because the experts have fought hard to give that "right" to her.

But, in the second-grade phonics classes in America which I tested in January, the same month I tested that little girl, 92% of the phonics-trained children passed the oral accuracy test. It is tragic that most American schools do NOT teach these phonics programs, but instead the sight-word basal readers that are producing our problem.

The REAL reason we have a reading problem today is because we do NOT teach reading in first grade. Ralph C. Staiger, Executive Director of the International Reading Association, gave an address to the New Jersey Teachers' Convention in 1978 with the title, "Reading: Still at the Top of the Curriculum." Nowhere in the world but in places where the basal reader sight-word method is used is reading at the top of the curriculum all through school. Reading should be FINISHED in first grade, as it is in Russia and many other places. The children then go on to study the grammar of their own language and its classic literature. But because we do NOT teach real reading in first grade, "reading" must remain at the top of the curriculum all through school, even, incredibly, in college!

In our classrooms we DO spent a good part of the day teaching so-called "reading comprehension." Yet that is not teaching "reading" but is only an abject exercise in futility since "reading comprehension" is only IQ plus attention, and IQ is unteachable. The motivation for engaging in this idiocy is the "silent reading comprehension test" on which schools MUST show "good" scores. So let's replace these "silent reading comprehension tests" with REAL reading tests, oral reading accuracy tests, to find out how bad our reading problem really is. Maybe then we can dump all those basal reading books that caused our problem and go back to teaching real reading with available texts like Lippincott's or Open Court or Alpha One or any of the other good phonics programs on the Reading Reform Foundation list in Scottsdale, Arizona.

Yet, if there is no good phonics program available for a classroom, rather than to continue with these monstrous present-day sight-word readers, I suggest, in all seriousness, that it would be far better to hand a first-grade teacher just a piece of chalk and a blackboard and to ask her to teach reading by using her own common sense.

ADDITION TO THE CASE FOR THE PROSECUTION
As of March 20, 1982

*T*he *Measuring Scale for Ability in Spelling* by Leonard P. Ayres (1915) appeared in two parts. One was the text section explaining the scale, and the other was a large, printed sheet with the scale itself. I was not able to get the scale (part 2) by interlibrary loan from Columbia Teachers College but was able to get the first part from Columbia, and it did list the words tested and the norms on them, based on tests given to 70,000 children in 84 American cities in 1914 and 1915.

Ayres' showed that 99% of children in mid-.third grade could spell these words in dictated spelling tests:

the, in, so, no, now, man, ten, bed, top.

At mid-fourth grade, 99% of American children could spell these words:

by, have, are, had, over, must, make, school, street, say, come, hand, ring, live, kill, late, let, big, mother, three, land, cold, hot, hat, child, ice, play, sea.

At mid-sixth grade, 99% of American children could spell these words:

became, brother, rain, keep, start, mail, eye, glass, party, upon, two, they, would, any, could, should, city, only, where, week, first, sent, mile, seem, even, without, afternoon, Friday, hour, wife, state, July, head, story, open, short, lady, reach, better, water, round, cost, price, become, class, horse, care, try, move, delay, pound, behind, around, burn, camp, bear, clear, clean, spell, poor, finish, hurt, maybe, across, tonight, tenth, sir, these, club, seen, felt, full, fail, set, stamp, light, coming, cent, night, pass, shut, easy.

See the previous comment on Ayres' 1909 study which showed that the vast majority of American school children of that period were in the right grade or only a year behind or above for their age, and virtually none were more than two years behind. Since children were generally forced to stay in school until age 14 in 1915, these 6th grade spelling scores should represent most children near sixth-grade age in America in 1915 except the retarded children.

At mid-eighth grade, 99% of American children could spell these words:

eight, afraid, uncle, rather, comfort, elect, aboard, jail, shed, retire, refuse, district restrain, royal, objection, pleasure, navy, fourth, population, proper, judge, weather, worth, contain, figure, sudden, forty, instead, throw, personal, everything, rate, chief, perfect, second, slide, farther, duty, intend, company, quite, none, knew, remain, direct, appear, liberty, enough, fact, board, September, station, attend, between, public, friend, during, through, police, until, madam, truly, whole, address, request, raise, August, Tuesday, struck, getting, don't, Thursday.

Except in rare cases, children who can spell words correctly in dictated spelling tests can read the same words. It is obvious that America had NO reading problem, as we know it with our high functional illiteracy now, back in 1914 and 1915.

About 1920, Ayres' spelling scale was well known, so its total disappearance from current literature is bizarre. I first heard of it from a few paragraphs in the 1938 book, *Psychology of Elementary School Subjects* by William Henry Gray (NOT William Scott Gray). In the 1957 book, *Introduction to Educational Measurement*, Victor H Noll said that Ayres' handwriting scale had been one of the most widely used scales ever made, with 600,000 copies prepared from 1917 to 1935. Yet it is obvious that Noll had never heard of Ayres' SPELLING scale, particularly since Noll made a point of referring to the Rice spelling scale, based on testing 33,000 children in 1895-96. Noll said, "...the significance of (Rice's) contributions is not always fully appreciated."

It was only from Noll's book that I learned of the existence of the once famous Rice scale, on which E. L. Thorndike himself wrote at great length in the *Teachers College Record* of 1901. But in Noll's 1957 book he did refer to the fact that Thorndike's student, B. R. Buckingham, prepared a spelling scale in 1913. Noll obviously did not know the further fact that, in 1919, Buckingham prepared an extension to Ayres scale. In 1914, William Scott Gray received his master's degree in oral reading tests directly under Thorndike's supervision, the year after Buckingham received his, and in 1915 Arthur Irving Gates started to study for his Ph. D. under Thorndike.[9]

---

9 Editor's Note in 2006: *The Measuring Scale for Ability in Spelling* by Leonard P. Ayres (1915) was republished in 1985 by Mott Media, Milford, Michigan. However, Mott's edition did not publish the scale separately from the text, but the data appears at the end of the text. (A copy of the original scale, a large, folded sheet, is available at the New York Public Library which has both the text and the scale. I saw several copies of the text at the Harvard libraries and several copies at the University of Chicago library. I believe, but am not sure, that the scale was inserted in those Harvard and University of Chicago copies.) Overall, Mott Media did a very nice job, although the book is different in appearance (but not in content) from the original. However, the Preface attributed to me was not written by me. I had sent Mr. Mott a longer preface, and, instead of using it, he had someone on his staff try to summarize my material. That summary is inaccurate in places and flatly wrong in other places. My name was signed to that erroneous summary even though I had never seen it.

BIBLIOGRAPHY

Adam, Nicolas.

Vraie Maniere d'apprendre une langue quelconque. *"Nouvelle maniere d'apprendre à lire aux enfants sans leur parler de lettres et de syllabes."* Paris, 1787.

Alpha Time and Alpha One Reading Program, by Elaine Reiss and Rita Friedman. Arista Corporation, Concord, California. 1970's. The program with the "Letter People."

Arnauld, Antoine.

Grammaire generale of Port Royal, France, VI (concerning Pascal's phonics). 1664.

Ayres, Leonard Porter.

The Binet-Simon Measuring Scale Intelligence: Some Criticisms and Suggestions, The Psychological Clinic, November 15, 1911. Reprinted by Russell Sage Foundation, New York, 1912.

The Public Schools of Springfield, Illinois. The Russell Sage Foundation, New York, 1914.

A Measuring Scale for Ability in Spelling, The Russell Sage Foundation, New York, 1915. p.58.

"A Review of the New Ayres Spelling Scale. "Educational Writings," Elementary School Journal, September, 1915.

The Cleveland School Survey, Summary Volume. Cleveland Foundation, Cleveland, Ohio, 1917.

Barnard, Henry B.

American Journal of Education. Articles from 1856 to 1864:

"Thomas Hopkins Gallaudet," by Henry Barnard. May, 1856.

"Letters to a Young Teacher," Gideon F. Thayer, 1857.

"Cyrus Peirce," 1857.

"Cultivation of the Reflective Faculties," 1857.

"Johann Bernhard Basedow and the Philanthropinum," translated for the American Journal of Education from the German of Karl von Raumer. 1857.

"Horace Mann," Abstract from Livingston Law Journal, December, 1858.

"John Locke," translated from the German of Karl von Raumer. 1859.

"Pestalozzi." 1859.

"Subjects and Methods of Early Education (Scotland Training College)." 1860.

"Quintilian." 1864.

"A-B-C Books and Primers." 1865.

"Catechism on Methods of Teaching," translated from Diesterweg's Almanac for 1855 and 1856 (printed in the 1865-66 Journal."

"Primary Instruction by Object Lessons of the City of Oswego, New York." 1865. (Establishes that what was called "phonics" there was only partial, supplemental phonic analysis of sight words.)

Barnum, Edith C.

"Reading," Teachers College Record, New York, January and September, 1906.

Bartusiak, Marcia.

"Beeper Man - A Thought Provoking Experiment with Some Signal Results." Discover the Newsmagazine of Science, page 57, November, 1980, Chicago, Illinois. (Reports on the work of Eric Klinger of the University of Minnesota on relative degrees of concentration or inattention to the matter at hand.)

Basedow, Johann Bernhard

The New Method, 1752.

Elementary Work, Dessau, 1774.

New Assistant for the Teaching of Reading for the Knowledge of God and for Necessary Correctness in Language, Hamburg, 1785.

Betts, Emmett Albert

An Index of Professional Literature on Reading and Related Topics (with Thelma Marshall Betts), American Book Company, New York, 1945.

Foundations of Reading Instruction, American Book Company, New York, 1946.

The Betts Basic Readers (with Carolyn M. Welch), American Book Company, New York, 1948. Revised 1963, and earlier.

Betts, George Herbert.

The Mind and Its Education, D. Appleton and Company, New York, 1906.

Outlines for Schools in Iowa, 1915.

Bobbs-Merrill Reading Series, Primer to Grade 6 (With Clara Baker), Indianapolis, 1923

Biographical Dictionary of American Educators, Edited by John F. Ohles, Greenwood Press, Westport, Connecticut, 1978. [10]

Includes biographies on Leonard Porter Ayres, Henry Barnard,

---

10 [Editor's note in 2006: This is an updated version of material originally prepared by the extraordinary publisher, C. W. Bardeen, Editor of *The School Bulletin*, published in Syracuse, New York from 1874 to 1920, which is of great historical interest, and also the publisher of *The Sentence Method of Teaching Reading*, by George L. Farnham. It is apparent, however, that Bardeen had no interest in or knowledge about beginning reading.]

Emmett A. Betts, George Herbert Betts, James McKeen Cattell, Stuart Appleton Courtis, John Dewey, Thomas Hopkins Gallaudet, Arthur I . Gates, William S. Gray, Joseph Mayer Rice, Nila Banton Smith, and Henry Suzzallo.

Biographie Universelle, J. F. Michaud, 1954. Republished by Akademisch Druckuverlagsanstalt , Graz , Austria.

Black, Hillel

The American Schoolbook, Mentioned in Samuel L. Blumenfeld's The New Illiterates, Arlington House, New Rochelle, New York, 1978

Blewett, John, S. J.

John Dewey, His Thought and Influence, Fordham University Press, New York, 1960.

Bloomfield, Leonard and Barnhart, Clarence L.

Let's Read - A Linguistic Approach, Wayne State University Press, 1961.

Blumenfeld, Samuel.

"Abirt ca folner sett Lindexh. To Many Bostonians, Everything Reads This Way - Thanks to the School System", Boston, November, 1978.

The New Illiterates, Arlington House, New Rochelle, New York, 1973.

Board of Supervisors for the Public Schools of Boston.

Method of Teaching Reading in the Primary Schools, An undated thirty-page brochure. Mitford Matthews, in Teaching to Read, Historically Considered, 1966, considered that this brochure contained Colonel Parker's ideas about reading.[11]

---

11 [Editor's note in 2006: As stated earlier, the author of this material could not have been Parker as he was incapable of writing lucidly, and this material is very lucid.]

Bogdanov, V. P.

Ot Azbukilvana Fedorovado Sovremennaug Bukvaria (Russian Primers, 1574-1974), 238 pages, Library of Congress Number Z 1033 H 8073, 1974. This book is available at the Library of Congress, Washington, D.C. It is a very large, white-leatherette-covered, coffee-table-type book with gold lettering and beautiful colored illustrations, but un-translated and apparently unknown to the American reading instruction community as of June, 1980, when I saw it at the Library of Congress. Obviously, if they had known of it, at least a part should have been available in translated form by that time, since it was stamped as received on March 17, 1975. In Admiral Rickover's book, Education and Freedom (1959), on page 44, he stated that the Russians had an excellent translating and abstracting service. He said it is so efficient and rapid that all major foreign technical articles reach the desks of every Soviet scientist in the field concerned in a few weeks after publication in their own countries. Yet, more than FIVE YEARS after reaching this country, this source book for American reading instruction languished, apparently untouched by reading experts, in our Library of Congress. I had portions translated at my own expense.

Bond, G. L. and Cuddy, M. C. (and others)

The Developmental Reading Series, Lyons and Carnahan, Chicago, 1950. Revised 1962.

Bond, Guy L. and Tinker, Miles A.

Reading Difficulties, Their Diagnosis and Correction, Third Edition, 1973. Prentice-Hall, Inc., Englewood Cliffs, New Jersey.

Borel-Maisonny, Suzanne

"Les Troubles du Langage dans les Dyslexies et les

Dysorthographies," <u>Enfance Magazine</u>, Paris, 1951 (On page 402, uses the term "psycho-linguistique," some years before either Goodman or Smith, apparently.)

Boscher, M.; V. Boscher; J. Chapron; and M. J. Carre

Methode Boscher de "La Journee des Tout Petits" reprinted by Oberthus at Rennes, 1974. (Phonics on syllables in words, and short sentences. Stories at end of book. Received Bronze Medal at Brussels International Exposition in 1958, apparently for excellence as a primer.)

Bowden, Josephine Horton

"Learning to Read," <u>Elementary School Journal,</u> September, 1911.

Braslavsky, Berta Pereistein de

<u>The Dispute on Reading Methods</u>, Editorial Kapelusz, S. A., Buenos Aires, Argentina, 1962. (Pages 10 to 17)

Brown, Herbert A.

"The Measurement of the Efficiency of Instruction in Reading", <u>Elementary School Journal</u>, June, 1914.

Brunswick Journal, Germany, 1788- 1789.

Editors: Campe, Struve, Trapp and Heusinger.

Buisson, Benjamin

<u>Enseignement Primaire a l'Exposition Columbienne de Chicago</u>, 1892. Pages 208-209. Librairie Hachette et Cie., Paris, 1896.

Buisson, Ferdinand

<u>Rapport sur L'Instruction Primaire a l'Exposition Universelle de Vienne en 1873</u>, Paris.

<u>Rapport sur L'Instruction Primaire a l"Exposition Universelle de Philadelphie en 1876</u>, Imprimerie Nationale, Paris, 1878.

<u>Dictionnaire de Pedagogie et d'Instruction Primaire</u>, Librairie Hachette et Cie., Paris, 1887.

Includes theseArticles: First Part: Lecture; Pascal, Blaise;

Pascal, Jacqueline; Epee, l'Abbe de l'; Epellation; Heinicke, Samuel; Olivier, Louis-Henri-Ferdinand; Philanthropinisme ; Sourds-Muets; Trapp, Ernest-Christian; Vogel , Jean-Charles-Christophe; Wolke, Christian-Henri; Bibliographie (de Pedagogie) Ecriture; Ecriture-Lecture; Edgeworth, Richard Lovell; Edgeworth, Maria; Supplement to Part I: Gedike, Frederic; Herbault; Second Part: Lecture; Pascal, Blaise.

Bunte Fibel

Hermann Schroedel Verlag, KG, Hanover, Berlin, Darmstadt, and Dortrnund, 1976. (German Analytic-Synthetic Primer, with Heavy Phonics.)

Buswell, Guy T.

Fundamental Reading Habits A Study of Their Development, Supplementary Education Monographs No. 21, The University of Chicago Press, Chicago, 1922.

The Silent Reading Hour (A Reading Series with William H. Wheeler), Wheeler Publishing Co., Chicago, 1923.

Caesar,F. B.

Zo Veilig. Leren Lezen, Uitgeverij Zwijsen bv, Tilburg, The Netherlands, 1976.

(Heavy analytic phonics after a very heavy beginning global approach for about the first three months, called the Structuuremethode.)

Bureau of Education, Washington, D. C.

Circulars of Information No. 1, School Systems in the United States, by John D. Philbrick, Washington, D.C., 1885.

Circulars of Information No. 2, Teachers Institutes, Washington, D. C., 1885

The Catholic Encyclopedia

The Encyclopedia Press, Inc., New York, 1913; Robert Appleton Company, 1909. (Articles: Analysis; Education of the Deaf and Dumb; Port Royal)

Cattell, James McKeen
"The Time It Takes to See and Name Objects", <u>Mind,</u> Vol. 11, pp. 63-65, 1886. (In 1921, Cattell founded the Psychological Corporation, currently at 757 Third Avenue, New York. It publishes many psychological tests today.)

Cherry, Laurence
"Can the Brain Understand the Brain?" <u>Family Weekly</u>, New York, November 9, 1980.

Chall, Jeanne S.
<u>Learning to Read: The Great Debate</u>, McGraw-Hill Book Company, New York, 1967.

Cornett, R. Orin
"What Is Cued Speech?", <u>Gallaudet Today</u>, Winter/1974-75, Volume 5, Number 2.
"Deafness and Reading - A New Approach", <u>The Reading Informer</u>, Scottsdale, Arizona, October, 1979.

Courtis, S. A.
<u>Then and Now in Education</u> (with Otis W. Caldwell), 1924.
<u>Picture Story Reading Lessons</u> (With Nila Banton Smith), 1920, World Book Company, Yonkers/Chicago, 1926.

Cunningham, Walter F., S. J.
<u>Notes on Epistemology</u>, Fordham University Press, New York, 1930.

Currier, Lillian Beatrice and Olive C. Duguid, Franklin, New Hampshire
"Phonics or No Phonics," <u>Elementary School Journal,</u> December, 1916.

Current Biography, H. W. Wilson Co., New York, 1941.
Article on E. L. Thorndike.

A Cyclopedia of Education, Edited by Paul Monroe, New York.
Vol. 1, 1911: Articles - Johann Heinrich (sic) Basedow (by

FM);

Campe, Joachim Heinrich (no author); Samuel Heinicke (by FM);

Thomas Hopkins Gallaudet (By Will S. Monroe, Montclair State Normal, N. J.)

Deaf, Education of the (author missing)

Vol. 3, 1913: Article - Teaching Beginners Reading (Henry Suzzallo)

Vol. 4, 1913: Article - Spelling, Teaching of (Henry Suzzallo)

Daniels, J. C. and Hunter Diack

The Royal Road Readers, Chatto & Windus, Ltd ., London, 1962.

Delaunay, Py-Poulain

Methode du sieur Py-Poulain de Launay, ou l'art d'aprendre lire le francois et le latin, Nicolas le Clerc et Jean Francois Herissant, Paris, MDCCXIX.

den Hollander, S., G. P. L. Steenwinkel, Tjits Veenstra

Leesfeest, Dijkstra's Uitgeverij Zeist bv, The Netherlands, 1976. (Effectively an analytic-synthetic phonics primer.)

Dewey, John.

School and Society, 1899.

"The Primary Education Fetich" (sic), Forum, Vol. XXV, p. 315, 328. (Dewey opposed using the period from 6 to 8 years of age to learn to read and write. In Popular Science Monthly, January, 1899 (the magazine owned after 1900 by Dewey's friend, James McKeen Cattell,) G. W. T. Patrick wrote an article, "Should Children Under Ten Learn to Read and Write?" in which Patrick had concluded, "No." Dewey had given the same general opinion in New York Teachers' Monographs, November, 1898, for children up to eight years of age.)

Dictionnaire Biographique et Bibliographique, By A. Dantes, Paris, 1875.

Dottrens, Robert.
Au Seuil de la Culture, les Editions du Scarabee, Paris , 1965.

Downing, John and Faith Graham.
The Downing Readers, Initial Teaching Publishing Co., Ltd., London, 1964.

Downing, John
Comparative Reading, The Macmillan Company, New York, 1973.

Particular Chapters by Franz Biglmaier, Germany; D.B. Elkonin, USSR; and Berta Perelstein de Braslavsky, Argentina.

Dumas
La Bibliotheque des Enfans, France, 1733. Three volumes, the first explaining his Bureau Typographique, the second l'abecedaire Latin, and the third l'abecedaire Francais.

Edgeworth, Maria and Richard Lovell Edgeworth
Essays on Practical Education, Ireland, 1798.

Eiter, Hans, Adolf Luchner and Hermann Gritsch
Komm, Wir Wollen Lesen und Schreiben, Verlag Leitner & Co., Wels , Vienna, Austria, about 1976. (A synthetic phonics approach in this primer.)

Elementary School Journal, University of Chicago, Chicago, Illinois.
"Educational Writings - Current Tendencies in the Construction of Spelling Books for Elementary Schools." 1918.

"Book Reviews: on A Cyclopedia of Education," 1911.

Elson, William H.
Elson-Runkel Primer, Scott, Foresman and Company, Chicago, 1914.

Encyclopaedia Brittannica, Inc., William Benton, Publishers, Chicago, 1962.

Biographies: Johann Bernhard Basedow; James McKeen Cattell, Etienne Bonnot de Condillac; John Dewey; Denis Diderot; Baron Friedrich Meichior Grimm; Charles Hubbard Judd; William James; John Locke; Jean Jacques Rousseau; E.L. Thorndike.

Articles: Accent, Alphabet, Consciousness, Logogram-syllabary, Pragmatism, Psychology

Encyclopedia of Education, Macmillan, New York, 1971.

Biography on E.L. Thorndike by G. J. Clifford.

Encyclopedia of Modern Education, Philosophical Library, Inc. (Printed by F. Hubner & Co., Inc. New York, 1943.

Editor: Harry N. Rivlin, Department of Education, Queens College; Associate Editor, Herbert Schueler, Department of Education, Queens College; Advisory Board: Dean Harold Benjamin, University of Maryland; Dean Francis M. Crowley, Fordham University; Prof. William F. Cunningham, University of Notre Dame; Dean Frank N. Freeman, School of Education, University of California; Prof. I. L. Kandel, Teachers College, Columbia University; Prof. William H. Kilpatrick, Pres., Teachers College, Columbia University; Paul Klapper, Queens College; Prof. Edward L. Thorndike, Teachers College, Columbia University.

Contains articles by the reading expert, Albert J. Harris. Harris's articles in this encyclopedia include "Phonics", "Reading", "Eye Movements", "Reading Interests", "Reading Readiness", "Reading Vocabulary" and "Reading - Methods of Teaching." In the last article, the statement appears:

"Systematic phonic methods have also fallen into

146

disfavor for teaching beginners because they tend to emphasize the mechanics of reading at the expense of comprehension and promote habits of excessive vocalization which later interfere with the development of speed and fluency in silent reading. Phonics (q.v.) is generally taught as a supplementary rather than as a basic technique in word recognition."

Under "Phonics," this statement is included:

"Phonic readiness is usually developed by giving practice in finding words that rhyme, words that begin with the same sound, etc. Letter sounds and phonograms are introduced by pointing out similarities and differences in words that have already been learned as wholes."

These comments by an authority in 1943 indicate that "intrinsic phonics" was the prevailing method by that date. (See other entries under A. J. Harris in this bibliography.)

Yet the idea of "intrinsic phonics" was first discussed in Arthur I. Gates' June, 1925, article in the Elementary School Journal, "The Supplementary Device Versus the Intrinsic Method of Teaching Reading." The article was a reprint of a speech Gates had given at the February, 1925, Cincinnati meeting of the National Society for the Study of Education. At that meeting, Part 1 of the society's 24th Yearbook had been discussed, "The Report of the National Committee on Reading". The committee's chairman had been William S. Gray.

Arthur Irving Gates indicated in a letter of November, 1965, to Dr. Jeanne Chall, which letter she quoted in her book, Learning to Read: The Great Debate, that he believed that most teachers were using very heavy phonics in the decade from 1920 to 1930. Gray's inrinsic phonics readers were published in 1930, and Gates's in 1931. So, American schools shifted from VERY HEAVY PHONICS IN 1930 BY Gates' own testimony, to almost exclusive use of the newly invented "intrinsic phonics" some time before the 1943 Encyclopedia of Modern Education article.

Encyclopedie ou Dictionnaire Raissonne des Sciences, des Arts et des Metiers, by Denis Diderot et al, 28 volumes. Published from 1751 to 1772 in France.

Fassett, James H. and Charles H. Norton

The Beacon Readers, Ginn and Company, Boston, 1912.

Flesch, Rudolf

Why Johnny Can't Read - And What You Can Do About It, Harper & Row, New York, 1955.

Why Johnny Still Can't Read - A New Look at the Scandal of Our Schools, Harper & Row, New York, 1981.

Feitelson, Dina

Cross-Cultural Perspectives on Reading and Reading Research, International Reading Association, Newark, Delaware, 1978. Article by Stella S. F. Liu, "Decoding and Comprehension in Reading Chinese;" Article by C. K. Leong, "Learning to Read in English and Chinese: Some Psycholinguistic and Cognitive Considerations."

Freeman, Frank N., Grace E. Storm, Eleanor M. Johnson and W. C. French.

Child-Story Readers, Lyons & Carnahan, Chicago, 1927-28.

Freeman, Frank N.

"Educational Writings - Reviews and Book Notes - Arithmetic and the New Psychology," Elementary School Journal, June, 1922. A Review of Edward L. Thorndike's The Psychology of Arithmetic.

Freinet, Elise

Naissance d'une Pedagogie Populaire, François Maspero,

Paris, 1949.

Fries, Charles. C.

Linguistics and Reading, Holt, Rinehart and Winston, Inc., New York, 1962.

Fries, Charles C., Agnes D. Fries, Rosemary Wilson, and Mildred K. Randolph.

A Basic Reading Series Based Upon Linguistic Principles, Charles E. Merrill, Columbus, Ohio, 1965.

Fuller, Sarah.

Illustrated Primer, D. C. Heath & Co., Boston, 1898.

Gallaudet, Reverend T. H.

The Mother's Primer, Daniel Burgess & Co., Hartford, Connecticut, 1835.

The Child's Picture Defining and Reading Book, 1830. It carries this notation on the copyright page, according to Samuel Blumenfeld: "This little volume, although originally prepared for the Deaf and will be found to be equally adapted to the instruction of other children..."

Gates, Arthur I.

Psychology of Reading and Spelling with Special Reference to Disability. Contributions to Education, No 129. Bureau of Publications, Teachers College, Columbia, New York, New York, 1922.

"A Test of Ability in the Pronunciation of Words," Teachers College Record, Teachers College, Columbia University, New York, 1924.

"Problems in Beginning Reading, "Teachers College Record, Teachers College, Columbia University, New York, March, 1925.

"The Supplementary Versus the Intrinsic Method of Teaching Reading," Elementary School Journal. University of Chicago, Chicago, Illinois, June, 1925.

"Flash Card Exercises in Reading," <u>Teachers College Record,</u> Teachers College, Columbia University, December, 1925.

"A Series of Tests for the Measurement and Diagnosis of Reading Ability in Grades 3 to 8", <u>Teachers College Record,</u> Teachers College , Columbia University, New York, September, 1926.

<u>New Methods in Primary Reading,</u> Bureau of Publications, Teachers College, Columbia University, 1928.

<u>Interest and Ability in Reading</u> , The Macmillan Company, New York, 1930.

<u>The Work-Play Books</u> (with Miriam B. Huber) (Primer through Grade 3), The Macmillan Company, New York, 1930. (Only the primer was published in 1930, and the rest in 1931).

"The Child's Reading Steps Made Easier," <u>New York Times,</u> March 27, 1932.

"Types of Materials, Vocabulary Burden, Word Analysis, and Other Factors in Beginning Reading," (With David H. Russell), <u>Elementary School Journal,</u> University of Chicago, Chicago, Illinois, 1938. (p. 27-35, p. 119-128, Vol. 39.)

<u>Methods of Determining Reading Readiness</u> (With Guy L. Bond and David H. Russell), Bureau of Publications, Teachers College, Columbia University, New York, 1939.

"Vocabulary Control in Basal Reading Material", <u>Reading Teacher,</u> November, 1961.

"The Word Recognition... of Second and Third Grade Children", <u>Reading Teacher,</u> 1962.

Gilmore, John V.

<u>Gilmore Oral Reading Test,</u> World Book Company, 1952. (Compare its norms in 1952 to Gray's oral test data on his Ph. D. thesis in 1917.)

Goodman, Kenneth S.

"A Psycholinguistic Guessing Game," Journal of the Reading Specialist, May, 1967.

Grashey, H. v.,

"Uber Aphasie Und Ihre Beziehungen Zur Wahrnehmung," Arch f. Psychiatrie u. Nervenkrankheiten, 12 (1885)

Gray, William Henry

Psychology of Elementary School Subjects, Prentice-Hall, Inc., New York, 1938.

Gray, William Scott

"Reading in the Elementary Schools of Indianapolis, III, Elementary School Journal, University of Chicago, Chicago, Illinois, March 1919. (Reporting on 1917 Survey.)

Studies of Elementary School Reading through Standardized Tests. Supplementary Educational Monographs, Vol. I, No. 1. Department of Education, University of Chicago, Illinois, 1917. (From his Ph. D. Dissertation.)

Summary of Investigations Relating to Reading, Supplementary Education Monographs, No. 28, The University of Chicago Press, 1925.

The Curriculum Foundation Program (by Wm. S. Gray and Others), Scott, Foresman and Company, Chicago, 1927 (according to Nila Banton Smith). Many revisions to 1965.

The Teaching of Reading and Writing: An International Survey, Scott, Foresman and Company, Chicago, 1956.

Great Soviet Encyclopedia, Vol. 4, The Macmillan Company, New York, 1974.

"Primer," page 423.

Gregory, C. A.

"The Reading Vocabularies of Third Grade Children," Journal of Educational Research, February, 1923.

Grimm, Baron Friedrich Melchior

Correspondence Litteraire, Published every other week in France from 1753 to 1773, to which Denis Diderot contributed. 16 volumes were bound and published in 1882.

Gueraud, 0. and Jouguet, P.

Un Livre d'Ecolier du IIIe Siecle Avant Jesus Christ, Publications de la Societe Royal Egyptienne de Papyrologie, Textes et Documents, II, Cairo, 1938.

Hall, G. Stanley

Educational Problems , Appleton and Co., New York , 1911.

Hamaide, Amelie, Collaborator with Dr. Ovide Decroly

The Decroly Class (Translated from the French), E. P. Dutton, New York. (1924?)

Harris, Albert J.

See entry under Encyclopedia of Modern Education, as well as entries below.

Harris, Albert J., Mae Knight Clark, and Others

The Macmillan Reading Program, The Macmillan Company, New York, 1965

Harris, Albert J., and Edward R. Sipay

How to Increase Reading Ability, 1940. Revised Editions to 1975. David McKay Company, Inc., 750 Third Avenue, New York 10017

Harris, J. H. and Anderson, H. W.

Measuring Primary Reading in the Dubuque Schools (Dubuque, Iowa), Ginn & Co., Boston, 1916. (See page 17 of Elementary School Journal, September, 1916, which reports on the superior results from the Beacon phonics of Ginn over the sentence methods of the Horace Mann Readers and the Aldine Readers)

Heartman, Charles F.

Bibliographical Check-list of the New England Primer, Third

Edition, 1934.

Heinicke, Samuel

Hanoverian Magazine ,1773, page 1485. The Biographie Universelle of J. F. Michaud, 1854, said, "Le Magasin Hanoverien, 1773, p. 1485, had published instruction on the manner of suggesting to deaf-mutes abstract ideas, and to teach them in very little time to read and to speak aloud."

Hildreth, Gertrude

"How Russian Children Learn to Read," The Reading Teacher, December, 1959.

Hilliard, G. S. and I. J. Campbell

The Second Reader for Primary Schools, Leigh's Pronouncing Edition, Brewer and Tileston, Boston, 1868.

The Horace Mann Readers, Longmans, Green and Company (about 1912)

Horn, Ernest and Grace Shields

The Learn to Study Readers, Ginn & Co., Boston, 1924.

The Houghton Mifflin Reading Series By William K. Durr, et al. Editorial Advisor: Paul McKee. Boston, 1976.

Huey, Edmund Burke

The Psychology and Pedagogy of Reading, The Macmillan Company, New York, 1908; The MIT Press, Cambridge, Massachusetts, 1968.

The New Iowa Spelling Scale State University of Iowa, Iowa City, 1954.

Johnson, Mary

Programmed Illiteracy in Our Schools, Clarity Books, Winnipeg, 1970.

Judd, Charles Hubbard

"Book Reviews," Elementary School Journal, June 1914, reviewing Edward L. Thorndike's Educational Psychology of 1913.

Reading, Its Nature and Development, The University of Chicago, 1918. (Reporting on work undertaken as a result of a grant by the General Education Board in June, 1915.)

Juredieu, J. and E. Mourlevat

Remi et Colette, Premier Livret, Editions Magnard, 122, Bld. Saint-Germain, Paris 6. 1975. (Entitled a mixed method but after 20 sight words in the first five lessons is an analytic-synthetic phonic method, Code 6, in my judgment.)

Kandel, I. L.

"Education and Social Disorder," Teachers College Record, Teachers College, Columbia University, New York, February, 1933.

Conflicting Theories of Education, Russell & Russell, New York, 1938. (Pages 108-9)

Kooreman, Dr. H. J.

Letterstad (with a "Letter Village"), Holland, early 1970's. A multi-sensory synthetic phonics program adapted from programs Dr. Kooreman saw while in Russia. Dr. Kooreman is with Pedagogisch Centrum Enshede in the Netherlands.

Lamport, Harold Boyne

A History of Teaching Beginning Reading, Ph. D. Dissertation, Department of Education, University of Chicago, 1935. Dr. W. S. Gray said, in The Teaching of Reading and Writing, in a footnote on page 76, that Boyne's dissertation was prepared under his supervision.

The Laubach Literacy News

A Quarterly Publication of Laubach Literacy International, Box 131, Syracuse, New York, 13210. Robert S. Laubach, President.

Leselehrgang des Padagogischen Zentrums - Materialien fur den Erst-Leseunterricht

Published by Verlag Julius Beltz, Weinhein, Berlin, Basel. I observed this as taught in a first grade Hamburg classroom in November, 1977, but did not test any class at second which used it. It was a global approach equivalent to American sight word readers without the concept of high-frequency words. (Published about 1971. The first grade teacher said he had been using it about five years.)

Lionni, Paolo and Lance J. Klass

The Leipzig Connection, Heron Books, Portland, Oregon , 1980.

J. B. Lippincott Company

Basic Reading Series, by Dr. Charles C. Walcutt and Dr. Glenn McCracken, 1963, revised 1975.

Locke, John

An Essay Concerning Humane Understanding, England, 1690.

Thoughts Concerning Education, England, 1693.

The London Times, Times Educational Supplement, London, England.

Letters to the Editor. Hunter Diack on May 7, 1954. J. C. Gagg on May 14, 1954, and the letter following. Frank Whitehead on May 21, 1954. (Originally listed in W. S. Gray's The Teaching of Reading and Writing, in a footnote on page 84. Diack's letter was titled, "First Steps in Reading: Phonics the Key." Gagg answered, "First Steps in Reading: Present Practice," and Whitehead, "Rival Reading Methods: Question of Timing." Gray did not refer to the letter which followed Gagg's, reading "...At first it is easy to know the words by the shapes. Bits of the shapes do not seem to do much. Other bits seem to do one thing one time and another thing another time. Look-and-say helps at first. Soon the boys and girls go mad..."

Makita, Kiyoshi

"The Rarity of Reading Disability in Japanese Children,"

American Journal of Orthopsychiatry, p. 599-614, July 1968.

Mann, Horace A.

Seventh Annual Report of the Board of Education, Together with the Seventh Annual Report of the Secretary of the Board . Boston, 1844.

(This brought on a violent answer, the "Remarks "of 31 schoolmasters.)

Reply to the "Remarks" of Thirty-one Schoolmasters, Boston, 1844.

(Mann's answer brought on the "Rejoinder" from the 31 schoolmasters.)

Reply to the Rejoinder to the "Reply" of the Hon. Horace Mann....,1844.

(Following this, the Boston schoolmasters published Penitential Tears, or a Cry from the Dust by the Thirty-one Prostrated and Pulverized by the Hand of Horace Mann, 1845.)

(Blumenfeld published much of this material in his book, The New Illiterates. It is also discussed in an appendix to the Walcutt-Lamport-McCracken text, Teaching Reading, a Phonic/Linguistic Approach to Developmental Reading.)

Marrou, H. I.

A History of Education in Antiquity, Paris, 1948. Mentor Books, New York, 1964.

Martin, Francis

Syllabaire Illustre, Brussels, Belgium, 1974. (Heavy phonics on syllables in words and stories.)

Mathews, Mitford

Teaching to Read, Historically Considered, The University of Chicago Press, Chicago 1966.

Mazurkiewicz, Albert J. and Harold J. Tanyzer

Early-to-Read i/t/a Program, i/t/a Publications, Inc., New York, 1963.

McCall, William A. and Lelah Mae Crabbs

"Standard Test Lessons in Reading," Teachers College Record, Teachers College, Columbia University, New York, November, 1925.

McDowell, Reverend John B.

"The Phonetic Method of Teaching Children to Read", The Catholic Educational Review, October, 1953. Pages 506-519.

McGuffey's Revised Eclectic Readers (Second Major Edition), 1879-1881

Henry H. Vail, Editor, Van Antwerp, Bragg & Co., Cincinnati, Ohio

McGuffey's Primer - The Eclectic Series

"Entered according to the Act of Congress in the year 1849 by W. B. Smith... District of Ohio," and "in the year 1867 by Sargent, Wilson & Hinkle... for the Southern District of Ohio." This was a sight-word primer.

McGuffey Readers (Original Series 1836-38, Republished 1982 by Mott Media, Milford, Mich.) McGuffey, William Holmes, Editor, and Alexander Hamilton McGuffey, published by Truman and Smith, Cincinnati, Ohio. This was a sight-word reading series but its 1838 spelling book by Alexander Hamilton McGuffey used phonics.

McNally, J. and W. Murray

Key Words to Literacy, Schoolmaster Publishing Co., Ltd., London. Discussed in The Ladybird Key Words Reading Scheme - Notes for Teachers, 1969, Wills & Hepworth, Ltd., Loughborough, Leicestershire, England. Reportedly also reviewed in "Educational Psychologist", Teachers

World, May 25, 1962.

Medici, Angela

L'Education Nouvelle, Presses Universitaires de France, Paris, 1940, 1948.

Messmer, Oskar.

"Zur Psychologie des Lesens bei Kinder und Erwachsenen", Archiv fur die Gesamte Psychologie, December, 1903, Bd. II, H. 2. u. 3, pp. 190—298.

National Society for the Study of Education

Yearbooks from 1914 to 1949.

New York Post

"Let's get the truth about reading tests." Editorial, June 15, 1981.

Noll, Victor H.

Introduction to Educational Measurement, Houghton Mifflin Company, Boston, 1957.

Nu laser vi A

Borrman Matthis Salminen Wigforss, A. W. Laromedel, Stockholm, Sweden, 1976. (Highly phonic primer. Its effect was weakened to a greater or lesser extent in some classes by the adoption of what is called LTG, an experience chart approach to reading, where children copy sight words and keep them in their own little file boxes, studying the alphabet from the sight words that appear in class experience stories. This text was still mandatory in all Swedish classes, as of 1977-78. The LTG method is reportedly greatly praised in teachers' journals, yet I heard it sharply criticized by several Swedish teachers, although some others used it. One said the LTG method "was not good for teaching reading." Another said, "I do not like it at all. I do not use LTG. " I found, where it was in use, a typical profile comparing LTG scores to Nu laser scores, lower accuracy in oral reading, far greater reversals, slower speed, and the effect on comprehension noted elsewhere: higher than one phonic class, but averaging lower the two best phonics classes. I tested five classes in Sweden: two LTG and three <u>Nu laser</u> emphasis, although all had to use <u>Nu laser</u> to some extent, so all were highly phonic classes compared to American sight-word basal readers.)

O'Hern, Joseph P., Assistant Superintendent of Schools, Rochester, New York

"Practical Application of Standard Tests in Spelling, Language and Arithmetic," <u>Elementary School Journal</u>, University of Chicago, Chicago, Illinois, 1918.

Open Court Language Arts Reading Program, 1976.

Open Court Publishing Company, La Salle, Illinois.

Orwell, George (English satirist whose real name was Eric Blair)

<u>Animal Farm</u>, 1946

<u>Nineteen Eighty-Four,</u> 1949

Orwell showed in his novels that he hated authoritarianism and feared the loss of individual liberty.

Painter, F. V. N.

<u>A History of Education</u>, D. Appleton and Co., 1886. Republished 1970, Scholarly Press, St. Clair Shores, Michigan.

Parker, Colonel Francis W.

<u>Tracts for Teachers - No. 1, Spelling</u>, Boston, 1882.

Patrick, G. T. W.

"Should Children Under Ten Learn to Read and Write", <u>Popular Science Monthly,</u> January, 1899, pp. 382-391. (After 1900, the magazine was owned by J. M. Cattell.)

Pearson, P. David

"A Psycholinguistic Model of Reading," <u>Language Arts Magazine.</u>

Pollard, Rebecca

Synthetic Method of Reading and Spelling, American Book Company, New York.

(E. B. Huey gave no date with this reference. Pollard's material was probably earlier than the 1889 edition Nila Banton Smith quoted from a different publisher, Western Publishing House, Chicago, in 1889, with this description: Pollard's Synthetic Method, A Complete Manual.)

Pinloche, Auguste

La Reform de l'Education en Allemagne au Dix-Huitieme Siecle, Basedow et le Philanthropinisme, Armand Colin et Cie., Editeurs, Paris, 1889.

The Reading Informer

G. K. Hodenfield, Editor. Published by the Reading Reform Foundation, 7054 East Indian School Road, Scottsdale, Arizona, 85251, Mrs. Raymond Rubicam, President. Volumes 1 to 8 (from 1973 to 1981). (An unparalleled clearinghouse for information on reading instruction.)[Editor's note in 2006: Stopped publication about 1990. Both Mrs. Rubicam and Mr. Hodenfield are deceased.]

Reeder, R. R.

Historical Development of School Readers and of Method in Teaching Reading, Columbia University Contributions to Philosophy, Psychology and Education, Volume VIII, No. 2, The Macmillan Co., 1900. (In his book, Teaching to Read, Historically Considered, Mitford Mathews implied that he was very unimpressed with the scholarship of Reeder on the topic of reading history.)

Rice, Joseph Meyer

The Public School System of the United States, New York, 1893.

Scientific Management inEducation, Publishers Printing Company, New York, 1913.

Rickover, Vice Admiral H. G., U. S. N.

Education and Freedom, E. P. Dutton & Co., Inc., New York, 1959, 1960.

Rollins

Supplement to Traite des Etudes, France, 1734.

Roudinesco, Mme., Jean Trelat and Mme. Trelat

"Etude de Quarante Cas de Dyslexie d'Evolution," Enfance, Paris, 1950.

Rousseau, Jean Jacques

Emile, France, 1762.

Rummell, Frances V.

"These Children Love to Read," Saturday Evening Post, November 9, 1961.

(On Mae Cardin's opposition to sight words and on her phonic method.)

Russell, David H.

Children Learn to Read, Ginn and Company, 1949.

The Ginn Basic Readers (By David H. Russell and Others) Ginn and Company, Boston, 1948. (Revised 1953, 1957, 1961, and 1964.)

Samuels, S. Jay

"Automatic Decoding and Reading Comprehension," Language Arts Magazine

"Automatic Decoding, Its Role in Comprehension," The Reading Informer, October, 1978.

What Research Has to Say about Reading Instruction (S. Jay Samuels, Editor),

International Reading Association, Newark, Delaware, 1978. Articles by Walter H. MacGintie, "Children's Understanding of Linguistic Units," and Frank B. Murray,

"Implications of Piaget's Theory for Reading Instruction."

Sasanuma, S. and O. Fujimura

"Selective Impairment of Phonetic and Non-Phonetic Transcriptions of Words in Japanese Aphasic Patients: Kana vs. Kanji in Visual Recognition and Writing," Cortex, pages 1-18, 1971. (Reported in C. K. Leong's article in Dina Feitelson's Cross-Cultural Perspectives on Reading and Reading Research, International Reading Association, Newark, Delaware, 1978.)

Schmitt, Clara

"School Subjects as Material for Tests of Mental Ability," Elementary School Journal, November, 1914.

"Developmental Alexia, Congenital Word Blindness, or Inability to Learn to Read," Elementary School Journal, May 1918.

Scott, Foresman Reading Systems

Glenview, Illinois, 1970. Kenneth Goodman was a co-author with others on this series and the one following, Reading Unlimited, 1976.

An advertisement from Scott, Foresman and Company on the 1976 series dates the earlier ones at 1970 for Systems, and 1960 for The Sixties Edition of the New Basic Readers, Open Highways and Wide Horizons. The Elson-Gray Basic Readers, introducing Dick, Jane and Baby Sally, is dated at 1930, and is reported as the first to use pre-primers. The Elson-Runkel Primer, which they state was the first to offer a teacher's manual [Ed. note, 2006 - This was not true.], is dated at 1914. A 1966 copy of The Wide Horizons Readers also carries the title, Curriculum Foundation Series.

Since Scott, Foresman themselves date the Gray reader at 1930, it is puzzling that Nila Banton Smith refers to "Gray, William and Others," as the authors of The Curriculum

<u>Foundation Program</u> in 1927, and not in 1930. Perhaps there was a pilot program on the materials at that earlier date.

Shankweiler, D. P. and I. Y. Liberman

"Exploring the Relations between Reading and Speech," in <u>The Neuropsychology of Learning Disorders: Theoretical Approaches</u>, R. M. Knights and D. J. Bakker (Eds.) University Park Press, Baltimore. (There is no date given in C. K. Leong's reference to this paper in Leong's article in <u>Cross-Cultural Perspectives on Reading and Reading Research,</u> by Dina Feitelson, International Reading Association, Newark, Delaware, 1978. Leong refers to a kind of voice print from another article by A. M. Liberman, "The Grammar of Speech and Language," <u>Cognitive Psychology,</u> 1, (1970) (301-323.)

Sholty, Myrtle

"A Study of the Reading Vocabulary of Children," <u>Elementary School Journal,</u> University of Chicago, Chicago, Illinois, February, 1912.

Simon, Brian and Joan Simon

<u>Educational Psychology in the U. S. S. R.</u>, Stanford University Press, Stanford, California, 1963. Translated the article, "The Psychology of Mastering the Elements of Reading," by D. B. Elkonin, page 165.

Simon, Dr. Theophile

Pedagogie Experimentale, Librairie Armand Colin, Paris, 1924.

Smith, Nila Banton

<u>Picture Story Reading Lessons,</u> (with Stuart A. Courtis), 1920, World Book Company, Yonkers/Chicago, 1926.

<u>Learning to Read Program,</u> Silver Burdett Company, 1940-1945. (From Pre-primer to Fourth Reader.)

<u>American Reading Instruction,</u> Silver Burdett Company, Morristown, New Jersey,

1934. Revised Edition, The International Reading Association, Newark, Delaware, 1964. (Based on Smith's Ph. D. from Columbia Teachers College, New York, NY)

Spaulding, Frank E. and Catherine T. Bryce

The Passaic Primer, A. L. Freeman Printing Company, Passaic, New Jersey, 1903.

The Aldine Readers, Newson and Company, New York, 1906.

On page 142 of Nila Banton Smith's American Reading Instruction, she said that The Aldine Readers were one of the many "sentence method" readers modeled after George L. Farnham's manual, The Sentence Method of Reading. On page 420 in her "Selected Bibliography", she listed Farnham's publishing date by C. W. Bardeen in Syracuse, New York, as 1890, but on page 122 in the body of her "history" she listed the publishing date as 1905. However, E. B. Huey in his 1908 book listed the same publisher and a publishing date of 1887, saying Farnham's sentence method had been in use in Binghamton, New York, about 1870. [Editor's note in 2006: The actual publishing date by Bardeen was 1881. It is true that the sentence method was in use by Farnham in Binghamton in 1870, and it is also more than curious that Smith omitted that fact which was clearly stated by Huey.] Smith said that in the sentence method, the child starts by memorizing sentences from stories first read aloud to them, and then read in print, and later the child breaks those sentences down into words, and finally, pays some attention to letter sounds. [Editor's note in 2006: This was not Farnham's method. "Stories" had nothing to do with his method. The meaning of a whole sentence written on the blackboard was implied silently by actions and props, and the children guessed its content. Later the sentence was broken down into words, and then letters.]

The Library of Congress has a copy of Spaulding's and Bryce's earlier primer, The Passaic Primer, showing the method described by Smith. A page reads, "To memorize," and has these lines:

"Fly, little birds, to the tall tree.
Fly to your nest and little birds three."

Some words are then shown in isolation: "birds, little, tree, fly, etc." This is followed by sentences made up of the words already used:

"Fly, little birds. Fly to your nest. Fly to the tall tree, little birds.

Fly to your little birds. Fly to your three little birds...."

Page 3 has the same kind of visual analysis as the Gallaudet primer. Sight words are broken into pieces: "t all" and the letter "t" written under it; "n est," and the letter "n" under it. The book has rhyming phonics, with words like "last, fast, past" written together, and visual analysis of phonograms as on page 23: "f all, c all ed." It is a forerunner to today's sight-word basal readers, without the use of high-frequency words. According to Nila Banton Smith, it was one of many such "sentence method" primers between 1909 and 1918, when they were at the height of their popularity. In Dubuque, Iowa, in 1918, the Aldine and Horace Mann sentence-method readers did poorly in tests against the Ginn Beacon phonic reader (see Harris.)

Starch, Daniel
The Measurement of Efficiency in Reading, Writing, Spelling and English, College Book Store, Madison, Wisconsin, 1914.

Stauffer, Russell G., Alvina Treut Burrows and Others
Winston Basic Readers, John C. Winston Co., Philadelphia, 1960-62.

Stockton, William

"Creating Computers that Think," The New York Times Magazine, The New York Times, New York, December 7 and December 14, 1980.

Suzzallo, Henry

See articles under Cyclopedia of Education on spelling and reading, and see entry below.

Suzzallo, Henry, George E. Freeland, Katherine L. McLaughlin and Ada M. Skinner

Fact and Story Readers, American Book Company, New York, 1930.

Taylor, E. A.

"The Spans: Perception, Apprehension, and Recognition." American Journal of Opthalmology, 1954, 44, p. 501-507. (Data on regressions in reading of 5,000 U. S. readers from Grade 1 to college. Found 23% regressions at first and 15% at college, in recording eye movements in reading. In Huey's 1898 work with American adults, reported on page 27-29, he cited "retrocals," presumably regressions, which work out to only 3%, when analyzed.

Teachers College Record, Teachers College, Columbia University, New York,

"Popular Appraisal of Dewey" (on his 70th birthday) (1929?)

"In Honor of Edward Lee Thorndike," February, 1926. Contributors included Stuart A. Courtis, James McKeen Cattell, Arthur Irving Gates, Henry Suzzallo, and a bibliography of Edward L. Thorndike's publications to that date. The May, 1926, issue included an address given by Charles H. Judd of the University of Chicago at the program honoring Thorndike on his 25th anniversary as a professor at Teachers College.

Thorndike, Ashley H. (Brother of E. L. Thorndike), Professor of English, Columbia University Everyday Classics Primer, written together with Fannie W. Dunn, Assistant Professor of Education, Teachers College, and Franklin T. Baker. Macmillan, New York, 1923.

Thorndike, Edward Lee

"A Pragmatic Substitute for Free Will," in Essays Philosophical and Psychological in Honor of William James, pp. 585-610, 1908.

Educational Psychology, three volumes, Teachers College, Columbia, New York, 1913.

"The Measurement of Ability in Reading," Teachers College Record, Teachers College, Columbia University, New York, September 1914. (With Gray's Oral Reading Accuracy Test.)

"Education for Initiative and Originality," Teachers College Record, Teachers College, Columbia University, New York, November, 1916. (pages 405-16)

"The Measurement of Achievement in Reading: Word Knowledge," Teachers College Record, Teachers College, Columbia University, New York, November, 1916 (pp. 430-5)

"The Psychology of Thinking in the Case of Reading," Psychological Review, May, 1917

"Reading as Reasoning: A Study of Mistakes in Paragraph Reading," Journal of Educational Psychology, June, 1917.

"The Understanding of Sentences: A Study of Errors in Reading," Elementary School Journal, University of Chicago, Chicago, Illinois, October, 1917.

"The Psychology of the Half-Educated Man," Harper's Monthly Magazine, April, 1920.

"On the Organization of Intellect," Psychological Review, pp.

141-51, March, 1921.

"Word Knowledge in the Elementary School," <u>Teachers College Record,</u> Teachers College, Columbia University, September, 1921.

Teacher's Word Book, 1921

<u>The Psychology of Arithmetic</u>, Macmillan Co., New York, 1922.

"Improving the Ability to Read," by Edward L. Thorndike, Professor of Education and Director, Division of Psychology, Institute of Educational Research, Teachers College," <u>Teachers College Record,</u> October, 1934.

<u>Teacher's Word Book of 30,000 Words</u> (with Irving Lorge), Teachers College Press, Teachers College, Columbia University, New York, 1944, 1972.

Time Magazine

"Review of the Year, 1955," quoted by Samuel L. Blumenfeld in <u>The New Illiterates:</u> "If 1955 was notable for anything as far as the U. S. public schools is concerned, it may be that it will be remembered as the Year of Rudolf Flesch... American education closed ranks against Flesch... his book (<u>Why Johnny Can't Read</u>) remained on the bestseller list for thirty-nine weeks.... In Louisville, a mother reported on her third-grader's typewriting: "He typed the letters very easily...But after typing the letters B-O-W-L across the page about ten times, he called it pot. To such parents, Flesch's book touched a sensitive nerve."

Toni Bim, Karin Leo, Ann - Witte Wir Lesen Fibe fur das Erste Schuljahr, Luxembourg,

In use in 1977. Heavy phonics after 50 sight words the first few weeks.

Tovey, Duane R.

"The Psycholinguistic Guessing Game," <u>Language Arts</u>

Magazine.

Trace, Arthur Jr.

What Ivan Knows That Johnny Doesn't. McGraw-Hill Book
Company, New York, 1968.

Twain, Mark (Real name: Samuel Clemens)

Life on the Mississippi, Copyright by H. 0. Houghton &
Company, 1874.

UNESCO

Practical Guide to Functional Literacy, UNESCO, Paris, 1973.

*United States Department of Health, Education and Welfare,
Office of Education*

USOE-supported "Cooperative Research Program in First
Grade Reading Instruction." Reported in the Summer, 1967,
Reading Research Quarterly of the International Reading
Association, Newark, Delaware, by Dr. Guy L. Bond,
Director of the Coordinating Center for the First-Grade
Reading Studies, and Dr. Robert Dykstra, Associate
Professor of Education at the University of Minnesota.
"Summary of the Second-Grade Phase of the Cooperative
Research Program in Primary Reading Instruction," by
Robert Dykstra, Director of the Coordinating Center for the
follow-up of studies in the USOE-supported Cooperative
Research Program in First-Grade Reading. Reported in the
Fall, 1968, Reading Research Quarterly of the International
Reading Association, Newark, Delaware.

Walcutt, Dr. Charles Child

Reading, Chaos and Cure (with Sibyl Terman), McGraw Hill
Book Company, New York, 1958.

Lippincott's Basic Reading (with Glenn McCracken) J. B.
Lippincott Company, Philadelphia, 1963. Revised 1975.)

Teaching Reading: A Phonic/Linguistic Approach to
Developmental Reading, By Charles Child Walcutt, Joan

Lamport, and Glenn McCracken. Chapters on Research and Evaluation by Robert Dykstra, University of Minnesota. Macmillan Publishing Co., Inc. New York, 1974.

Tomorrow's Illiterates. The State of Reading Instruction Today, Little, Brown and Company, Boston, 1961. (Charles C. Walcutt, Ed.)

Waldo, Karl Douglas

"Tests in Reading in Sycamore Schools," Elementary School Journal, University of Chicago, Chicago, Illinois, January, 1915.

Ward, Edward G.

The Rational Method in Reading Manual of Instruction, Silver Burdett & Company, New York-Boston-Chicago, 1896.

Webster, Noah

The American Spelling Book, 1783

Wickersham, James Pyle

Methods Instruction, J. B. Lippincott, Philadelphia, 1865.

Wiswell, Phil

"The Name of the Game Is Electronics," Parade, New York, November 23, 1980.

Witty, Paul A.

Reading for Interest (Primer to Fourth Reader), D. C. Heath and Company, Boston, 1942, Revised 1955.

Worcester, Samuel

Primer of the English Language, Hilliard, Gray, Little and Wilkes, Massachusetts, October 9, 1826.

Zeitler, Julius

"Tachistoskopische Versuche uber das Lesen." Wundt's Philosoph. Studien, Bd. XVI, H. 3, pp. 380—463, 1900.

THE WARY READER'S GUIDE TO PSYCHOLINGUISTICS: SUBJECTIVE VS. OBJECTIVE READERS

BY GERALDINE E. RODGERS

JULY 6, 1982

Prepared for the Workshops Given July 10 and 11, 1982, at the Toronto Meeting of the Reading Reform Foundation

Added Comments in 2006

The following paper, written in 1982, suggests that the completion of the alphabet, which dated from about 800 B.C., was the gift of a single Greek whom I dubbed Anonymous I. I had suggested that it was only one Greek (not a group) who was responsible for adding the vowels to the incomplete Phoenician "alphabet" and so completing it. Yet that earlier Phoenician "alphabet", as I. J. Geib pointed out, had not really been an alphabet, but only an incomplete syllabary which lacked vowel sounds. Each character stood for any whole syllable that contained its sound (as for "b": ba, be, bi, bo, bu, ab, eb, ib, ob, ub, bau, aub, boo, oob, etc.) but the vowel sound in each syllable had to be provided by the reader, obviously by guessing. Although it was a strange one, the Phoenician series of sound-suggesting symbols was still a kind of syllabary. The Phoenician symbols are presumed to have been developed from earlier sound characters, the earliest of which had appeared in ancient Egypt.

Prior to the arrival about 800 B. C. of the incredibly efficient, short, and completed Greek alphabet, which was the very first to have true vowels and true consonants, (and in many places after its arrival), writing systems had to depend on the far less efficient and lengthy syllable systems or on word systems. That is for the very good reason that there really is no spoken unit smaller than a syllable (and words are composed of syllables). Actually, even our completed alphabet is a kind of abbreviated syllabary, because consonants plus vowels are used to produce syllables (and vowels by themselves are also syllables). Since there really are no such things as consonant "phonemes" (consonant letter sounds) that can stand alone (except for a few like m and s) and since most free-standing consonant phonemes are strictly imaginary, it is not surprising that the ancients did not try to write down "phonemes" (vowels and consonants) but concentrated instead on syllables. Because the Phoenician script was only meant to suggest syllables, it seems apparent that the Phoenicians could have had no understanding of consonants and vowels.

It is true, as Diane McGuinness related in *Why Our Children Can't Read* (1997, Simon and Schuster: page 62) that the Brahmi script from India in the 5th century B.C., which I would call a syllabary and which appeared in a matrix table, showed true vowels in a line across the top and true consonants in a line down the left side. That matrix, when filled in from those "givens," produced symbols for vowel-consonant syllables like the ba-be-bi-bo-bu units of the Greek alphabet syllabary, the Brahmi material giving a different written character for each syllable. That certainly demonstrates that, by the 5th century B. C., the true alphabet (consonants + vowels = syllables) had to be known in India or it could not have been used to devise that syllable matrix. However, that does not mean the Brahmi scribes independently arrived at the consonants + vowels = syllables concept of Anonymous I. That is because, by the 5th century B. C., the Greek invention from over 300 years earlier (consonants plus vowel letters produce syllables) would long since have reached India.

Furthermore, since the Brahmi system seemed to appear full blown in the 5th century B. C., it obviously had to have been derivative and not original, and it almost certainly was derivative of earlier Indian syllabaries. India had an earlier script (now undecipherable) as old as those from ancient Sumer and ancient Egypt, so it seems likely that the highly organized Brahmi syllabic script from the 5th century B. C., instead of having appeared full blown, had been derived from some such earlier material. It seems likely that the Brahmi 5th century use of the imported consonant/vowel categories in a matrix of their own devising was to expand on such an earlier syllabary which, like the Phoenician, had lacked vowel sounds. Even a casual examination of the few samples shown on page 62 of Diane McGuinness's book strongly suggests that pre-Brahmi characters had merely been "completed" by the addition of various, consistent short lines or dots to indicate vowels. Apparently, the reason for the use of a matrix was that its neat organization made it easy for users to learn how to place those added vowel markings on the syllable characters.

However, in Diane McGuinness's *Why Our Children Can't Read*, she also made an interesting comment about the ancient writing system from Crete, Linear B. It now seems probable that Anonymous I about 800 B. C. must have been drawing on that far older Linear B system, although using it in a new way, because of his discovery of the fact (so obvious to us now but obviously unknown back then) that consonants plus vowels produce syllables. Diane McGuinness called the Cretan syllable system "diphonic". It was a two-sound syllable system, such as in the two-sound syllables, ba, be, bi, bo, bu, etc. However, unlike the incomplete Phoenician syllabary (where a single symbol, such as "b" stood for many syllables, - ba, be, bi, bo, bu, etc.), Linear B had a unique symbol for each syllable. However, Linear B also used characters at the beginning of some words which could be called "monophonic" syllables. Those "monophonic" syllables were, by today's understanding, five true vowel sounds. Vowel sounds uttered by themselves are also, of course, syllables, which the Cretans obviously understood. It therefore seems self-evident that the Cretans would have regarded those five symbols simply as syllables, and no different from the rest of their syllables, and that the Cretans would have found nothing particularly noteworthy about them.

As Diane McGuinness commented, it is presumed that the Greeks about 800 B. C. were familiar with that earlier Cretan syllabary. Therefore, that wonderful Greek, Anonymous I, would presumably have known about that Cretan syllabary with its five monosyllables that we now know were isolated vowels. He also would have understood that, for instance, the Phoenician "b" meant ALL the unbreakable syllables using that symbol, ba, be, bi, bo, bu, etc. He also would have understood, better than we do, that such syllables are unbreakable.

It must suddenly have dawned on him that he could take those five Cretan monosyllable sounds used at the beginning of some Cretan words and put them before and after those existing Phoenician syllable-suggestive characters. The Cretan monosyllable sounds provided the missing parts of the Phoenician syllables which previously had to be guessed from a text's context. By using those Cretan vowel sounds, it suddenly became possible to write out most Greek syllable sounds very precisely and to do away with the need to guess exactly which syllable was meant.

With his inspiration, Anonymous I had realized that it was

possible to build syllables, and that the two elements that were necessary to build syllables were his newly invented vowel sounds borrowed from Crete (the voiced element) and his newly invented consonant or consonants (the Phoenician characters which immediately lost their appended "guessing" baggage and became what we call consonants, those together-with letters that can seldom exist without a vowel).

It was a positively earth-shattering discovery, that it was possible actually to build all the multitudinous syllables from only a very few symbols, even though those syllables were (and still are) unbreakable. Using those few consonant/vowel building blocks together, Anonymous I could make the indefiniteness of the Phoenician "b" disappear, and replace it with multiple syllable sounds for "b" (ba, be, bi, bo, bu, ab, eb, ib, ob, ub,). The same thing could be done with all the rest of the Phoenician symbols. (At some point, two-vowel "special" vowels and diphthongs arrived, such as au, oi, eu, ou, etc.) It was now also easy to perceive consonant blends (spla, sple, spli, etc.) All that Anonymous I had left to do was to make some of the more useless Phoenician letters stand for the five Cretan vowel sounds.

Now it would never be necessary to devise a special symbol for each Greek syllable as had been done in other syllabaries, because almost the whole Greek syllabary could now be written out simply by using most of the 22 existing Phoenician symbols, and adding two new ones. (Diane McGuinness gives a helpful table, Figure 4 on page 69, comparing the 1050 B. C. Phoenician, the 8th century Greek, the reportedly 8th century Etruscan, the 5th to 4th century Classic Greek, and the Old Latin alphabets.)

I did not know of the Cretan proto-vowel material when I wrote the following 1982 paper, but I now think it is probable that Anonymous I must have been drawing on those Cretan proto-vowels when he added the vowels to the incomplete Phoenician syllabary. Even though he did not just invent the vowels out of thin air himself but most probably drew on the Cretan syllabary, he still deserves enormous credit for his creative idea of tacking those five Cretan proto-vowels, in before and after positions, onto those incomplete Phoenician proto-consonant syllables so as to produce clearly spelled out syllables. By doing so, he had discovered that there are two distinctly different building blocks for syllables, consonants and vowels, and for that discovery he deserves the most enormous credit. Because of his discovery, it is no longer necessary to memorize long syllabaries, or, as an alternative, to use "guessing" from such things as those abbreviated Phoenician syllables which failed to indicate vowel sounds (although Kenneth Goodman, the promoter of "psycholinguistic guessing," still has not received that good news from 800 B. C.). Anonymous I's 800 B. C. consonants-plus-vowels-equal-syllables alphabet, the only true alphabet that has ever been invented anywhere on earth, was certainly a magnificent, planet-rattling, one-time achievement. Its descendant variations are in use all over the world today, 2,800 long years later.

Because of Anonymous I's discovery, it has become possible to write down any thought of which mankind is capable by using only a little over 20 symbols, and to teach that simple writing and reading skill from those 20-plus symbols, not just to geniuses like Aristotle, but to the simplest and the poorest of children.

"Kilroy was here" inscriptions from ordinary people have not been reported in the parts of the ancient world which used those earlier and far more complicated syllabaries before the 800 B. C. invention of the simple, short Greek true alphabet. It is probably no accident that the first such graffiti of which I ever heard came, not from those earlier Egyptians or Sumerians, but from Greek soldiers in the time of Alexander the Great, who casually scribbled "Kilroy was here" types of comments on surfaces. That must have been because literacy had become easy to obtain in Greece after 800 B.C.

with the advent of that enormously abbreviated syllabary, the Greek alphabet. Literacy was also easy to obtain for Viking sailors about 1,600 years later, in the 9th century A. D. Vikings used the runes to write (which runes were descendants of the original Greek alphabet). Some of those Vikings inscribed rocks, apparently while winter-bound on an island near Scotland, with such things as boasts of their prowess with women. Those Greek soldiers in Alexander's day in the 4th century B. C., and those Viking sailors in the 9th century A. D. were not intellectuals, but they were most certainly literate, and literacy was a skill that had been unavailable to ordinary people before Anonymous I's invention of the consonant-plus-vowel-equals-syllable Greek alphabet, the ancestor of our own alphabet. With Anonymous I's gift of that simple alphabet, which, properly taught, can produce near universal literacy, civilization had taken a massive leap forward.

Geraldine E. Rodgers December 8, 2006

WHAT ARE SUBJECTIVE AND OBJECTIVE READERS?

One of the best kept secrets in history has been the early psychologists' discovery that there are different kinds of readers. They knew that the kind of readers people become usually depends on how they are taught to read in the first half of first grade: either by sounding-and-blending phonics on all the letters in every syllable, or by sight words and guessing from the context. What is more, the kinds of readers people become as a result of how they are taught at the beginning appear to be as permanent as their fingerprints. After the "perceptual-type" mold has finally been set (the conditioned reflex), usually at the very beginning of school, the evidence powerfully suggests there are no returns, no refunds and no exchanges.

One of these kinds of readers is what is currently called "psycholinguistic" (originally called subjective), and the other (though never mentioned any more) is the "objective". The objective readers turn printed syllables into sounds with great accuracy, automatically and rapidly, which syllables then automatically produce syntax-generating-words, and the objective readers then can consciously choose to "listen" to the print as they can choose to listen to speech. These two levels, (Level 1 - syllables, and Level 2 - syntax-generating-.words), apparently operate not only automatically but in concert, balancing and correcting one another, as do so many of the other automatic body systems such as walking. But consciousness, the third level, at which the ultimate message in reading or speech is understood, should be voluntary. The objective reader, like the reader with normal hearing, can choose to pay attention or not to pay attention to the stream of language he is receiving.

That reading can follow the same kinds of pathways as does speech and can operate on the two levels of syllables and then syntax-generating-words is shown by the existence of two rare kinds of aphasics, those people who are unable to talk. One rare kind of aphasic has normal hearing except for his being incapable of distinguishing the differences in syllable sounds at Level 1. Yet he IS capable of using written language at Level 2, syntax-generating-words. So that kind of aphasic must be taught language as some deaf-mutes are taught language: with printed sight words instead of sound. He makes use of Level 3, ultimate meaning, to help him figure out the syntax and unknown words, so by definition his reading cannot be automatic.

The other rare kind of aphasic is the precise opposite. He CAN make perfect syllable sounds at Level 1, but can neither produce nor receive language at Level 2, whether it is spoken or written, so he is incapable of understanding ultimate meaning at Level 3.

Some of this latter type of aphasic, who can operate at Level 1 but not Level 2 (and not at Level 3, either) are described by Dr. Hilde Mosse in her great work, *The Complete Handbook of Children's Reading Disorders*. This rare kind of aphasic who is limited to Level 1 can, amazingly, sometimes read the sounds of print off the page, and so obviously can operate at the syllable step. But, since he cannot operate at Level 2, syntax-generating-words, he has no understanding of the meaning of what he is reading and makes no use of language except for this parrot reading. This type of aphasic is able to do this in any alphabetic language, and not just that of his own country, at about a 60% accuracy rate.

Requires   (
Conscious   (Level 3 - Consciousness of Meaning
Attention   (

                    (
                    (Level 2 - Syntax-Generating-Words
Automatic Levels   (
Not Requiring   (
Conscious Attention (
                    (Level 1 - Syllables
                    (

> If conscious attention IS focused on Level 2, the result is
> stammering and stuttering. Correspondingly, if conscious
> attention is focused on the automatic action of walking,
> the result is an altered gait and stumbling.

The objective reader, however, is like the healthy normal listener and can "listen" to printed syllables because he can operate on BOTH these automatic levels, syllables and then syntax-generating-words, and both levels DO operate automatically and very probably in concert. For the objective reader, reading is a completely automatic act, but understanding - paying attention - is completely voluntary.

By contrast to the objective, the subjective "psycholinguistic" reader, like the first kind of aphasic, just mentioned, skips the syllable step at Level 1, and turns only part of the print directly into whole, meaning-bearing sight words at Level 2, NOT sound-bearing syllables. He then has to guess consciously at Level 3 about the syntax and the rest of the words from the context of the selection, which means he has to use Level 3 to figure out Level 2. In an article in the May, 1967, *Journal of the Reading Specialist*, Dr. Kenneth Goodman does a fine job of describing this kind of psycholinguistic reading. Such a reader does this conscious guessing from the context with the help of only some of the letter sounds, and he makes frequent errors. Since such a reader is guessing consciously, his reading, therefore, is not automatic and effortless. He reads the way a partially deaf person has to listen, by consciously guessing from the MEANING of the context. That is, of course, very trying and divides his attention between decoding words at Level 2 and the ultimate message at Level 3. This divided attention, with only part of it on the ultimate message, lowers his understanding.

Teaching subjective readers real phonics after they have learned to read DOES make them better readers, better SUBJECTIVE readers, that is. They use the real phonics consciously to work out and then to "store" the meanings of new sight words in their memories. As their banks of meaning-bearing sight-word memories grow, they can read more sight words at Level 2 and therefore may have to do somewhat less conscious guessing at Level 3. However, they apparently never change their perceptual type, which is to read by "meaning," and become able to operate automatically at Level 1, which is to read by "sound." As Dr. Rudolf Flesch said in his book, *Why Johnny Can't Read*, back in 1955, while he taught Johnny phonics, he still had to keep telling Johnny not to guess.

HOW CAN WE TEST READING?

Many subjective, psycholinguistic readers can give the illusion of reading even when they can barely read at all, because the 100 commonest words which are taught as sight words in first grade, out of half million or so words in English, compose about 50% of almost ANYTHING in print. About 300 of the highest frequency words, most of which have usually been taught by the end of first grade, compose 75% of the different words in children's books, as shown by J. McNally and W. Murray in their *Key Words to Literacy*, London, reported in *The Ladybird Key Words Reading Scheme - Notes for Teachers*, publishers Wills & Hepworth, Ltd., Loughborough, Leicestershire, England, 1969. So if a child knows only about 300 of the highest frequency sight words and has been trained to guess, he may already score in an oral reading test in a child's book at 75% accuracy! But actually he will probably score far better because psycholinguistic readers are taught to make the initial consonant sounds of unknown words and then to guess from the meaning of the context of the selection, so the probability is he will score closer to 90% (or "passing" according to most reading standards) on such an oral test in an easy book.

It should be obvious that with this kind of "word attack skill," the child also can guess his way through silent reading comprehension tests and get "good" scores even when he cannot TRULY read, in the objective sense of listening to syllables at Level 1, at all! It is obvious that with this kind of reading his reading comprehension scores will drop in high school when he is faced with difficult vocabulary. Therefore, he will probably never be able to handle difficult textbooks, although Dr. Kenneth Goodman, the psycholinguist, co-author of a Scott, Foresman reading series, and president for 1981-82 of the International Reading Association, covers such difficulties nicely by having spoken about the right NOT to read, in the cassette offered in the *National Council of Teachers of English Catalog* for 1978-79 from their 1975 NCTE Convention. The cassette is titled, *The Disabled Reader: The Right Not to Read*, by Ken Goodman, Dewayne -Triplett and Frank Greene. Significantly, it was NOT offered in print, but only on tape. That is where Goodman and all his followers may lead us, I am afraid, away from print and back to the spoken word.

By 8th grade, these silent reading comprehension tests correlate statistically with IQ tests in very much the way one IQ test form correlates with another. In other words, reading comprehension tests ARE IQ tests, except at higher levels when they contain many more lower frequency words. So such silent reading tests do NOT test reading, but only IQ plus attention, for those students who have learned enough of the highest frequency words as sight words. Yet, for 70 years, these silent reading comprehension tests have masked the sight-word method's reading failures in American schools, which the reading of oral word lists - and, I repeat, ORAL WORD LISTS, and dictated spelling tests which were normed nationally, would have unmasked.

On the connected oral reading of texts, sight-word-trained children can context-guess when they can only recognize about 300 of the highest frequency words that compose 75% of texts, and so can score at least at 75%, but probably far higher by guessing from those words which they do know. That is why reading ability can only be tested by the ORAL reading of word lists, and by dictated spelling tests. Such tests MUST be done in our schools to expose the abject failure of the sight-word basal readers currently in use.

Such sight-word basal readers are presently used in about 85% of American schools. The scores from sight-word-trained students on such tests should be compared to the scores of children trained on phonics series like *Lippincott, Open Court, Alpha One, Sing-Spell- Read and Write*, or *Spaulding*, or any of the other good programs on the approved list of Reading Reform Foundation of Scottsdale, Arizona. [Editor's note from 2006: Not only is the Reading Reform of Scottsdale gone, which operated nationally, but so are all of the phonics series just listed except the last two.

However, since writing this, I have concluded that Spaulding is not a desirable program.] Such test results should reveal the worthlessness of the sight-word basal readers and make it possible to forbid the use of sight-word method by law, as we forbid the use of ANY injurious products like thalidomide. As a matter of fact, that is exactly what a German headline called the sight-word method in Germany back in the 1960's, "The Thalidomide Case in Education." Geneva, Switzerland had the good sense back in 1955 to ban the global method, which is its European name.

But it is not reasonable to expect any cooperation in such a campaign for testing from "reading experts" because they would only be putting themselves out of business. Reading experts exist almost solely because we have a reading problem. The United States had virtually NO reading experts before 1914 (honestly!) because, as I will show, we had no reading problem even in 1914, and Russia apparently has almost no experts now, although their psychologists do write about reading. But there is literally an army of such reading experts from Coast to Coast in America who have an understandable vested interest in protecting their livelihoods. Therefore, the lobbying for such tests and laws will have to be done by an informed general public (plus the exceedingly few maverick experts who MAY favor true phonics). It is necessary, however, to give a warning to any new entrants into the field of "reading reform." The opposition always manages to SOUND very good. It rattles its Ph. D's and foundation grants and professional associations and books and large meetings of "experts" and news releases, and generates an altogether dandy aura of professionalism. They have behind them, of course, the megabucks of the publishing companies who have so much invested in their basal reader products. And they have influence. I have seen an educational journal in the past record an education leader's conversation with a high-ranking Government official on a first-name basis. Yet proponents of true phonics (not phony phonics) often cannot get in the front door of such offices. I know, because I have tried to contact Government officials by phone and by mail with my research findings and have received what I consider only "bedbug" letters in response.

For instance, Senator Dole's name was in the papers, along with Senator McGovern's, about their inquiry into America's reading problem, about two years ago. I sent Dole all my materials. In response, I received courteous letters apparently written by some one on his staff, but that ended the matter. After the big publicity, Dole has apparently dropped the subject.

There was something else in the papers not long ago about Secretary of Education Bell's making an inquiry into our educational problems in America. I called his office and announced to a secretary that I was SURE my research had uncovered the explanation for our reading problem, and pleaded to speak to Secretary Bell PERSONALLY. In due course, I received a call from someone far down the line who was disinterested (you can always sense this) in what the loquacious woman on the other end was trying to explain to him.

I tried again and sent Secretary Bell my book and again received a courteous letter from someone far down the line, who obviously was not going to do anything with my material. You can imagine my reaction when I read Secretary Bell's answer in *Family Weekly* on June 6, 1982, in the "Ask Them Yourself Column", to someone's question about the drop in children's reading levels. Bell's explanation for our increased illiteracy was non-school factors like television and poor home discipline, plus the school factor of poor school discipline. His solution was for the schools to set high standards (NOT, you will note, to change the method of teaching reading) and for parents to read to their children. His answer included this saying, "The child who is read to, reads." That is like saying the

185

child who has music played to him, plays music. I have been listening to classical music with great appreciation since childhood, but I STILL cannot even play *Jingle Bells* on the piano, not even with one hand. An occasional Mozart can sit down at the piano and play spontaneously at three years old but such rare prodigies are in no danger of putting piano teachers out of business. As a first-grade teacher with 19 years of primary grade school teaching experience, who knows that teaching children to read is exactly (AND I MEAN EXACTLY) like teaching them how to type or to play the piano, Bell's apparent recommendation of this last "teaching method" of imitation really appalls me. Hasn't Secretary Bell heard ANYTHING about what in 1967 Jeanne Chall called The Great Debate, the question about whether or not initial teaching methods in first grade basal reading books ARE the cause of our literacy problem?

But many experts now say, after Chall's 1967 book, *Learning to Read: the Great Debate*, that they DO support phonics. Apparently, the reading experts found they were outflanked, and many of them adopted the policy, "If you can't beat them, join them." This is the probable reason for the phony phonics in sight-word basal readers today and for experts announcing that they do not support sight-words any longer but believe in phonics. But don't press them for a definition of phonics, though, or ask them why they are so busy stating now that the "decoding" issue has been "solved" in the primary grades when there has been almost no published valid testing of oral reading accuracy comparing the results from sight word approaches to phonics approaches in America for almost 70 years! If you ask WHY there has been almost no testing of oral reading accuracy comparing phonics to sight words in 70 years, you are getting unpleasantly close to what was so carefully buried long ago, the fact that there are different KINDS of readers, which such testing would reveal.

So, because of their vested interests, almost every "reading expert" is INCAPABLE of seeing straight on the subject of reading. If we were discussing reading and a reading expert walked in and said. "Good morning," I would look out the window to confirm that it was daylight. To try to walk with "reading experts" is to try to walk in quicksand. Currently, there are seeming fields of agreement between reading experts and some reading reformers, such as teaching reading early to little children at about four years of age. The very fact that the experts approve makes me very doubtful and inclined to believe that the Russians, like the ancient Greeks and the modern Swedes, must be right to wait until children are seven!

It reminds me of a title of a book that came out about 1939, *You Can't Do Business with Hitler*. You can't do business with reading experts, either, and when nation-wide testing of oral reading and spelling is finally done to uncover the extent of our reading problem (which such testing WILL be done, sooner or later), it absolutely MUST NOT be handled through reading experts, if the results are to mean anything. I suggest such tests might be carried out by concerned nation-wide companies willing to cooperate with the Government in such a study. For example, perhaps the highly professional and competent customer representatives of the local telephone companies, which reach into every community, could do the actual testing, and perhaps the data could be processed through the equipment of AT&T, with their enormous know-how.

There would be a certain fitness to all of that. Alexander Graham Bell, like his father, was concerned with teaching the deaf, and the route he used was PHONICS, the same as that for those with normal hearing. But the sight-word method as it is used in America, with its dependence on context guessing, as Samuel Blumenfeld brilliantly discovered, originated in a book *The Mother's Primer* written by the Reverend Gallaudet, also a famous teacher of the deaf. Gallaudet, unlike Bell and Bell's father, believed in sight-words for the deaf and then came to recommend sight words for ALL students. Gallaudet was wonderfully influential as his method was in use in almost all American schools from about 1840 into the 1890's, despite Nila Banton Smith's fairyland history to the contrary, and again after 1930. [Editor's note from 2006: Gallaudet's associates had promoted simple sight-word materials without deaf-mute context guessing, from 1826. *The Mother's Primer* which used the deaf-mute method with context guessing, like the 1930 Dick and Jane materials, came out in 1835 and was highly successful. However, the installation of sight-word teaching in America was 1826, not 1840, and it never totally disappeared after that.]

So, in trying to remove Gallaudet's sight-words and trying to reinstall Bell's phonics for normal children in American schools, perhaps it WOULD be appropriate to ask the assistance of the Bell Telephone companies in this ancient, sight-word/phonics war. As Blumenfeld pointed out, the war between phonics vs. sight words for the deaf originated in the 18th century, between Samuel Heinecke of Germany for phonics and the Abbe de l'Epee of France for sight words and sign language. It was a violent, emotional war from its very beginning, but now it concerns not just deaf children, but ALL children. The turning point came in 1930-1931 with the introduction of W. S. Gray's Scott, Foresman and A. I. Gates' Macmillan sight word readers. Gates actually admitted his approach was tried out on little five year-old deaf-mutes at Columbia in the 1920's. The Gray and Gates readers are actually deaf-mute readers, but of course were never described that way.

HOW SHOULD WE TEACH READING?

Surprisingly, we SHOULD be playing the child's game of "Simon Says" with Russia on the subject of teaching beginning reading. Whatever Russia does in teaching reading, we would be wise to imitate precisely as in the child's game "Simon Says" because Russia HAS no reading problem (and no reading research community comparable to ours, either.)

But Russia teaches real phonics in first grade and is DONE with reading ever afterward! In M. Kashin's report, "Concerning the Results of the Soviet School's Adoption of the New Curriculum," (from the M. E. Sharpe, Inc., White Plains, New York, May, 1977 issue of their periodical, *Soviet Education*) the Russian Kashin stated:

"The adoption of the new primary grade curricula raised the question of teaching first-graders how to read and write. After long study, the conclusion was drawn that the period for instruction in reading and writing could be shortened somewhat. It was found that 3 to 3.5 months (from September 1 to December 1-15) are quite long enough for the development of correct reading skills and habits. The practice of the mass school has confirmed the correctness of this conclusion, and today, at the end of the period of reading and writing instruction, over 95 percent of the pupils meet the established demands in reading."

So "reading" ENDS in Russia by December of first grade! The outline of the Soviet curriculum after first grade made NO mention of "reading comprehension" which we "teach" not only through high school but even in college. The Russians do teach literature and spelling, and Kashin was appalled that "20% of third-graders misspell unstressed vowels." But the 1952 *New Iowa Spelling Scale* showed that 75% of the American third graders they tested then missed a word with an unstressed vowel (the word was "number,") and 77% even missed a word with a STRESSED vowel (the word was "pin.") The other scores were little better. There has been some improvement since then in spelling because of the largely phony phonics of the newer basal readers since Chall's book, *Learning to*

Read, The Great Debate, but I suspect it is not much.

The Russian Kashin said about their students, "By the end of the third grade, the vast majority of pupils read fluently and expressively, and correctly understand what they read," and that promotion rates in Russia were 98.7% in first grade, 99.2 % in the second grade, and 99.4% in the third. It has to be remembered that he was talking about pupils who were not asked to learn reading until they were seven years old, so that the reversals of letters (d for b, etc.) which is so characteristic of younger children would have largely disappeared.

A January, 1959, issue of *The Instructor* magazine on visits their American editors had made to Russian schools reported that they saw reading taught entirely by the phonetic method, that each child had a small wooden pointer to point to the syllables as he read, which the child keeps if necessary THROUGH THIRD GRADE, and that reading was taught to the entire class, not to groups. But OUR children are forbidden to point, as it might interfere with reading fluently "for meaning" and have been so forbidden since about the time of J. McKeen Cattell's 1880's experiments. In contrast to our schools, it is obvious that the Russians are aware of the importance of the syllable in developing objective readers, when they even give their children pointers to point to them!

Make no mistake about it. The Russians with their emphasis on the syllable and their uncontrolled vocabulary ARE developing objective readers. The very essence of our basal reader instruction, "reading for meaning," with a controlled sight-word vocabulary which develops psycholinguistic subjective readers, has NOTHING to do with their approach. To prove it, here is the definition of reading given by D. B. Elkonin of the Union Of Soviet Socialistic Republics, as reported in Brian and Joan Simon's *Educational Psychology in the USSR*, 1963:

"In the present paper we start from the proposition that reading is a reconstitution of the sound forms of a word on the basis of its graphic representation. Understanding, which is often considered as the basic content of the process of reading arises as a result of correct recreation of the sound forms of words. He who, independently of the level of understanding of words, can correctly recreate their sound forms is able to read."

Obviously, Elkonin is describing objective reading. Elkonin's view of reading is also obviously based on the Russian Pavlov's psychology, with its "conditioned reflexes" applied to the automatic processing of print to speech, instead of on E. L. Thorndike's American psychology which grew out of Thorndike's work with his former professors William James and James McKeen Cattell. The latter was the man who performed the famous sight-word experiments in the 1880's purporting to prove that we read by whole words and not by letters.

WHO IS RESPONSIBLE FOR OUR READING MESS?

It was Cattell who appears first to have recognized, on what was considered to be a scientific basis, the existence of two different kinds of reading, with his high flashing of words and letters. He first did his experiments in 1883 at Johns Hopkins University in Baltimore, and two of his subjects were his fellow graduate student, John Dewey, and his professor, G. Stanley Hall. Hall almost immediately tried to pirate young Cattell's work and to publish it under his own name, earning Cattell's enmity. Cattell finished his work under the psychologist Wilhelm Wundt in Germany, after his fellowship at Johns Hopkins was not renewed but was given to John Dewey. Cattell remained Dewey's friend but made great trouble over his loss of the fellowship. This uproar was the first of the many battles in which Cattell was engaged over the years, resulting in his great personal unpopularity. Cattell's unpopularity outside his own sphere of influence was increased because he also was an outspoken atheistic materialist and a socialist, possibly of the radical variety. Ultimately, Cattell was fired from Columbia in World War I because he had written to Congressmen opposing the draft, on Columbia University letterhead, after a public warning from Columbia President Nicholas Murray Butler not to oppose the war effort. Until then, Butler had put up with Cattell's notoriety and personal attacks on Butler because of Butler's dedication to academic freedom, and once even interceded for Cattell.

The triangle shown in the illustration on the following page most probably grew directly out of Cattell's psychological experiments done first at Baltimore and finished in Germany. It was taken from an article in the 1913 *Cyclopedia of Education* by Professor H. J. Suzzallo, then of Columbia Teachers College, who had been a student of E. L. Thorndike about 1901, as Thorndike had himself been a student of Cattell about 1898 (and of the psychologist William James at Harvard just before that).

The psychologist, William James, and Francis Galton of England (who was Charles Darwin's first cousin), with whom Cattell had been friendly while in England, were both concerned about the formation of habit patterns, or associations, in thought. These came to be known as conditioned reflexes after Pavlov. Such habitual thought patterns, or stimulus-response connections, were shown in diagrams in James' 1890 psychology book. Suzzallo's triangle, shown on the following page (which most probably originated with Cattell) [Editor's 2006 correction: It probably originated with William James] was just such an "association" diagram as appeared in James' book, and in Galton's work as described by James.

The psychologists of Cattell's early day were interested in how fast we think and flashed stimuli at subjects and then timed their reactions. Cattell did this with words and with letters. But Cattell apparently wrongly saw what he called perception-apperception as a one-step process (stimulus-conscious response). When the letters or words were flashed, he apparently thought the viewer almost immediately became consciously aware of EITHER the whole word OR the letters. Cattell apparently thought if it were only letters, the reader then had to perform a conscious step (what he called "willing") to turn the letters into a word.

THE READING TRIANGLE

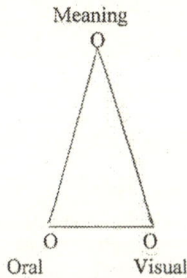

Meaning

Oral   Visual

Source: Article entitled, "Reading, Teaching Beginners" by Henry Suzzallo, on page 118 of the 1913 volume of A Cyclopedia of Education, edited by Paul Monroe, Columbia University. Suzzallo was also with Columbia, at Teachers College, and had been a graduate student of the psychologist, E. L. Thorndike ,at Columbia about 1901. Thorndike had been a graduate student of the psychologist, James McKeen Cattell, at Columbia in 1898, and of the psychologist, William James, at Harvard, before that.

But Cattell did NOT mean "willing" in the sense of a voluntary action but only a conscious action. "Will" in the sense in which it is usually used did not exist in Cattell's brand of psychology. (Nor did consciousness in the time-honored sense, but that is another story.) To keep the matter as simple as possible, the evidence indicates that

Cattell thought that people who read by phonics make an automatic response from print to letters, and then have to take a conscious step to turn the letters into words. But Cattell apparently thought that people who learned to read WHOLE words make an automatic step to WHOLE words, which draw up meaning association bonds with them. The conclusion apparently was that teaching children whole words means they will AUTOMATICALLY read with meaning. Cattell is on record saying that reading is a completely automatic process (per M. M. Sokal, in *An Education in Psychology* (1981), the MIT Press, Cambridge, Massachusetts.)

Bizarrely, Cattell appeared originally to be completely unaware of the existence of the syllable in learning to read, probably because he learned to read in America at a time when sight words were almost universally taught, so Cattell himself was probably a psycholinguistic, subjective reader. (His terrible spelling in his journals certainly suggests that, as psycholinguistic readers tend to be poor spellers, unless they have photographic memories.). Cattell's work concerned the reading of phrases, pure words or pure letters, but no such thing as pure words or pure letters exists. Words have meaning only as PARTS of speech (syntax), which is why dictionaries define words as nouns, verbs, adjectives, and so on. Letters cannot exist outside of syllables any more than words can exist outside of syntax. To recite a letter name (or its "sound") is actually to recite a syllable. We do not "read" letter names (or sounds) but whole syllables composed of such letters ("cat," not kuh-ah-tuh, or see-aye-tee).

But since Cattell did not recognize the syllable, but only "whole words" or "letters," the choice for Cattell, obviously, on the triangle diagram was between EITHER whole words which would draw up meaning bonds with them, or letters which would draw up only sound bonds. If the reader had been initially conditioned to go from "visual" or print to "oral" or sounds, that one step would be automatic, but the next step from "oral" to meaning would presumably be conscious - and therefore slower and less reliable. Cattell apparently did not believe that perception could have TWO automatic steps, first syllables, and then syntax-generating-words, before conscious awareness arose. But Pavlov and his Russian psychologists apparently figured out Cattell's mistake (that there is not ONE automatic step but TWO automatic steps) about 1929, after they had attended the Ninth International Congress of Psychology at Yale University, the first such congress Russian psychologists attended. Cattell was president of this congress, one of the many indications of his enormous influence.

Russia had made some use of sight words before 1929. Probably Celestin Freinet of France, the famed European exponent of sight words along with Ovide Decroly, discussed sight words when he visited Krupskaya, Lenin's widow, in 1925, who was then in charge of Russian education . Freinet was with the first group of Western educators to visit Russia after the Revolution.[12] Nevertheless, by 1930 Russian primers were reportedly again dividing words between syllables, and by 1932 Russia had swung back to the analytic-synthetic phonics method, the same as that used by Tolstoy in the readers he wrote about 1872.

Yet America in 1929 and later was saddled with Cattell's one-step psychology errors, which Cattell was apparently able to propagate through his enormous influence. This was not only through his highly influential ex-student and close personal and professional friend, E. L. Thorndike, who was acknowledged as the

---

12 Cattell and John Dewey also visited Russia in the summer of 1928. At a dinner for John Dewey at the University Club, New York, given by the Aristogenic Society on May 17, 1933, Cattell said, "At the invitation of the Soviet government I was asked to organize and lead a party to visit that modern purgatory, half way between heaven and hell. When we got there I was nowhere, for St. John was worshipped everywhere." (meaning John Dewey)

leader in American educational thought for 50 years, but through John Dewey, also his friend. According to Sokal, both Thorndike and Dewey visited Cattell at his home after he had been fired from Columbia in 1917. Cattell must have had enormous influence in his position as Chairman of the Executive Committee of the American Association for the Advancement of Science from 1924 to at least 1941(and possibly to his death in 1944) and through Cattell's control and ownership of many publications, including the major American educational magazine, *School and Society*, the major American scientific magazine, *Science*, the directory of leaders in science and the directory of leaders in education, his ownership of other magazines, his co-founding of The Psychological Corporation, and his activity in other groups.

After performing his 1880's experiments which apparently proved to Cattell's satisfaction that readers must instantly see EITHER whole words OR letter sounds, because he did not recognize the importance of the syllable[13] and because he did not recognize that a reflex action can have TWO steps, Cattell was faced with the apparent dilemma of teaching children to read either whole words for meaning (but being fuzzy about sounds and spelling because they would have to do the sound step consciously) or to read letter sounds perfectly (but to be fuzzy about meaning, because the meaning step for them would be conscious). Cattell apparently opted for the first kind of reader, the child who reads for meaning. But that meant, of course, that he knew from the very

---

13 Addenda 1/83: Cattell had to be aware of the importance of the syllable after Hermann Ebbinghaus published his 1885 German work, *Memory A Contribution to Experimental Psychology* on his study of completion tests and nonsense syllables. James referred to it in his 1890 book, *The Principles of Psychology*. Ebbinghaus's work on memory was used by A. Binet of France in constructing the first successful intelligence tests about 1905. Yet Ebbinghaus's work on nonsense syllables, meaningful material and memory appears NOWHERE in American reading instruction literature!

beginning, back in the 1880's, that children who read words for meaning, BY DEFINITION, would be weaker in oral reading and spelling than phonics readers.

Cattell had given a talk on how we read to the Aristotelian Society in London on February 21, 1887, according to Sokal, which had aroused great interest at that meeting. He had previously used the material under the title, "The Time It Takes to Think," but changed it to "Recent Psychophysical Researches" for the London meeting. One of the Aristotelian group was G. J. Romanes, who according to W. S. Gray in his 1917 research summary had written on the results of an investigation with practiced readers to determine the speed of silent reading and the factors conditioning it. Gray cited pages 136-137 in Romanes' 1884 book, *Mental Evolution in Animals*, as his source, but I suggest the real source was Cattell who must have known Romanes from the Aristotelian Society in London in 1887. Cattell's final conclusions on reading very probably arose from the discussion on his paper at this February 21, 1887 meeting, which most probably would have referred to Romanes' ideas on silent reading speed from his book three years before. Cattell's paper WAS of great interest to the men at the meeting, as Cattell reported, according to Sokal, "They seemed to like it better than I had expected, and the discussion was kept up until nearly eleven."

As a result of that meeting, Cattell then wrote a new paper, "The Way We Read," which was accepted for publication by the prestigious magazine, *The Nineteenth Century*. Instead, Cattell sent them another manuscript with the title he had used originally, "The Time It Takes to Think." *The Nineteenth Century* offered to publish both, but only the latter article ever appeared in print. Cattell told his parents in a letter of December 3, 1887 (his paper was published in November), "My name has been a good deal in the papers in connection with the paper before the Aristotelian Society & the article in the Nineteenth Century." His unpublished paper, "The

Way We Read," is listed in the manuscript files of the Library of Congress, but when I sent for a copy I was told they only had the first page and had apparently never received the rest.

However, Cattell's probable view of reading put him squarely into the ancient war of the teachers of the deaf, phonics vs. sight words, and it put him on Gallaudet's and the Abbe de l'Epee's side, the counterclockwise route on the triangle, and not on Alexander Graham Bell's and Samuel Heinecke's side, the clockwise route.

I suggest the first scientific awareness of the existence of two types of readers based on conditioned reflexes, on the triangle, originated with J. McKeen Cattell in 1883, and that from the very beginning the subject of reading types has been hushed up. I suggest that THIS is the reason that Cattell's second paper was never published, because the public would not "understand" how necessary it was supposed to be to trade in oral reading accuracy and good spelling for the presumed benefits of increased "reading comprehension."

Cattell trained Thorndike, who trained Gates and Gray. Gray is on record saying that reading words is automatic but the use of phonics is conscious, confirming Cattell's probable ideas on the counterclockwise route. The pattern of one expert training another has remained unchanged to this day, but now it is only custom which keeps sight words in use. Cattell's early psychology was apparently buried long ago by sanitizing the literature.

[Editor's note in 2006: Cattell did his original experimental work at Johns Hopkins under G. Stanley Hall in 1883 and the inspiration for his experiments very likely came from having heard Hall's lectures on Wundt's experimental equipment, which Hall had seen in Germany, and having heard Hall's comments on James' ideas on language, which ideas Hall would have know from close contact with James. Per Gay Wilson Allen in William James, A Biography, page 211, while an instructor in English at Harvard in the mid 1870's, Hall "often took walks" with William James and Hall later graduated as James' Ph. D. student in 1878. Hall must have thought Cattell's 1883 findings were of real importance since he apparently tried to steal credit for them. Therefore, it is very likely that Cattell's findings were communicated by Hall to William James, whom Hall knew very well, as early as 1883.]

Gray's authoritative 1925 summary of reading research was doctored to omit the two studies which appeared to support Cattell's probable view of two types of reading. One was Oskar Messmer's in Germany in 1903 who discovered by high-speed flashing of words the two kinds of readers, and it was Messmer who named these reading types the subjective and objective. Nor did Gray discuss at all Myrtle Sholty's 1912 study at the University of Chicago. Sholty saw the two types in three little second grade girls she tested, and she referred to them by Messmer's labels, subjective and objective, and she cited Messmer as a reference.

Gray, amazingly, did not omit just Messmer, and Sholty's REAL conclusions, from his earlier 1917 summary of research. He even omitted Cattell! In Gray's 1925 summary, he only listed W. F. Dearborn's 1914 summary of Cattell's work in the bibliography, omitting any listing of writings by Cattell himself, and he totally omitted Cattell in the 1925 index! The omission of Cattell completely in 1917 is made even more incredible since Gray obtained his master's degree under Thorndike at Columbia Teachers College in 1914, at the same time that Cattell, Thorndike's associate and close friend, was still teaching at Columbia!

A back-up to Gray's faulty research "summaries" is Nila Banton Smith's "history" of reading, but it is a classic case of Orwellian unthink. Smith wrote her "history" as her Ph. D. dissertation at Columbia Teachers College and it was published in 1934, and Thorndike was still teaching at Columbia Teachers College when she studied there and when she published her thesis.

As mentioned, James McKeen Cattell had been fired from Columbia University in 1917 in a scandal over his opposition to the World War I draft, which had been reported on the front page of *The New York Times*.

WHAT PROOF IS THERE OF DIFFERENT KINDS OF READERS?

Dr. Hilde L. Mosse, the late German-American psychiatrist/ pediatrician, referred specifically to Russian Pavlovian psychology in connection with establishing the proper automatic "conditioned reflexes" in reading. Dr. Mosse said:

"Reading disorders can be caused by an inability to form the necessary conditioned reflexes or by the establishment and practice of wrong reflexes."

So, if the Russian Elkonin's view of reading is correct, the clockwise route on the triangle, then to teach children to read in exactly the OPPOSITE fashion to Elkonin's view, the counterclockwise route, would INDUCE such wrong reflexes, i.e., reading disorders or artificial dyslexia. But this is exactly what the new psycholinguists, like the older experts Gates and Gray, are now recommending.

Frank Smith, in his book, *Psycholinguistics and Reading*, spoke of phonics as the "great fallacy" of beginning reading instruction and said, "I shall argue that sound, if it is produced at all, comes only after the comprehension of meaning in reading." Smith is obviously going counterclockwise on the triangle, the path used to teach some deaf-mutes language, ALL the way around the triangle, where readers learn sounds AFTER knowing meaning.

What is so striking about Smith's definition of reading is that it is the EXACT OPPOSITE of the definition of reading given by D.

B. Elkonin of the Soviet Union. Smith is counterclockwise on the triangle, and Elkonin is clockwise. But if the Russian Elkonin is correct in his definition of reading, then to teach children to read in exactly the OPPOSITE way would interfere with the proper conditioned reflexes and would induce dyslexia. Smith's psycholinguistic reading should therefore CAUSE dyslexia, to a greater or lesser degree.

They have no reading groups inside the classrooms in Russia, but we do here, and teachers have to teach them separately, wasting most of the primary school day. Three groups is normal here but there can be as many as five or six. A little simple arithmetic shows that each child, therefore, receives only 1/3 or 1/5 or 1/6 of the teacher's lessons.

Yet, in Russia where the teacher teaches the WHOLE CLASS, each child receives ALL of the teacher's lessons. I use whole class instruction myself in reading and it makes an enormous difference in the amount that children learn. I found in visiting primary grades in Germany, Luxembourg, Sweden, France and Austria in 1977 that whole class instruction was the norm in those countries, too, and there was not such an enormous waste of teaching time. Obviously, in whole-class instruction, allowances have to be made for differences in ability, but such differences CAN be taken care of without reading groups, though children may practice their reading orally with the teacher individually or in small clusters.

Experienced and dedicated teachers who limit the oral reading of their children to reading groups, using basal readers with their controlled vocabulary, and who then limit their reading tests to silent reading comprehension tests, are often completely unaware of severe reading disabilities right in their own classrooms. It is asking too much of human nature to ask such teachers who have been using these sight-word basal readers for years, with the honest conviction that they were teaching little children to read, to recognize that they have been doing something wrong all their professional lives. But such teachers are reassured by something called "reading levels", by which a child is supposed to know successively his handful of first-grade words and then a few more second-grade words and then his third-grade words, ad nauseum, and his reading books only use the few words he has learned. The reality is that outside the never-never land of "reading experts" who invented such "controlled vocabulary", there is no such thing as a third-grade word, as a simple reading of the Mother Goose rhymes demonstrates. These-were written for six-year-olds, but no subjective six-year-olds can read them. But I DO enjoy hearing so many objective first-grade students rattle them off. One little girl in my class, just turned 7, brought up to me a selection of Mother Goose rhymes from our classroom library this June and announced, "THESE were funny ! I read ALL of them." She had, of course, added enormously to her literary background because English literature can be said to start with Mother Goose, and the little girl is on her way now to conquer all of it. (Incidentally, she had Chinese spoken at home.)

Some few children taught to read subjectively DO manage to figure out the phonic code by themselves early in first grade and so become objective readers. They are the "miracle readers" in such first grades, who astonish everyone by doing only what is normal for an objective first grader. But the other first graders in that room, who become subjective readers, are doomed to a blighted reading development.

Above the level of beginning readers, books are written in a different language from the spoken language, at what Dr. Charles C. Walcutt called Reading Level 3, to distinguish it from beginning levels. For instance, starting with books far easier than Lang's fairy tales, a syntax and vocabulary is used which is more difficult than spoken language. Children who CAN really read, the objective readers, learn this higher level syntax and vocabulary through "hearing" it in their reading, as they learned their spoken language through hearing it spoken aloud. But most subjective readers who are limited to their few memorized sight words and guessing are unable to do this, because they are hard of hearing when faced with print. THIS is the reason for our dropping SAT scores in high school, the fact that these partially deafened children have not learned the language of books, not the fact that "higher level reading skills," as the experts would say, are not taught enough in high school! But fourth and fifth graders back in 1920 DID read the Lang fairy books, for example, and Lang's books work out today with our readability formulas at NINTH GRADE LEVEL! So 4th and 5th grade in 1920 equals 9th grade in 1982! No greater blight ever hit American schools than "psycholinguistic" subjective reading.

In my sabbatical oral reading research in 1977-78, I tested the oral reading of approximately 1,000 children in America, Sweden, Germany, France, Luxembourg, Austria and Holland (using a copyrighted test with the permission of IEA in Sweden for the second graders). My second-grade testing of about 900 second graders revealed that there is a gradual scale from the objective readers to the subjective readers, depending on the relative emphasis that was given on sight words in first grade.

The illustration shows the copyrighted IEA test portion I used. It consists in English of 144 words, of which 64 are different words. Of these 64 different words, 40 are among the 250 commonest words in English, according to *Key Words to Literacy*. Only 11 are above the 500 frequency. The test was given in the fall and in January of second grade in Europe and America, and should have been very easy for sight-word trained American readers, but ONE QUARTER OF THEM FAILED IT IN JANUARY! It did not even begin to test the ceiling of the phonics-trained children, nor did it even begin to reveal the word attack problems of the sight-word children, other than those who did not even know the 500 commonest sight words. For instance, one Houghton-Mifflin-trained second-grader scored 99% in word accuracy but could not read the word that was printed over and over on her own shirt. The word was "outrageous" and when I asked her what it said, she said "Australia."

I scored the children at 95% accuracy, at 90% accuracy, on the per cent of readers who made reversals, on the per cent of children who read slowly and who read quickly, and on the per cent of children who passed the comprehension questions. I then totaled the scores for American phonics vs. American sight words in the months of September and October, European phonics vs. European sight-words emphasis in October and November, and American phonics vs. American sight words in January. I also compared the Scott, Foresman January scores to the Houghton Mifflin January scores, since Houghton Mifflin is somewhat more phonic in its approach than Scott, Foresman.

To my surprise, I found that the relationships between phonics and sight words on all these scores was absolutely uniform. The heavier phonics programs scored higher in accuracy and speed but lower in reversals, and might score on comprehension lower or higher than the sight-word programs because of relatively greater freedom of attention when reading. They were not reading with the forced but divided attention of the heavier sight-word programs who were using the context to figure out unknown words.

The following is the beginning portion of a much longer
copyrighted speed-reading test for 10- and 14-year-olds,
from the International Association for the Evaluation of
Educational Achievement (IEA), Stockholm, Sweden.
Permission was granted to Geraldine E. Rodgers to use
these first five items from that test if IEA were
acknowledged in any written material and if, when
possible, a copy were sent to IEA.

1. Peter has a little dog. The dog is black with a white spot on
   1   2   3   4   5   6   7   8   9   10   11 12   13   14

his back and one white leg. The color of Peter's dog is mostly
15 16   17   18   19   20   21   22   23 24   25 26 27

            black   brown   gray
            28   29   30

2. When Peter got the dog it was a small puppy. Now the dog is
   31   32   33   34   35 36 37 38 39   40   41   42 43 4

a little more than two years old. How many years has
45 46   47   48   49   50   51   52   53   54   55

Peter had the dog?
56   57   58 59

            one   two   three
            60   61   62

3. Peter's dog has a spot on his back. That is why Peter named
   63   64   65 66 67   68 69   70   71 72 73   74   75

the dog Spot. The dog was named after the spot on his
76 77   78   79   80   81   82   83   84 85 86 87

            back   ear   leg
            88   89   90

4. The dog has learned to do two tricks. One trick is to catch
   91   92   93   94   95 96 97   98   99   100 101 102 103

a ball. To stand on its hind leg is the second
104 105 106   107 108 109 110 111 112 113   114

            story   trick   way
            115   116   117

5. When he was a puppy Spot was fed three times a day. Now
   118   119 120 121 122   123 124 125   126   127 128 129   130

he is fed only once. The number of times is now
131 132 133 134   135   136   137   138 139   140 141

            often   less   many
            142   143   144

Fascinated with this discovery, I then compared American
phonics to European sight words, and European phonics to
American sight words, and found that the relationship STILL held,
despite the differences in languages and the difference in time, the
European being done two to three months earlier than the January
American scores. Only on one score did the earlier testing affect the
profile in comparing European to American.

I am convinced that this phonics/sight word profile will show
up whenever large enough groups of readers are compared. Those
who learned with more phonics will show the phonics profile; those

with a greater sight word emphasis will show the sight-word profile, as a result of the relative differences in the conditioned reflexes they formed at the time they were taught to read.

It should be evident from these scores that the relatively more stable comprehension scores of the sight-word groups are a function of their crippled decoding, their lower oral reading accuracy, slower speed, and greater reversals. Sight-word trained comprehension scores fell into a narrow band, higher than the worst phonics scores but lower than the best. But the phonics scores went from terrible to marvelous, showing that the teaching method had not controlled the comprehension scores but left the readers free potentially to score very high. In the American scores, three of the phonics classes had EVERY CHILD who scored above 97% word accuracy pass the reading comprehension portion of the test, and since half of those classes scored at that level, that was a very large group, and obviously indicated superb comprehension scores.

The point remains: the phonic-trained reader is FREE when he is reading. Whether he pays attention or not depends on his training - AND on his mood, just as it does at home when his mother tells him to close the front door when he goes out. He may or may not leave it swinging. But the sight-word trained child can only read BY paying attention - divided attention, it is true. He will score lower than the best phonics children but higher than the phonics child who is not interested. This, I am convinced, is the reason school systems still buy sight-word basal readers. They may yield more consistent "reading comprehension" scores. A large sales job needs to be done to convince administrators that "reading comprehension" does NOT test reading but only intelligence plus attention, once the children know the high-frequency words.

Since the relationship in scores between lesser and greater sight-words teaching emphasis was absolutely consistent when large numbers of classes were compared, it proved the presence of a force acting to produce that profile. It also showed there is not a clear-cut "subjective" type compared to an "objective" type but a scale running from black to white with all shades of gray in between, depending on the relative emphasis on sight words and phonics in first grade. I labeled programs from Code 1 for total sight word emphasis to Code 10 for total phonics emphasis, and most fell somewhere on the scale in between. So readers are therefore not normally pure subjective or pure objective, but a mixture of each, depending on the way in which they were first taught to read and the resulting establishment of conditioned reflexes.

However, my "profile" showed clearly that there are two different and opposite types when methods are compared. When I returned from my sabbatical- research, I thought I had a discovery with my data on two different and opposite kinds of readers, and I wrote a short article in all sincerity announcing my "discovery." But some time afterwards, I ran across the work of Oskar Messmer and then Myrtle Sholty in 1903 and 1912 and found that my discovery of two different and opposite types of readers was ANYTHING but new. W. S. Gray is the famed "summarizer" of reading research, and we apparently have him to thank for burying the research of Messmer and Sholty, which I discuss in my book, *The Case for the Prosecution*. Gray did NOT publicize the fact that there are two different and opposite kinds of readers, despite oblique references in his 1956 *The Teaching of Reading and Writing* about different paths in reading development because of different emphases. Nor in 1922 did Buswell at the University of Chicago clearly differentiate reading types, despite his mention of differing paths of development.

Yet, "In Vino Veritas," in wine is the truth, and sometimes in anger. William Scott Gray was apparently angry when he visited a Bloomfield phonics-type classroom about 1940 and saw how accurately and easily the children read. So Gray broke his studied silence on the existence of two permanent types of readers, and what he said became a matter of record, reported in Mitford Mathews *Teaching to Read, Historically Considered.* Mathews reported that Gray:

> "...explained to the other visitors that what the children were doing was in no sense remarkable. He said that reading experts had long known that children could rather quickly be taught to pronounce words with remarkable glibness, but that real reading with understanding of what was read was another matter entirely. He pointed out that these children were mere word-callers, that they were pronouncing well beyond their mental ages, and that they were heading straight for serious trouble later in their reading development."

What makes this quotation so remarkable is that it is the ONLY clear reference I have ever been able to find from any reading expert to explain why they jettisoned a teaching method with almost 3,000 years of history behind. It was to protect that non-existent "skill," so-called "silent reading comprehension." To do that imaginary thing, they imposed on our nation a teaching method for children with normal hearing which had never FORMALLY been used for them before in recorded history.

The Gates and Gray deaf-mute-method readers of 1930-1931 which were based ONLY on whole high-frequency sight words and context guessing WERE new and outdistanced anything Gallaudet had ever done. That is because Gallaudet's *Mother's Primer* of 1835 only took hearing children through the first-grade, after which some kind of "sound" eventually became necessary to identify unknown words. Yet the Gates and Gray deaf-mute-method readers of 1930-1931 which took hearing children through grade 3 were constructed so that no real sound ("phonics") would ever be necessary, all through a child's life (or so Thorndike's *Teachers College Record* 1934 article seemed to indicate). The writing of the deaf-mute-method readers only became possible after 2,000 or so of the highest frequency words had been identified by E. L. Thorndike, because it is those words which account for about 95% of any almost any text and make "successful" context-guessing possible. (However, since our present-day "reading comprehension" problems start at the high-school level, it is obvious that history has demonstrated that the deaf-mute context-guessing method has not been "successful" all through life, after all.)

E. L. Thorndike identified 10,000 of the highest-frequency words after ten years of personally counting about three and a half million words in children's literature, and published his *Teachers Word Book* listing the 10,000 highest-frequency words in that material in 1921. He must have had a very powerful motive (obviously to make it possible to construct deaf-mute-method materials for hearing children) to undertake such an exhausting, tedious, ten-years-long job as tabulating the relative number of occurrences of the different words in that three and a half million words, so the claim that Thorndike was not personally involved in the teaching of beginning reading is utter nonsense. Furthermore, the fact that the deaf-mute method readers were published by Thorndike's ex-graduate students, Gray and Gates, in 1930-1931 was obviously far from being a coincidence.

The European global methods did not use the high-frequency word approach, which is essential if hearing children are to be taught to read like deaf-mutes, without sound, but by context guessing from the meaning of the stories. Therefore, the pure deaf-mute-method for hearing children which is totally dependent on context guessing originated right here in the United States. However, the fact that there are no clear references in the literature from reading experts on the replacing of objective phonics with sight words about 1930 proves that the deaf-mute, context-guessing, subjective method was sneaked into America's schools, the public being considered too dull-witted to be let into the secret that, with the deaf-mute subjective method, oral reading accuracy and good spelling were going to be traded in by the psychologists for the fancied improvement in "silent reading comprehension."

But there are many OBLIQUE references in the literature to the existence of two opposite types of readers. Consider Arthur I. Gates' remarks in the *Teachers College Record* of October, 1926, which obliquely confirmed that perceptual types are established at the very beginning of reading instruction:

"The use of phonetic analysis by a pupil in the course of ordinary reading should be subordinate to the method of "guessing" the word from the context. It is very important that the pupil does not develop the habit - as many do -of forgetting the thought and making a phonetic attack on an unfamiliar word...."

The same kind of oblique confirmation on the existence of perceptual types was given by Dr. Guy L. Bond of the University of Minnesota, who worked with Arthur I. Gates, Thorndike's ex-student, at Columbia in the 1930's, and who was, like Gates, the author of a sight-word basal reading series and a reading expert. Bond was also Director of the Coordinating Center for the First Grade Reading Studies, that massive USOE Government-funded study on first-grade reading in 1967, almost all of which was based on silent tests. The few oral tests did show the superiority of phonics.

In Bond's 1955 book, *Teaching the Child to Read*, he said:

"The teacher's major tasks during this time are to introduce the words in a meaningful fashion so that the children have contextual clues to aid them in "guessing" the word and to give repetition of the words so that these words become the nucleus of a sight vocabulary. The words should be recognized as whole words. It is detrimental indeed to have the children spell or sound out the words at this stage."

Apparently, it was "detrimental indeed" because they would become objective, not subjective, readers, if they were exposed to phonics at the beginning, though there is no indication that Bond himself ever heard of this term at Columbia, any more than Mae Carden did, who left Columbia in horror to found a phonics movement in the early 1930's. By the early 1930's, the reading experts were saying NOTHING clearly, while they churned out rivers and oceans of expertise "literature." To wade through this drivel is to drown, and it is necessary to go back BEFORE 1930 - preferably back before 1920, to find any reason or continuity in "reading instruction literature."

The difference in the kinds of readers that teaching methods produced was noticed in Europe, too, despite the fact that deaf-mute-method context guessing was not emphasized there. Take the 1939 remark of J. E. Seegers of the Netherlands, reported in W. S. Gray's *The Teaching of Reading and Writing*. While Russia had gone back to phonics by 1932 after only a very brief partial use of the global sight-word method in the 1920's, Europe in general made heavy use of the global method during the 1930's, as did Argentina and, of course, the United States. Concerning the effect of the global sight-word method in Europe, Seegers referred to comments by T. Simon in 1924, who had worked with Binet in France earlier:

"As already pointed out by Simon, the results of children who have learned to read by the global method are completely different from those who learn to read by the synthetic method. We even admit that we have frequently been most embarrassed to evaluate these results, and we have preferred not to point out those referring to time spent and pauses during reading.

"Here are the reasons our subjects used to recognizing known words by their ensemble (general configuration, gestalt) make little effort to decipher meaningless syllables and words alien to their vocabulary. During the reading of sentences they omit unknown words.... One could consider this fact as a grievance against the global method, but we think with Vaney that the child learns to read only after several years."

Vaney was an educator from Paris, on whose work Simon reported in his 1924 book, *Pedagogie Experimentale*, Librairie Armand Colin, Paris.

Robert Dottrens of Switzerland also commented on the differences in the results from the global and phonic methods, in his *Au Seuil de La Culture,* (Les Editions de Scarabee, Paris, 1965). Dottrens said, concerning what he considered the awful effects of straight phonics, which he nevertheless confirmed DOES rapidly produce accurate readers:

> "To have learned to read by the letters and the combinations of syllables is to have acquired a mechanism in which comprehension [has no part] and it is probably the most grave reproach that one can address to the synthetic method. A child can learn to read rapidly without understanding."

But, concerning the global method, he said a "danger" had to be avoided, the danger of guessing (and I have rearranged his comments here):

> "...the tendency the children have to invent when they do not know. Some of them are past masters in this art. To

avoid this fault, which is grave, it is absolutely necessary that the exercises with sight words... and the work of analysis be executed in a rigorous manner .... all must be put to work to avoid the child's inventing, and reading something other than has been written... (under the) menace of veritable catastrophes ..."

But a far earlier reference to psycholinguistic "guessing" which Dottrens said resulted in "veritable catastrophes" occurred in France in the 17th century. This was when the syllable method was still the standard method for teaching reading. Buisson's 1887 *Dictionnaire de Pedagogie et d'Instruction Primaire* quoted Pere Charles Demia, who ran schools and a normal school in Lyons, France, in 1672. At that time, children first learned to read regularly formed series of syllables (ba, be, bi, bo, bu, ab, eb, ib, ob, ub, etc.) and then learned to read their prayers in Latin, and later in their own language. After having learned to read, for instance, In Nomine Patris, the children in Demia's class then read it again, each child reading one syllable. The first would read "in," the second "no," the third "mi," the fourth "ne," the fifth "pat," and the sixth "tris." Children practiced their letters and beginning syllables with dice, as Locke had suggested and as was suggested earlier in England in 1653 in a book by Sir Hugh Plat. Pere Demia said, concerning such dice:

"...where should be printed the letters or the syllables, with which the children will play, being given a pupil more capable to settle their differences..."

But the psycholinguistic serpent was producing different kinds of readers then, too. That they showed up in Paris in 1654 is clearly seen by this comment by another 17th century author, I. D. B., Priest, who wrote *The Parish School*. The author warned concerning the teaching of beginning readers:

> "Not to undertake to make them fly in reading before they know how to spell the letters because, wishing to advance them teaching them so many things at one time, one makes their reading so confused that further they are a long time learning; (and) they never know to read well, neither in Latin or in French.
>
> "To proceed, therefore, by order, it is necessary (1) to teach the little children to know the letters, (2) to assemble them to make syllables, (3) to spell the syllables to make some words, and afterwards to read...."

Obviously, Pere I. D. B. recognized two types of readers and thought they were permanent, since he said concerning the poorly taught:

> "...they never know to read well, neither in Latin or in French."

The famous ancient Roman educator, Quintilian, also saw the existence of different types of readers back in the first century A. D. He said:

> "For learning syllables there is no short way; they must all be learned throughout. Nor are the most difficult of them, as is the general practice, to be postponed, that children may be at a loss, forsooth, in writing words. Moreover, we must not even trust to the first learning by heart; it will be better to have syllables repeated, and to impress them long upon the memory; and in reading, too, not to hurry on, in order to make it continuous or quick, until the clear and

certain connection of the letters become familiar, without at least any necessity to stop for recollection. Let the pupil then begin to form words from syllables, and to join phrases together from words. It is incredible how much retardation is caused to reading by haste; for hence arise hesitation, interruption, and repetition, as children attempt more than they can manage; and then, after making mistakes, they become distrustful even of what they know. Let reading, therefore, be at first sure, then continuous, and for a long time slow, until by exercise a correct quickness is gained."

It is obvious that Quintilian was recommending "objective" teaching, but with his comment that the general practice was to postpone the learning of the most difficult syllables and his further comment, "It is incredible how much retardation is caused to reading by haste," it seems fairly certain that Ancient Rome also was turning up some subjective psycholinguistic readers.

But we have to go back even further for some of the VERY earliest psycholinguistic readers. The ancient Egyptians used an advanced form of picture writing with pictures equaling specific words, but they also used some syllable writing. With this, they must have had a problem like that in our own language, where there are too MANY different syllables to make a different symbol for each one, so one of their very cleverest scribes had a brilliant idea. He decided to make only one syllable sign for each of those syllables that sounded a good deal alike (such as ba, be, bi, bo, bu, and so on) and people could then GUESS from what they were reading WHICH exact syllable sound was correct . It would look something like this:

TH CW JMPD VR TH MN

Do you recognize what is being said? It is, of course, "The cow jumped over the moon." I. J. Gelb in his *Encyclopedia Britannica* article (and he IS a major authority) maintains that these ancient Egyptians considered their symbols to be incomplete syllables, NOT consonant letters. It was not until much later, after these symbols had traveled to Greece from Phoenicia, that some brilliant Greek we can call Anonymous I invented the vowels to complete these indefinite syllables. By so doing, he had invented BOTH the consonants AND the vowels, or our alphabet as we know it, so that it instantly became possible to record WHOLE syllables very precisely (ba, be, bi, bo, bu, etc.).

It was Blaise Pascal of France, the famed scientist and mathematician, who first split these syllable atoms by recommending in 1655 that we teach children the 40 or so phonemes in their native languages and how to sound and blend these phonemes into syllables. Of course, most consonants cannot exist OUTSIDE of a syllable, so in asking children to make such consonant sounds, and then to try to blend them, Pascal was introducing for the first time an imaginary step in reading. But once he had introduced this imaginary step, it then became possible for the first time in recorded history to SYNTHESIZE syllables from phonemes, instead of merely to ANALYZE syllables as wholes. Pascal, as a scientist, was used to both these paths of the sciences, synthesis and analysis, which probably explains his invention of sounding-and-blending phonics which used synthesis for the first time.

Once Pascal had introduced synthesis, it was only necessary to teach children the 40 or so phonemes in their native languages and the skill of blending. Pascal had removed forever the former necessity of memorizing those long tables of regularly formed syllables (dab, deb, dib, dob, dub, etc.) which had been used since

216

about the time of Anonymous I to teach reading. Because of Pàscal's invention, learning to read was reduced from an exercise which had taken a very long time to one which was much shorter, if the child were old enough to learn reading easily (7 years or so).

But, long before Pascal's invention in 1655, and before Anonymous I's invention of the vowels back about 800 B.C., the only way the ancient Egyptians could read THEIR incomplete syllables was by CONTEXT GUESSING. So THAT'S where our psycholinguistics really originated, back there at the pyramids in ancient Egypt about five thousand years ago. But the ancient Egyptians did not use psycholinguistics because it was better. They just HAD no other way! The rest of our society may be marching forward into a space-age future, but the psycholinguists are marching reading instruction straight back to the pharaohs and their tombs.

Which gets an. "oh, hum," reaction from a lot of people because they just cannot believe that what happens in first grades from September to February could POSSIBLY matter that much, and we probably ALWAYS had reading problems, if the truth were known. What PROOF is there that things were ever any different, that we once had a different KIND of mature reader? By the time children are adults, most catch up, don't they?

They DO seem to catch up in many cases. But most people do not know that is because only about 100 of the commonest words compose half of almost anything written, and about 300 of the commonest words compose about three-quarters of simple material. If people have learned to read with these common sight words and what the sight word people call "phonics" (which means to guess an unknown word from the sound of the first letter or so plus context, with almost no attention to vowels - which therefore means NO ATTENTION TO SYLLABLES), they SEEM to be reading, if they are faced only with words that they already have in their spoken vocabulary. But ask them to read out loud, though, and count their errors. Most "successful" American readers under 50 today who learned to read with sight word basal readers are probably subjective readers and many are incapable of reading ANYTHING that is unpracticed without frequent errors - in the order perhaps of 5 for every running 100 words (10 or more would be at the "frustrational" level) . Besides, having to read subjectively and consciously BY MEANING instead of objectively and automatically BY SYLLABLES is such a disagreeable and exhausting activity for them that many avoid reading and so never learn to read the more complicated vocabulary and syntax used in good literature. As mentioned, THIS is the reason our SAT's are dropping, because our students have never learned the different and complex language of books, which Dr. Charles C. Walcutt calls Reading 3 to distinguish it from the lower levels of language.

This is what has happened to our SUCCESSFUL readers, the ones who are managing to show up in college, but, even so, many of them can neither spell nor write sensible compositions, according to widespread reports.

But, what happens to our unsuccessful readers - to our illiterates and functional illiterates? These are most often the ones on unemployment, or turning to crime (studies show most criminals are functionally illiterate) or ruining expensive equipment in the military services because they cannot read the directions for running it.

IT WAS NOT ALWAYS LIKE THAT, before we got these psycholinguistic subjective reading books which were sneaked into the schools by Gates and Gray, Thorndike's graduate students, to protect what they thought was "reading comprehension", because of Cattell's erroneous one-step psychology. Before that disastrous development, we had a DIFFERENT KIND of reader, the kind of reader the Russian Elkonin talked about, a reader for whom decoding print to sound was an automatic two-step operation, a "conditioned reflex."

How many of our students were successful then, when we had the SAME IQ ranges that we have now, and when massive numbers were immigrant children or the children of immigrants? The record shows, BEYOND ANY SHADOW OF A DOUBT, that the American schools succeeded so successfully in teaching reading in 1914 and 1915 that (excluding the mentally defective),

NINETY-NINE PER CENT OF THE PUPILS COULD READ!

But the document that PROVES it is something else that comes up missing in most libraries. It is Part 2 of A Measuring Scale for Ability in Spelling, by Leonard Porter Ayres, published in 1915 by the Russell Sage Foundation, New York, and at one time so famous that another of E. L. Thorndike's graduate students, E. R. Buckingham, later wrote an extension to this Ayres spelling scale. In 1913, Buckingham had made his OWN scale directly under Thorndike's supervision, so the fact that it was AYRES scale that Buckingham extended, and not his own, shows which was the more successful.

There is virtually no doubt whatsoever that Thorndike knew of Ayres' work, since Thorndike and Ayres gave two papers jointly in 1912 titled "Measuring Educational Products and Processes," at the Harvard Teachers' Association, dealing with measurement in education, and reported in *School Review,* Vol. 20, 1912. According to Elwood P. Cubberly in *Public Education in the United States* (1919, 1934), Ayres had published his first spelling scale in 1912, which was the very year that Ayres and Thorndike gave their joint papers at the Harvard Teachers' Association. Since Thorndike had his graduate students work with him on various topics, it seems highly likely that Buckingham's original scale, appearing in 1913, only a year after the 1912 meeting, probably originated from Thorndike's having suggested that topic to Buckingham.

Victor H. Noll in his 1957 book, *Introduction to Educational Measurement,* referred to Ayres' handwriting but not his spelling scale, and said that the Ayres' handwriting scale was one of the most widely used scales ever made, with 600,000 copies prepared from 1917 to 1935. Yet it is obvious that even by 1957 Noll had never heard of Ayres' 1912 or 1915 spelling scales, since Noll made a point to refer to an earlier (and also forgotten) scale, the Rice scale, based on testing 33,000 children in 1895-1896. Noll said:

"...the significance of (Rice's) contributions is not always fully appreciated."

It was only from Noll's book that I learned of the Rice scale, which also showed fine spelling in American schools, and which I had never seen referred to elsewhere. Yet later I found that Thorndike, himself, wrote an extensive article on the Rice scale in the 1901 *Teachers College Record.*

When Rice toured American schools in the early 1890's, he found about half still teaching sight-words, for which he had contempt, but he ALSO had contempt for what he called the daily spelling "grind." In the 1880's, after enormous reading and spelling failures, spelling books were introduced into the schools which taught spelling (and therefore reading) phonically. That they WERE successful in curing the awful spelling failures reported in the 1880's is shown by Rice's fine scores when he gave his tests in 1895 and 1896. Phonics gradually found its way back into reading instruction in general about 1900, although there was an enormous amount of time wasted on the "sentence method", to which "supplemental" phonics was attached in most places after 1900.

I first learned of the Ayres' spelling scale from a few

paragraphs in a 1938 book, *Psychology of Elementary School Subjects*, by William Henry Gray (NOT William Scott Gray). Yet it is evident that the Ayres' scales of 1912 and 1915 HAD to be well known, not only to Thorndike, but to the major reading expert, Arthur Irving Gates, since Gates got his Ph. D. in 1917 from Columbia Teachers College and later wrote a well-known paper on spelling. When I tried to get Ayres 1915 *A Measuring Scale for Ability in Spelling* at the Library of Congress, the Library of Congress had only the cover, but inside was Ayres' handwriting scale. Elsewhere on the shelves, however, the librarian showed me MANY copies of the Ayres' handwriting scale. Yet, I could see inside the single copy of the Ayres' spelling scale cover where the original spelling contents had been removed from the binding, where it had been stitched in, in three places.

I was finally able to get Part I of the Ayres' work, the text from Columbia University Teachers College by interlibrary loan, but not Part2, the single page, folded-paper scale itself. But Part 1 listed the grade rankings on the scale on page 28 and the words and where they fitted in to fill those grade rankings on pages 51-56. Ayres' earlier 1909 work, *Laggards in Our Schools*, had shown that the vast majority of the students at that time were in the right grade for their age or only a year ahead or behind, and virtually NONE were more than two years behind. In 1914 and 1915, when Ayres gave his spelling tests to 70,000 children in 84 American cities, most children had to stay in school until age 14 or at least to sixth grade, so his scores, therefore, for 6th grade should be representative of almost every child at or near sixth grade age in America in 1915 except the mentally retarded. His results showed that NINETY-NINE PER CENT of those sixth-grade children in 1915 could spell these words in DICTATED, not printed recognition spelling tests:

became, brother, rain, keep, start, mail, eye, glass, party, upon, two, they, would, any, could, should, city, only, where, week, first, sent, mile, seem, even, without, afternoon, Friday, hour, wife, state, July, head, story, open, short, lady, reach, better, water, round, cost, price, became, class, horse, care, try, move, delay, pound, behind, around, burn, camp, bear, clear, clean, spell, poor, finish, hurt, maybe, across, tonight, tenth, sir, these, club, seen, felt, full, fail, set, stamp, light, coming, cent, night, pass, shut, easy

Except in rare cases, children who can spell words in dictated spelling tests can READ those words, and can read a very great many more words than they can spell correctly. It is obvious America had NO reading problem, as we know it, in 1914 and 1915. We were in the same fortunate position THEN that the Russians are NOW, because we obviously were developing objective readers. That is because children in most American schools from 1900 to 1930 either learned by phonics or by what was called "supplemental phonics" which meant fooling around with reading for meaning with sentences for a month or so in the first grade classrooms and then finally teaching the children to read by real phonics.

It is small wonder that Arthur Irving Gates who received his Ph. D. in 1917 under James McKeen Cattell and Edward L. Thorndike, and Walter Scott Gray who received his Ph. D. from the University of Chicago on oral reading tests which he had started as his Masters' degree work at Columbia directly under Thorndike, NEVER tested the results of their deaf-mute 1930 and 1931 sight word readers against their very own spelling and oral reading tests. They KNEW the terrible results they would get. That is the REAL reason there have been virtually no oral reading accuracy comparisons between phonics and sight words in American schools for SEVENTY YEARS! (By 1982, I had only turned up about ten minor comparisons in the literature since 1912.) Yet Gray, who got his Ph. D. on oral reading accuracy tests, was the leading reading expert in America for 40 years, and the major summarizer of what is laughingly called "research."

Psycholinguistic, subjective readers can neither spell properly nor read accurately, and large numbers of them become functional illiterates. If we WANT such psycholinguistic, subjective readers in our schools, as Gates and Gray obviously did, then oral reading accuracy and dictated spelling accuracy do not matter. But if we do NOT want psycholinguistic subjective readers with their enormous failing rate and their enormous reading inefficiency, then it is high time we reinstituted DICTATED spelling tests (from the Ayres list would be ideal) and the reading of oral WORD LISTS to uncover the failure of sight-word reading instruction. We should COMPLETELY forget about using "reading comprehension tests" which are really only tests of IQ plus attention when the child knows the 300 or so highest frequency words. With the results from these dictated spelling tests and oral word list tests, it should be possible to show the enormous gap between objective phonics-trained children and subjective psycholinguistic, sight-word trained children. With this demonstration of the great harm done by the psycholinguistic sight-word reading books, it should be possible to forbid their use in our schools, as was done by an edict in Geneva, Switzerland, almost thirty years ago, in 1955.

But such testing and such edicts will not come because they are needed, but only because they are fought for. The sad truth is that we have not even begun that fight.

Geraldine E. Rodgers

July 6, 1982

THE FLAT EARTH OF AMERICAN READING "INSTRUCTION"

By Geraldine E. Rodgers
July 20, 1983

Prepared for the Workshops Given July 23 and 24, 1983
At the Indianapolis Meeting of the Reading Reform Foundation

Reading in America is in the bad state it is because of very severe attacks of the "flat earth syndrome," beliefs in fundamental facts which in reality do not exist. The condition can only be appreciated if we back away far enough in space and time to see things in their proper setting. Yet America's reading "experts" have been floating along for generations above their imagined flat earth in their own little bubble of the "here" and "now." They have almost completely ignored the "there" and "then" in reality which make real understanding of any situation possible.

Besides ignoring the "there" and "then" in reading instruction, which is to say its geography and history, "experts" have effectively ignored the real science of reading. Obviously, this must be based on the structure of the brain. As long ago as the 1860's, Broca published his research on aphasia, or inability to speak, showing a specific location in the brain controlling speech, which should have had obvious connections for anyone wishing for an understanding of the teaching of reading.

It is inconceivable that James McKeen Cattell, the psychologist whose research has so often been cited for generations as the basis for the sight-word method, did not view his 1883 Johns Hopkins experiments, completed in Germany in 1885, in the light of that kind of brain research which was so widely known at the time. This is particularly so since articles by Cattell were published in two of the best known scientific periodicals of the 1880's, named, significantly, *Brain,* and *Mind.* Also, Cattell's journals and letters in M. M. Sokal's book, M. M. Sokal, in *An Education in Psychology* (1981), the MIT Press, Cambridge, Massachusetts, record Cattell's heavy reading and study of literature on nervous physiology and the brain.

Cattell is presumed to have proved (with experiments begun with John Dewey, G. Stanley Hall, Joseph Jastrow and others at Johns Hopkins as subjects in March, 1883) that people read words more quickly than letters, and sentences more quickly than words. In William James's 1890 psychology book, James quoted Cattell extensively in his chapters on association of ideas and on attention. On page 263, James quoted the following comments by Cattell in *Philosophische Studien:*

"The sentence was then apprehended as a whole. If not apprehended thus, almost nothing is apprehended of the several words, but if the sentence as a whole is apprehended, then the words appear very distinct."

Cattell considered this to be so because of the association of ideas in the sentence, which formed a whole. The same idea is used to explain the fact that we can perceive the "five" pattern on a dice much more quickly than we can count five randomly placed dots. But later studies of eye movements showed that Cattell was wrong in applying this idea to reading, since the eye can only see clearly a word or so at a glance. It is obvious that people who read a sentence at a glance are context-guessing. Cattell actually confirmed this, in a quotation from Cattell in Edmund Burke Huey's *The Psychology and Pedagogy of Reading* (page 73):

"...the observer constructs an imaginary sentence from the traces he has taken up."

Cattell's "sentence" ideas tied in with fellow psychologist William James' ideas on the "stream of consciousness" which James invented as a substitute for the soul. At any given point of time, the stream of consciousness contained some idea, which is to say, some sentence idea. James has some rather silly diagrams in his book explaining this ersatz soul, and Huey copied one in his book.

I believe Cattell and James wedded their psychology to work done by Hermann Ebbinghaus in Germany in 1885. Ebbinghaus had done research on memory, on the memorizing of meaningless syllables (which would be a reflex action not involving higher thought processes). Ebbinghaus also did research on the memorizing of meaningful material and found that could be done more quickly, which supported both Cattell's and James's sentence ideas.

I believe this research of Ebbinghaus's is the reason that the bottom, horizontal line on the triangle reading diagram in the 1913 *Cyclopedia of Education* article is shorter than the other two vertical lines meeting at the top point. The author of the article, Henry Suzzallo, was trying to show that children, in making associations of ideas, could go from the sight of the print (visual) in the lower right hand corner of the triangle, straight to meaning at the top point

227

of the triangle, if they read whole sight words by their meaning. But, if they read the sight words by their phonic sounds first, they would go from the sight of the print (visual) in the lower right-hand corner, to oral (the sound of the print) in the lower left-hand corner, before going to meaning at the top. That bottom horizontal line, from the sight of the print to the sound of the print, is Ebbinghaus's syllable step, and it would be a simple reflex action since it would not use the higher centers of the brain that deal with conscious meaning. But the line going from the sight of the print to meaning at the top of the triangle would be longer, since that association would not be a simple reflex action but would be a complex reflex action.

THE READING TRIANGLE

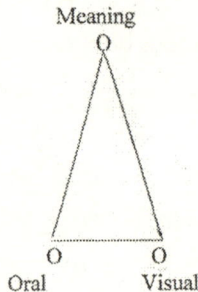

Meaning
O

O   O
Oral   Visual

Source: Article entitled, "Reading, Teaching Beginners" by Henry Suzzallo, on page 118 of the 1913 volume of A Cyclopedia of Education, edited by Paul Monroe, Columbia University. Suzzallo was also with Columbia, at Teachers College, and had been a graduate student of the psychologist, E. L. Thorndike ,at Columbia about 1901. Thorndike had been a graduate student of the psychologist, James McKeen Cattell, at Columbia in 1898, and of the psychologist, William James, at Harvard, before that.

However, Cattell was convinced that reading is an automatic act, and said so. He was equally convinced that perception is a one-step process: stimulus to response. Cattell had argued with Wundt in Germany, denying the existence of two steps, which two steps were what Wundt had proposed: perception, apperception. However, if Cattell were right, then to teach children phonics would mean that children would go, on this triangle diagram, from print to its sound, but they could drag up no meaning association bonds because the automatic step would go only as far as to the sound of print, in the bottom left-hand corner, and would not take the long step up to meaning at the top of the triangle.

Therefore, to avoid the "peril" of making a dead stop at "oral" (sound) and not proceeding to "meaning" at the top of the triangle, children would have to be taught whole sight-words - and preferably whole sentences - so that they could go automatically straight from "visual" to "meaning."

However, these early psychologists obviously knew very well that children taught to go straight to meaning would be doing so at a cost, because they could not then, automatically, have the sound and spelling correct. Oral accuracy and spelling for them would always be far more difficult, just as they obviously reasoned (incorrectly) that children reading by "sound" would always find it far more difficult to get the "meaning." For this reason, I believe, (and the record supports me) that Cattell and his close associates buried his research. With public relations methods (Cattell's subsequent life history revealed he was a genius at the use of influence), Cattell promoted the "sentence" approach to reading, to protect so-called "reading comprehension." But, to do so, it means he had to bury the truth. I am convinced that this is where America's reading instruction flat earth really started.

Cattell and James were close friends and professors of E. L. Thorndike. Thorndike was the reading experts' A. I. Gates and W. S. Gray's teacher, and so the family tree goes, down to the present day, very commonly showing the close influence of one "expert" upon another developing "expert."

James's philosophy was "pragmatism." Truth was what worked. The sentence method "worked," or so they thought. So the sentence method automatically became "truth."

Of course, Cattell was wrong about reading. Reading IS an automatic act, or it should be, but it is not one stimulus-response step. There are at least TWO automatic steps, or should be, from Visual, the sight of the print, to Oral, the sound of the syllable, and only then to Meaning. (It is actually a lot more complicated than this, but the simple outline is nevertheless fundamentally correct.) When the steps are completed, the mind can then "listen" to a printed page, just as it "listens" to speech. However, Cattell's route, from the sight of the print to its meaning, or whole sentences, is the route that was used for centuries to teach deaf-mutes language. Signs were hung on things, which signs themselves had no sounds, and then words were strung together in sentences, the meanings of which the deaf child could guess from the known words and the context.

My historical research, which must wait to be reported in full elsewhere, has convinced me that James McKeen Cattell is the eye of the reading instruction problem hurricane with which America has been buffeted for almost a century. [Editor's note in 2006: As outlined in my 1998 book, *The Hidden Story*, William James was the probable eye of that hurricane, but from 1870, and Cattell probably joined James before 1890, because of James' interest in Cattell's 1883 and later reading research, which James discussed in his 1890 psychology book.] (Without taking time to discuss the details, I would like to caution all to disregard Nila Banton Smith's so-called reading history. For example, she cut out, effectively, the years from about 1846 to about 1894 from American reading history, using only a few buckshot references, as a chronological listing of all her references makes clear. Most meaningfully, as will be seen, she cut out Gallaudet.)

The Reverend Gallaudet passed on the deaf-mute, sight-word, context-guessing method into American reading instruction, as Samuel Blumenfeld has so brilliantly researched. At the time of the founding of America's normal schools about 1840, both Gallaudet and Horace Mann were active in promoting their establishment. Horace Mann was also an apostle of the sight word method and promoted it extensively. But massive reading failures in the 1860's were bringing a return of phonics into the schools. The return was opposed by some, one of whom was presumably G. Stanley Hall, who wrote *How to Teach Reading* in 1874, still being reprinted by D. C. Heath as late as 1899. Hall had given public lectures on pedagogy in January, 1882, which resulted in his appointment at Johns Hopkins in 1883. At the urging of Johns Hopkins President Gilman, Hall repeated the lectures in 1883 (page 64, M. M. Sokal, *An Education in Psychology*.)

Arthur I. Gates confirmed Hall's opposition to practices in the late 19th century. In the May, 1962, issue of the *Reading Teacher*, "Word Recognition Ability...," Gates objected to current books by Arthur S. Trace, Jr., *What Ivan Knows That Johnny Doesn't*, and by Dr. Charles C. Walcutt, *Tomorrow's Illiterates*, because he said they thought reading problems could be solved by returning to reading books with uncontrolled vocabulary and phonic drill. Gates said that some leaders in education and psychology had "vigorously" criticized that practice before 1900, and listed G. Stanley Hall, John Dewey, James McKeen Cattell and E. B. Huey, citing Huey's 1908 book as a reference. Gates did not have to depend on Huey's book, though, as a reference on Cattell's point of view, as Gates lived with the Cattell family in the summer of 1917, working with Cattell on psychology. When Cattell was fired from Columbia for opposing the draft that year, Gates lost his draft exemption, presumably because of this association. Thorndike had it reinstated (G. Joncich, *The Sane Positivist*, page 378).

G. Stanley Hall had been Cattell's and Dewey's professor at Johns Hopkins in 1883 and had been, with Dewey, Jastrow and others, one of the subjects in Cattell's reading experiments that began the night of March 17, 1883. Cattell's experiments, wedded to William James's psychology, seemed to support the Gallaudet context-guessing, sight-word approach, based on the faulty understanding that these people had of the structure and psychology of the brain.

A "sentence" method of reading had been promoted by Farnham in 1870 but was "not widely adopted until 1885-1890" (Huey, page 273). Not surprisingly, it was promoted extensively in America after 1890, I believe through the influence of the small group of psychologists around Cattell and James. [Editor's note in 2006: See *The Hidden Story* for the ties of the sentence method to William James, who, I believe originated it.]

Shortly after 1890, the sentence method was used in a series of readers written by Charles Eliot Norton of Harvard, the *Heart of Oak Books*.[14] Norton said:

"Mother Goose" is the best primer.... the mere art of reading is the more readily learned, if the words first presented to the eye of the child are those which are already familiar to his ear."

From "Mother Goose," the children graduated to fables, fairy tales, and then:

"entrance into the wide open fields of literature, especially

_____

14 Editor's note in 2006: Norton was a close friend of the novelist, Henry James, William James' brother, and had published materials by both brothers as early as 1868 or so.

into those of poetry."

Norton's books contained only literary selections of the highest quality. Norton said, in his preface:

"It will be plain to every teacher, after brief inspection, that these books differ widely from common School Readers."

Norton said, in his acknowledgments:

"I regret that I am not allowed to mention by name one without whose help the Books would not have been made, and to whose hand most of the Notes are due."

The copy of the fourth grade book I have (copyrighted in 1895) includes these unusual and elaborate notes on the backgrounds of the selections. The notes are actually advanced literary research. They are, to put it mildly, MOST unusual for a fourth-grade reading book! It is also interesting that these books were published by the same company, D. C. Heath, which published G. Stanley Hall's *How to Teach Reading*, and Sanford's *Experimental Psychology,* both of which were advertised on a publication list at the back of the reader. Both Hall and Sanford were at Clark University, and, like Cattell and James, were members of the very small American Psychological Association at that time.

The author of the *Heart of Oak* readers, Charles Eliot Norton, was a highly influential and well-known man in his own right. So the one he could not mention by name who wrote the extraordinarily literary notes for his readers and "without whose help the Books would not have been made" must have had at least equal stature. William James's home had been built on a subdivision of Norton's estate, as had Josiah Royce's, James' close friend and neighbor. G. Stanley Hall was a personal friend of James, Norton and Royce, and had lived close to Cambridge, in Somerville, Massachusetts, before his move to Baltimore (*The Letters of Josiah Royce*, Edited by John Clendenning) . But it is unthinkable that G. Stanley Hall could have been the one whom Norton was "not allowed to mention by name" because the quality of Hall's own writing is so poor and because, in it, he showed little interest in literature. But James's psychology book is chock-full of literary quotations, and James, himself, wrote beautifully. (His brother, of course, was the famous novelist.) The record suggests that William James or Henry James may have been Norton's anonymous editor.

At the time Norton's readers were published, many at Harvard were interested in the improvement of schools. As C. H. Judd put it at the Thorndike honorary program at Columbia on February 19, 1926 (*Teachers College Record*, May, 1926):

"The decade of the 90's was a decade of agitation. It was during this period that J. M. Rice went up and down the land writing about school systems. This was the period of great committees, of the Committee of Ten and the Committee of Fifteen. This was the decade of... the institution of sweeping educational reforms under Charles W. Eliot and William Rainy Harper... The decade of the 90's was in an important sense of the word a period of experimentation in ways of dealing with educational problems. It was a period of restlessness. It closed with that striking manifestation of genius, the measurement of school results in spelling and arithmetic by J. M. Rice."

J. M. Rice, of course, is one of the flat earth casualties, because his results showed excellent spelling in American schools in the late

1890's, when phonetic spelling was once again being taught.

I suggest that the promotion of the sentence method was the joint work of both Cattell and William James, but they wanted to be dissociated from it because they knew, from the beginning and by the very definition of their psychological theory of association of ideas, that children who learned "whole words" and "sentences" would be weaker in spelling and oral reading accuracy than who learned phonics.

E. B. Huey' s famous quotation in his 1908 book should be remembered (the one which so fascinated Rudolf Flesch back in 1955, who regarded it with amazement on page 51 of his book, *Why Johnny Can't Read*:

> "Even if the child substitutes words of his own for some that are on the page, provided that those express the meaning, it is an encouraging sign that the reading has been real....it is well to place the emphasis strongly where it really belongs, on reading as *thought-getting*."

A most interesting series of letters in the Library of Congress suggest very powerfully that Huey was recruited to psychology by Cattell himself and was his protégé, and that his book, *The Psychology and Pedagogy of Reading,* was written in payment of that debt. After writing it, Huey immediately dissociated himself from any further connection with reading instruction, which strange occurrence has been noted by many. Huey wrote Cattell on June 8, 1897, from the academy at which he taught Latin, where he said he had just handed in his resignation:

> "I have finally decided to try to begin in earnest with psychology next fall.... I will only have about $150 to begin with next fall. If it seems possible for me to earn my

way at Columbia I would like to begin there.... Is it possible for me to get a scholarship at this late day? I did not feel free to apply for one before. Am afraid I cannot enter if have tuition to pay.

"If I am not troubling you too much, would you let me know about the possibilities for a scholarship, and what would be the best (or a possible) means of earning money in the University? Am willing to do anything.

"Have been much interested in the little book by Jastrow and hope you will pardon me if I keep it just a little longer."

Jastrow had been one of Cattell's subjects in his reading experiments in 1883 at Johns Hopkins University, and was later at the University of Wisconsin (from which Starch came, who worked on reading comprehension tests about 1915). The book which Cattell had obviously lent to Huey may have been a small book, *Epitomes of Three Sciences,* 1890, that contained a section by Jastrow, "Aspects of Modern Psychology." The reference to Jastrow's material on modern psychology suggests that Cattell was recruiting the Latin teacher to the field of psychology. Huey had graduated from Lafayette, Cattell's alma mater, and the school where his father had been president for years.

I believe Cattell and James were using public relations techniques in promoting the "meaning" method to teach beginning reading, emphasizing the positive and ignoring the negative. (William James died in 1910, but his influence persisted in Thorndike, who had been both James' and Cattell's student and friend.)

It was not William James of Harvard, but President Charles W. Eliot of Harvard, who wrote an essay in 1890 violently opposing the current school readers. In a magazine article in July, 1891, he advocated literature in place of school readers. Eliot was completely outspoken on the subject, so hardly would have opposed the use of his name, if he had helped compile the *Heart of Oak Books.*

In Rex Reeder's 1900 history of reading, he referred to Norton's *Heart of Oak Books:*

"The problem of method in teaching beginners is scarcely recognized.... the first book is entirely Nursery Rhymes...and Jingles.... The most radical departure from the conventional lines of textbook publishing...."

Nila Banton Smith quoted Charles Eliot, but omitted the *Heart of Oak Books.* Book four which I have was copyrighted in 1895, and printed in 1899, but Smith said (on page 143) that the first literary readers were Arnold and Gilbert's *Stepping Stones to Literature* in 1897. Since I have come to the conclusion that most of Smith's many historical omissions were carefully tailored for very specific effects, her omission of the *Heart of Oak* readers and her assertion that the first literary series was a later one have convinced me that my reconstruction of the history is close to the truth.

Concerning William James's interest in language and therefore interest in reading, in his 1890 psychology book he told the story of a Mr. Ballard of Gallaudet College, deaf from infancy, who did not learn language until being taught written language at the age of 11. Yet, before he acquired language, he was capable of thinking the most complex thoughts, without language, such as "How came the world into being?" (James, page 172). James had given other quotations to show the possibility of using elaborate language, yet arousing no thought. Obviously, it was the whole thought that mattered for that deaf-mute child, and not the words, and enshrining of the whole thought is the rationale for the sentence method.

By 1911, the date of the publication of the first volume of the

Cyclopedia of Education, articles from elsewhere had shown that the human brain had been clearly mapped on speech. Types of aphasia had been identified as originating from defects in certain parts of the brain. William James in his 1890 *Principles of Psychology* went into detail on the subject of aphasia and brain injuries and related them to reading and writing.

Yet, other than in James's 1890 work, in some pre-1912 sources, and in Dr. Hilde Mosse's great 1982 work, *The Complete Handbook of Children's Reading Disorders*, a brain-based explanation for the act of reading is never discussed clearly, particularly by "reading experts." With fair regularity, "reading experts" do produce Rube-Goldberg-types of diagrams which attempt to explain reading. But where is the kind of clarity to be found in William James's and Hilde Mosse's works, where statements are concretely based and therefore verifiable, instead of being just confused waterfalls of words?

Observed types of aphasia have shown clearly that separate areas of the brain relate to speech. One area concerns the ability to reproduce syllables. Others concern the abilities for processing syntax and words. These abilities, for the production of syllables and what I will call syntax-generating-words, are automatic functions. But processing the MEANING of language is always conscious.

So the acts of listening (and therefore its closely related function, reading, which deals with frozen speech) are done on three consecutive levels, the first two of which are automatic. Level One is that of syllable sounds. Level Two is that of syntax which includes what we call words. Level Three is conscious attention. It is possible for computers to operate at the first two automatic levels, and so can the human mind, without using conscious attention. We can be said to hold computers inside our heads, as we can hold them with our hands, because our brains automatically process these syllable sounds and syntax-generating-words, balancing one with the other, to produce the stream of language which is automatically presented to Level Three, the level of consciousness, attention, or life itself. It is this level, however, which cannot be duplicated by a machine computer. No matter how clever computers can be made to perform at finding calculus solutions and programming space stations, they can never reach the independent thinking level even of my old cat, Blackie, because Blackie is conscious and alive and they are not.

THE FIRST FLAT EARTH FACT

Our reading "experts" have invented an illusion, or flat earth fact, for each of these three levels of reading, and it is with these illusions that all discussion of reading is carried out in America today. Let us examine each of these illusions in turn.

The first flat earth "fact" of many reading experts, their first illusion, is on Level One, syllables, when they talk about using "letter sounds." Yet voice prints show clearly that there IS no such thing as a pure letter sound, except for vowels (and semi-vowels). What we produce instead when we speak (or read properly) are syllable sounds. This was recognized in the ancient Greek and Roman worlds and almost universally in countries using the alphabets descended from them until long after the time of Leonardo Da Vinci and Shakespeare.

The ancient Greek Dionysius of Halicarnassus wrote:

"We first learn the names of the letters, then their forms
and length, then syllables and their usual variations Then
we begin to read and write, but syllable-wise and slowly,
until we have acquired some facility, and then connectedly

and as we choose."

(From "A-B-C Books and Primers," page 594, Vol. XII, 1865?, *American Journal of Education*, Henry B. Barnard, Editor. This version differs from that cited by Mitford Mathews on pages 6 and 7 in his *Teaching to Read, Historically Considered*, The University of Chicago Press, 1960, which Mathews quoted from W. Rhys Roberts' book, *Dionysius of Halicarnassus*, London, 1910, page 269.)

The ancient Roman Quintilian said:

"For learning syllables there is no short way; they must all be learned throughout."

In *Love's Labor Lost,* Shakespeare says of the schoolmaster, Holofernes, "....he teaches boys the hornbook." The hornbook was a page covered by transparent horn, which had the alphabet to be memorized, followed by strings of regularly formed syllables (ba, be, bi, bo, bu; ab, eb, ib, ob, ub, etc.) to be practiced, and then the *Lord's Prayer*. The expression "Fe, fi, fo, fum," from the English fairy tale probably arose from children's practicing the syllabary, as may have also been the case with the invention of the musical scale: "do, re, mi, fa, sol, la, ti, do."

A little earlier than Shakespeare's reference, in 1496, Leonardo Da Vinci made miniature illustrations for a similar ABC book in Milan. Presumably the prayers following the syllabary in this ABC book were written in Latin, as all ABC books had been in Europe before the Reformation.

So, at that time, about the 16th century, syllables were still being taught as the "atom" of reading, just as they had been in the third century B. C., as shown by the *Papyrus Gueraud Jouguet* (discussed in *A History of Education in Antiquity*, by H . I. Marrou, pages 210-218, 496, 520). This papyrus was a teacher's guide dug up from the sands of North Africa where a Greek-language school's wastebaskets must have been emptied some two thousand years before. This third century B. C. scroll was an astonishing discovery just before the start of World War II. It outlined in great detail the study of sequential tables of syllables, where the regularity of the syllables in the tables demonstrated their sounds. The children spelled them as they learned them: beta—alpha, ba; beta—epsilon, be; etc.

It was Blaise Pascal, the famous scientist and mathematician, who finally split this syllable atom in France in 1655. Pascal was a sympathizer of the Jansenists, the grim heretical French Catholic sect preaching predestination. His sister Jacqueline was a nun at the even grimmer Port Royal Jansenist School. Even little four-year-old students there led a life so devoid of normal childhood pleasures that the author of an article in Ferdinand Buisson's *Dictionnaire de Pedagogie et d'Instruction Primaire* almost cried on the page for them. But the author of the 1887 article on Jacqueline Pascal for Buisson's *Dictionnaire* quoted a letter Jacqueline Pascal wrote her brother in 1655. She questioned Blaise Pascal on the proper use of the method he had invented.

The Pascal method was to give different names to the consonants instead of their usual names, consisting of the phoneme plus what we call a schwa, a vowel said so quickly it is almost indistinguishable. We show schwas in our dictionary pronunciation guides with a kind of upside-down "e".

The names of the letters had been a source of trouble in beginning reading ever since the Greeks borrowed them from the Phoenicians about 800 B. C. On page 343 of *A History of the Art of Writing,* (1920), William A. Mason said:

"The early Greeks also may be credited with other substantial contributions to the alphabet. At the time when the earliest known Thera inscriptions were written there already had been evolved out of the Phoenician characters five true vowels: alpha, epsilon, iota, omicron, and upsilon."

Mason said that these earliest inscriptions found at Thera dated from the 8th or 7th century. That certainly makes it appear likely that the vowels were a once-only invention, at Thera sometime in the 8th century B. C., and it was a stroke of genius by an old Greek we can call Anonymous I. The Phoenician letters originated in Egypt, where they had been invented as a sort of short-hand syllable writing. As I. J. Gelb said, the letters originally meant, for B, all the syllables formed from B plus any possible vowel sound. Old Anonymous I had made it possible to write out those syllables very precisely by the invention of the vowels.

Yet the Greeks who first borrowed the alphabet missed the whole point of the Phoenician names for the letters. The Phoenician letter names simply were whole words meant to demonstrate the letters' sounds but were certainly not meant to be put together in sequence to form new words. It was as if we call "h" "house," and "u" umbrella and "b", "ball." Those words, recited in sequence, certainly do not produce "hub." When the Greeks borrowed the Phoenician words as letter names, instead of using Greek words that could function the same way, they began the problems in reading instruction that are still us, the illusion that the names of the letters, recited in sequence, can suggest words. Yet that is manifestly false. See-aye-tee does NOT suggest the name "cat."

However, the *Alpha One* program does use the ancient Phoenician letter-naming method. It calls "c" "Cotton Candy," "a" "Ah, Ah, Ahchoo," and "t" "Tall Teeth." The letters are Letter

People, and their names demonstrate their sounds, just as the original Phoenician letter names did about three thousand years ago. But reciting such names in turn is not sounding and blending phonics.

The Pascal letter names made sounding and blending phonics possible, the synthesis of letters into syllables instead of the analysis of syllables into letters. Cuh - ah- tuh recited in sequence does suggest the word cat, but it should be clearly understood that the Pascal letter names can only SUGGEST a word, since it is absolutely impossible to blend such shortened letter sounds together. The Pascal letter names are, and must remain, syllables themselves.

However, with Pascal's new abbreviated letter names, it became possible for the first time in history to suggest synthesis in reading, instead of analysis. As a scientist and mathematician, Pascal was used to both paths, synthesis and analysis, which may explain his invention, which was the first real improvement in reading since the time of Anonymous I.

Ickelsamer of Germany is usually credited with originating phonics in Germany in the previous century before Pascal's, but Ickelsamer did not rename the letters and synthesize them, but only had his students analyze their sounds in assorted syllables which were not arranged in the regularly formed sound tables that had been used from antiquity.

Buisson's *Dictionnare de Pedagogie et d'Instruction Primaire*, in its article on Blaise Pascal, includes a letter from Antoine Arnauld in January, 1656. Arnauld was in hiding in Paris because of government persecution of the Jansenist sect. Arnauld's letter was addressed to his niece, the Abbess of Port Royal:

"You will laugh at what gives me the occasion to write you. There is a little boy here around 12 years old who does not know how to read. I want to try [to see] if he can learn it by the method of

243

Mr. Pascal. This is why I beg you to finish what you should have begun to put in writing and send it to us."

The Pascal method eventually showed up as a page in the 1664 *Grammaire Generale* of Port Royal, which book is commonly attributed to Arnauld. After falling into obscurity, the method was found again by Py-Poulain de Launay in 1719 and eventually found its way into Diderot's *Encyclopedie ou Dictionnaire Raissonne des Sciences, des Arts et des Metiers* in the last half of the 18th century.

The author of the 1887 *Dictionnaire de Pedagogie....* article added to his account on Pascal:

"Assuredly, this invention does not add any big thing to the glory of Pascal. It attests at least his care for clarity and rigor which is proper to his genius, and that he carried it out in little things, as big ones."

But it was a VERY big thing! No longer did children have to be taught to recite misleading letter names and then to memorize the syllables they formed in long strings of regularly formed sound patterns: ba, be, bi, bo, bu, bab, beb, bib, bob, bub , etc., as they had done even from the days of the Etruscans. It is known that the Etruscans had a syllabary in 600 B. C., and it is mentioned by H. I. Marrou in *The History of Education in Antiquity* (page 336). After Pascal's invention in 1655, children could figure out the syllable sounds for themselves, without reference to their places in a systematic sound table. Children had only to recite the abbreviated names for the letters, which, recited in sequence, suggested the syllables.

An article, "Syllabaire" appeared on pages 713-715, Volume XV, of the_*Encyclopedie ou Dictionnaire Raissonne des Sciences des Arts, et des Metiers*, (18 volumes, 1752-1772, Paris). The author of that article, who was very possibly the *Encyclopedie's* editor,

Denis Diderot, did realize the value of Pascal's invention, unlike the author of the *Dictionnaire...* article a century later. He totally endorsed Pascal phonics and recognized that Pascal phonics meant the renaming of the consonants of the alphabet, and wrote:

"I will not say further that it is necessary to name all the consonants with this scheva or e muet, conforming to the view of the Grammaire Generale, adopted since by Messrs. Dumas and de Launay, and by the masters the most wise. This spelling to me appears so true, so simple and so useful; and the old to the contrary, so inconsequential, so encumbering and so opposed to the progress of children, that I think it is no longer necessary to insist on this.

"But I shall remark, as something important, that for the syllables of which I have indicated the detail and the divisions, it is necessary not to omit a single one in the tables that one will set up: 'Syllabis nullum compendium es, perdiscendae omnes.' This is the opinion of Quintilian (Inst. I, j. 5) and he wished that one stopped the children there until one had all the certitude possible that they were no longer confused in the discrimination of a single syllable. I am persuaded that they scarcely ever will be, if they name the consonants by the scheva, because it is easy to make them conceive, instead of the scheva, to put the sound which follows the consonant."

The last sentence, of course, is the author's description of blending. So this author, very possibly the *Encyclopedie's* editor, Dennis Diderot, who was one of the most brilliant though controversial men of the 18th Century, did NOT agree with I. Carre, the author of the *Dictionnaire...* article, that Pascal's contribution was unimportant, or that beginning reading was unimportant. The "Syllabaire" article's author (Diderot?) actually said:

> "I seem to hear some of the proud philosophers of whom I come to speak to find fault with disdain the high tone [with] which I report here a kind of work which, in their eyes, perhaps is not dignified enough to be indicated in the *Encyclopedie*. I believe that reading is the least of the necessary parts of an education; but at least it is one, and one could even say that it is fundamental, since it is the key of all the other sciences, and the first introduction to the Grammaire; 'quae nisi oratori futuro fundamenta fideliter jecerit, quidquid superstruxeris, corruet. It is Quintilian who has spoken so. (Inst. I, jv. 1.)"
>
> "He himself, from his first chapter of his excellent work, occupied himself in enough great detail with this which offends here the false refinement of our grave philosophers and I can only answer them by the very words of this sage rhetor, who in his time had to forestall similar objections...."

The author then reminded his readers that Quintilian referred to the fact that King Philip of Macedonia obtained Aristotle, himself, as the tutor for his son, Alexander the Great, when Alexander was a child. He added:

> "One sees that it is not to the most unskillful that Quintilian abandons the care of showing the first elements.... He judges that the man the most perfect is not too much for this first culture...."

Pascal's invention provided a watershed date. From having had to learn the lengthy sound tables of regularly formed syllables by practicing them in regularly formed sound patterns, children were freed after that date to learn the sounds of the syllables from the basic 40 or so phonemes in their own languages, through the new Pascal alphabet. But the *Encyclopedie* author made it clear (though he probably was unaware that it was possible to doubt it) that phonics was meant ONLY to help the children learn by heart their SYLLABLES, not their words. This was apparent even in his comment on the reading matter children eventually would receive, after practicing the new letters and the syllables they formed. He wrote:

"When the children are firm on their letters and on their syllables, it is necessary to make them read something, but this should be prepared. I find nothing better conceived than the "expedient" that I have seen used in some syllabaires. The discourse which must serve as the material of the first reading is printed at the right on the page "recto" under the ordinary form and vis-a-vis, to the left on the "verso, " the same discourse is printed in similar characters, but with a separation and a dash between each of the syllables of each word."

It was apparently through Diderot's widely circulated *Encyclopedie...* in the last half of the 18th century that Pascal's idea of true, synthetic, sounding-and-blending phonics finally entered the Western World's intellectual mainstream, over a hundred years after it had been invented for Port Royal. Synthetic phonics in different variations showed up in widely separated places shortly after Diderot's encyclopedia volumes began to appear. In Germany, phonics appeared in Heinecke's work with the deaf in 1773. Phonics showed up in Johann Bernhard Basedow's famed school in

Germany, the Philanthropinum, in 1774, where Basedow married phonics to his newly invented word method, skipping the syllable step that the author of the Encyclopedie article correctly believed to be so essential.

Basedow was a follower of John Locke and adopted in his school the ideas Locke expressed in England in 1690 and 1693, in Locke's books, *An Essay Concerning Humane Understanding*, and *Some Thoughts Concerning Education*. Following Locke's advice, Basedow began instruction with objects or their pictures, then moved to words, and finally to phonemes in words. Basedow then immediately put the phonemes (the Pascal letter names) back together to make new words. Basedow is the probable father of the German analytic-synthetic phonic method. But Basedow had moved the initial teaching of reading up from Level 1, the syllable, where it had always been, to Level 2. Although his method was highly successful, he left the door open for ultimate confusion on the nature of reading.

The idea of true synthetic phonics showed up in Ireland where Richard Edgeworth recorded in his *Practical Education* in 1798 that he had used points and marks on letters to indicate pronunciation in teaching children to read. Edgeworth said this was before he had seen the work of the Anglo-Irish dictionary author, Thomas Sheridan. Edgeworth said:

"These marks were employed by the author in 1776, before he had seen Sheridan's or any similar dictionary; he has found that they do not confuse children as much as figures."

In England, Thomas Sheridan had added figures (numbers) over vowels to indicate their sound. Thomas Sheridan, the Anglo-Irish actor, had been the friend (and later enemy) of the dictionary author, Samuel Johnson. Thomas Sheridan was also the father of the famed playwright and member of Parliament in England, Richard Sheridan, who wrote *School For Scandal*. Thomas Sheridan,

248

himself, was the son of another famous Sheridan, at whose home in Ireland Swift stayed while he wrote *Gulliver's Travels*.

Samuel Johnson had not included a pronunciation key in his famous dictionary, as such a thing was unknown at the time. However, the *Encyclopedia Britannica* said Lord Bute was so impressed with Sheridan's scheme for a pronouncing dictionary that he gave Sheridan also a 200-pounds-a-year pension, which would appear to confirm that Sheridan's was the first dictionary which used phonics to indicate pronunciation. In 1760, Sheridan had been acting under David Garrick at Drury Lane. It is possible that he saw there the *Encyclopedie* article mentioning Pascal's phonics sometime before he left for France in 1764, where he might also have seen the *Encyclopedie* article. Sheridan returned to England from France after his wife died in 1766. Diderot's *Encyclopedie* was apparently well known in Sheridan's group in Drury Lane, since in 1766 David Garrick subscribed for the last ten volumes and plates (according to John Lough in 1970, *The Encyclopedie in Eighteenth Century England and Other Studies*, Oriel Press, Ltd., Newcastle-upon-Tyne, England).

The actor, Thomas Sheridan, was interested in education like his father who had been a highly regarded schoolmaster. Sheridan had been concerned for years not only with teaching elocution but with education in general. In 1769 he published *Plan of Education for the Young Nobility and Gentry*, and in 1780 his *General Dictionary of the English Language*. As stated, this was apparently the first dictionary with a pronunciation key. Presumably, it was through his interest in teaching elocution that he eventually discovered Pascal phonics and invented his own pronunciation key for the vowels in English.

In 1783, only three years after the publication of Sheridan's dictionary, the young Noah Webster published his *American Spelling Book*. It used the precise method to indicate pronunciation that Sheridan had used three years earlier in England, numerals over the vowels, with a key to explain the numerals. This was not the method which had been used by Edgeworth in Ireland in 1776 and seems to confirm that Webster modeled his 1783 method after Sheridan's dictionary. This is particularly so since Webster mentioned Sheridan in his "Preface."

Horn book paddles, that had contained the alphabet, the syllabary up to "f" (fa, fe, fi, fo, etc.) and the Lord's Prayer (originally in Latin), in use from the 14th century but only for rank beginners, had begun to die out at the start of the 18th century, and were gone by about 1830. Originally, they had been followed by what were called ABC books, but the English spelling books which arrived at the end of the 16th century were dominant by the end of the 17th. (These spelling books were often called primers, but the true English primers were prayer books, although they also included syllable tables after the Reformation.) In the spelling books, words of progressively longer syllables were listed for spelling after the syllabary had been gone over. Webster's 1783 spelling book largely replaced other spellers that had been in use in America, such as Dilworth's, and it added the concept of true phonics.

However, despite Webster's carefully explained pronunciation key to be used on the words in his book, Webster still realized the value of the syllable. He wrote:

"In nine-tenths of the words in our language, a correct pronunciation is better taught by a natural division of the syllables, and a direction for placing the accent, than by a minute and endless repetition of characters."

As all first-grade teachers should know and teach their children (and as Webster obviously knew), the sound of a vowel is most commonly determined by how a word is divided into syllables (su -

per, sup - per, for instance).

Walker, like Sheridan, was an actor in England and he wrote a highly successful dictionary after Sheridan with its own pronunciation key. That both Walker and Sheridan may also have written spelling books (as Perry did) which used phonics is suggested by a note in the preface to an 1807 edition of Webster's:

"The multitude of characters in Perry's scheme render it far too complex and perplexing to be useful to children, confusing the eye, without enlightening the understanding. Nor is there the least necessity for a figure over each vowel, as in Walker, Sheridan, and other authors."

Webster solved this problem by arranging his words in similar sound tables, with the sound indicated at the head of each list of words.

Concerning the invention of phonics, it is no accident that this abstract idea, to think of the consonants as something apart from syllables, and then to invent new shortened names for them which, by an imaginary blending of sounds produce the syllables, came from one of the most abstract thinkers in history, the scientist and mathematician Blaise Pascal. Just as it took a Greek genius to invent the vowels about 800 B. C., it took a French genius to invent real phonics. Yet this invention, meant only to help in the initial learning of the syllables of words, was to be distorted. Most people totally forgot that there IS no such thing as an isolated. letter sound, except for the vowels. Consonant letters, when used without vowels, are still syllables today, just as they were in Egypt about 5,000 years ago when they were first invented. Yet sight-word basal readers teach children to use "consonant sounds" as "clues" in guessing at unknown words all through school, resulting in permanently crippling habits. To believe in such PURE letter sounds is to believe in an illusion, or to believe in the first flat earth "fact" of the reading experts.

THE SECOND FLAT EARTH FACT

The second flat earth fact of the reading experts, or their second illusion, is on Level Two, syntax-generating-words. It is the illusion that there IS such a thing as a pure word which can be used apart from syntax. Yet the dictionary does not make this error, as every word is defined in terms of syntax, as a noun, or a verb, or an adjective, and so on.

The ancient Greeks taught children to read separated syllables, not words, and, even after the very early stages, all print was run together without separation into words. It was not until the first century B.C. that Dionysius Thrax produced the first grammar, defining eight parts of speech (again, defined in terms of syntax) so it should be evident that the ancient Greeks were not spending much time thinking about "words." Yet even Dionysius Thrax did not get around to deal with the proper use of his parts of speech, or "words" in syntax, although the Romans did later.

The Romans also generally ran printed matter together without separating the syllables or words. Alcuin, the English scholar in Charlemagne's court about 800 A. D. is the man generally credited with introducing lower case letters, punctuation and word separations in ordinary texts. Before this, words had been separated occasionally as on Roman monuments, and Roman schoolboys separated them laboriously on texts they had to prepare.

Almost all reading in the ancient world was done aloud. Mitford Mathews referred to the fact that St. Augustine in the fourth century A. D. was amazed to find St. Ambrose reading silently. This puts the great "push" on silent reading in America since the late

19th century in rather a silly light, because, if silent reading were essential for comprehension, then almost no one in the ancient world "comprehended" what he read.

Concerning "pure words," the ancients did have Latin to Greek translating dictionaries for schools, as in the Middle Ages we had Latin to vernacular translating dictionaries, but it should be evident that "words" for the Greeks and Romans were NOT the atom of printed matter, as they are in our schools today. To the ancients, it is obvious that the syllable, as read in syntax, was more important. Isn't it to us, even now, as we listen to oral speech? Think about the comic strip question, "Ya gonna GO?" Words collide and are destroyed in that use of syllables in syntax. Yet the sentence is perfectly understandable to any American. The truth is that it is syllables in syntax which generate words, but the reading "experts" have it backwards, thinking that words generate syntax.

After the advent of the English scholar, Alcuin, in Charlemagne's court about 800 A. D., when print was finally separated into words, words assumed a new emphasis. This was the beginning of a long evolution in which people in English-speaking and German-speaking countries gradually but mindlessly forgot that it is the syllable which is the atom of speech and reading, not the word. But in Latin languages like French which have many open syllables that are not words (ve - lo), unlike English and German which have many closed syllables that ARE words (dog, hund) , people were relatively immune to that trend. That is so even though true dictionaries with word definitions, which mindlessly seem to stress the existence of pure "words" became widespread in Europe in the 17th century. Yet dictionaries tacitly acknowledge that words can never exist outside of syntax, or the syntax-dependence of words, when they identify all words as parts of speech: nouns, verbs, adjectives, and so on. One of the ancient Roman writers did not even call them words, but, more accurately, parts of speech.

Nevertheless, the syllabary in earlier times was the method for teaching beginning reading all over Europe and America as well until almost the 19th century. Ferdinand Buisson's *Dictionnaire de Pedagogie et d'Instruction Primaire*, Paris, 1887, speaks of the book, *Rules for the Schools of the City and Diocese of Lyon*, by Charles Demia, which was presumed to be published in the last half of the 17th century by Andre Olyer, publishers. This showed that children learned to read in Latin and only later learned to read French. All over Europe before the Reformation, children first learned to read in Latin and only afterward in their native languages. Of course, since Latin breaks easily into syllables, this was additional drill on the syllable in beginning reading.

In the 17th century in Lyon, France, Charles Demia's book said that, after having learned to read, for instance, "In nomine Patris," meaning "In the name of the Father," the children would read it again, but with each child reading a syllable in turn. One read "in," "the next "no," the next "mi," the next ne, and so on. Demia mentioned the use of dice in beginning reading:

"One could also use squares in the form of dice, where would be printed the letters or syllables, with which the children will play, being given a pupil more capable to settle their differences.... those who shall know the most will gain a good point, or something else that might be designated."

Buisson referred to another book, <u>The Parish School,</u> by I. D. B. Priest, published in Paris in 1654. Pere I. D. B. warned concerning beginning readers:

"...not to undertake to make them fly in reading before they know how to spell the letters because, wishing to advance them teaching them so many things at one time, one makes their reading so confused that further they are a long time learning; (and) they never know to read well, neither in Latin or in French.

"To proceed, therefore, by order, it is necessary (1) to teach the little children to know the letters (2) to assemble them to make syllables (3) to spell the syllables to make some words, and afterwards to read."

Tuer's *History of the Horn Book* tells of the paddle-shaped horn books which were in common use in England from at least the end of the 15th century until the early 19th century. A horn book was a piece of wood on which a sheet of paper had been placed, which paper was then covered and protected by transparent horn. Horn books were about three by five inches in size, and sometimes had a hole in the handle of the paddle for a string to tie the paddle to a child's waist so that the horn book would not be lost. The paper sheet had on it, first, the alphabet; next, the vowels a, e, i, o, and u; and then alphabetically-ordered sample syllables up to fa, fe, fi, fo; af, ef, if, of, uf. The child was expected to complete that alphabetically ordered syllabary by himself, from ga, ge, gi, go, gu; ag, eg, ig, og, ug, up to "za, ze, zi, zo, etc.", with the help of his fescue pointer, going in turn from each of the consonants in the alphabet after "f" to each of the vowels.. The rest of the horn book page, below the alphabet and sample syllabary, contained the Lord's Prayer.

Little children were sent off to dames' schools (which meant to an old neighborhood woman who sewed, minded toddlers, and listened to them recite their horn -book lessons) . Children were sent to such "schools" at the ridiculous age of three in England. Diderot confirmed that children began reading at about the same age in France. Since, today, we know that most children of three years of age cannot distinguish geometric figures such as squares and triangles so as to draw them consistently, the silliness of teaching "letters" at that young age should be apparent.

Children at the age of three were expected to learn their alphabet and syllables from the paddle horn book, and then to practice their newly learned syllables in reading the Our Father, the Lord's Prayer. The Our Father was written in English from about 1545 in the reign of Henry VIII, instead of in Latin as the Pater Noster. That change about 1545 from the regularly spelled Latin syllables of the Pater Noster to the irregularly spelled English syllables of the Our Father placed an enormous barrier in front of those three-year-old beginners. (It is interesting that the pre-Reformation term for the Lord's Prayer was Pater Noster, and that it was only after Henry VIII's move away from Latin that the name, the Lord's Prayer was coined.) After they used the hornbook, apparently until about the middle of the seventeenth century, children graduated to the primer, which also began with syllables and progressed to further prayers. The famed *New England Primer* of the late 17th century was a variation on this. However, the spelling books which had been invented in the late sixteenth century appear to have generally replaced the prayer-book- primers before the beginning of the 18th century, but the history is muddied by the fact that books which were manifestly just spelling books, not prayer books, were often called primers.

William Hornbye wrote *Hornbye's Hornbook* in London in 1622, and it was reprinted by Andrew W. Tuer. The poem is clear on the practices of the time, as some of the following excerpts from the very long poem can show. It should be remembered, however, that Oliver Cromwell's unpleasant arrival on the scene not very long after so disrupted England that it obviously also derailed some of the practices reported by Hornbye in 1622:

"For three or fower years space, like to a lamb,
He spends his time in sporting, and in gam,
His wanton courage somewhat then to coole,
His Parents put him to a petty Schoole,
Then after that, he takes a pritty pride,
To weare the Horn-book dangling by his side.
"And, was it not well arm'd with plate and horne,
'Twas in great danger to be rent and torne....
"And having so the child's affection won,
(He faith) Sweet Lad, come and thy Horne-booke con.
"And so the A B C he first is taught;
From that to spelling, he is after brought;
And, being right instructed for to spell,
He learns his Sillables and Vowells well.
Then, with due teaching he doth well consider,
By's Master's rule how he may put together.
The Horn-booke having at his fingers end,
Unto the Primer he doth next ascend."

Children were given a fescue, or pointer to use in reading, to point to the letters and syllables. Buisson's *Dictionnaire de Pedagogie et d'Instruction Primaire* quotes Demia in Lyon, France, in the 17th century, writing about fifty years after Hornbye, who said about pointing for beginners:

"Each should look and hold his finger or touch it on the word that is read."

Citing the same practice in 20th century Russia, a January, 1959, *Instructor* article on visits to Soviet schools said:

"Each child has a small wooden pointer that he uses to

point to the syllables as he reads. This is used through the first three grades and higher if the child requires it. Reading is taught to the class as a whole with no recognition of individual differences."

The last sentence is of great interest in contrast to our practices.
According to the *Encyclopedia Brittanica,* in John Locke's 17th century *Essay on Humane Understanding*, he did deal with the use of words, not syllables, but inconclusively, it was said. Locke considered words to be signs of ideas, and much use was made of this view in the 19th century teaching of object lessons, which grew out of Locke's general philosophy, after being filtered through the writings of Basedow and Pestalozzi, among others.

But John Locke, himself, testified that syllabic hornbooks were the normal route for beginning to read in the late 17th century. In his 1693 *Thoughts on Education*, when recommending Aesop's fables as a book which would interest children in reading, he said:

"Nothing that I know has been considered of this kind, out of the ordinary road of the horn-book, primer, psalter, Testament and Bible."

However, even in Locke's time, true primers (prayer books) could not have been normally used to teach beginning reading. As far back as the reign of Henry VIII, the primer Henry VIII published was to be preceded by the ABC book - and the hornbook was essentially only the first page of the ABC book. When the ABC books faded away, their place was taken by spelling books, which were, as has been said, sometimes called primers. Eventually even the hornbooks were wiped out by the spelling books.

Concerning the syllabary in the horn-books and "primers," Andrew Tuer said:

"The syllabarium, as we know it in the horn-book, figures in the earliest primers, and if not quite as old as the hills, must go back in some form or other to the time of the invention of a written alphabet."

Things began to change in the 18th century. Noah Webster said in a letter to Henry Barnard in 1840:

"When I was young, the books used were chiefly or wholly Dilworth's Spelling Books, the Psalter, Testament, and Bible."

Noah Webster was born in 1758. By the end of the 18th century, the syllabic hornbooks had all but disappeared, having been replaced by the new spelling books and the new readers, like Webster's *Third Part.*

But awareness of the syllable as the atom of speech, and not the word, still managed to persist in the teaching of reading in English until well into the 19th century, despite the fact that "spelling" meant the invariant use of particular syllable spellings in certain words. But gradually the teaching of whole words, particularly after the advent of Gallaudet's deaf-mute sight-word readers in America, made people lose sight of the function of the syllable.

Awareness of the syllable as the atom of reading is still present today in the French language. I have copies of a Belgian French language primer printed in 1974, *Syllabaire Illustre,* a very meaningful title. It DOES teach syllables, but from phonic synthesis. The importance of the syllable in French reading instruction is shown by something else, apparently well known even today in France. It was reported in "French Research in the Teaching of Reading and Writing," by J. Simon, in the *Journal of*

Educational Research, February, 1957, and by T. Simon in Pedagogie Experimentale, Paris, 1924. Back in the first decade of the 20th century, the psychologist Binet of France, and Vaney, who was a primary school principal near Paris, composed the first reading test. (Most American "experts" apparently still have not heard about it. Instead, Thorndike in 1914 gets the credit for that in American sources.) Vaney divided reading into four meaningful levels:

A. sub-syllabic reading, when a child could only read a few letters.
B. syllabic reading, when a child reads syllable by syllable.
C. hesitating reading - with stops.
D. fluent reading -no stops, and punctuation observed.
E. expressive reading.

Therefore, with his test, Vaney obviously acknowledged that it is the syllable which is the basic atom in reading, and NOT the word.

So the concept of syllabic reading is very alive in the French language. I saw such syllabic reading (although with phonic synthesis) in almost all the schools which I visited in France in 1977.

Yet the concept of syllabic reading no longer exists in America, even among phonics proponents. Children are thought to read - or not to read - "whole words," even though it should be obvious that words can have no existence outside of syntax. The fact that English has variant spellings for the same syllable sounds (ate, eight) does not alter the fact that in English, as in French, the ultimate task should be to teach children to read the printed syllables of their own language automatically, which syllables then produce syntax-generating-words. If any phonically trained adult doubts this, let him pick up a child's book printed in ITA phonetic print which dispenses with dictionary English spellings, and which even adds new letters. He will find that he can read the ITA phonetic print with almost as great ease as normally spelled English. At a New Jersey Teacher's Convention some years ago, an ITA representative told of American kindergarten children, trained in ITA print, who read ITA German selections as fluently as they could American ones, which was very fluently indeed. What they were reading, obviously, were syllable sounds.

Rudolf Flesch made the point that reading should be translating symbols to sound when he commented on page 27 in his original 1955 *Why Johnny Can't Read*:

> "I once surprised a native of Prague by reading aloud from a Czech newspaper. "Oh, you know Czech?" he asked. "No, I don't understand a word of it," I answered. "I can only read it."

Flesch's comment, of course, drove the reading "experts" mad. They contend that people are supposed to read "psycholinguistically," which means to guess upcoming words from the meaning of what has already been read. But how could anyone possibly "psycholinguistically" guess Czech if he did not even know the language, but only its pronunciation rules? (Flesch said he had learned these in a short course as a teen-ager.)

Phonically-trained children eventually learn the arbitrary English spellings, the use of certain syllable spellings for certain words, through their reading. It is through reading practice that they learn to attach these correct spellings to words, and they learn it to the level of automaticity. Two-thirds of my phonically trained first-graders astonished me in the late spring of one year by having correctly spelled on tests almost all of the 250 commonest words in English. Yet they had only the most casual actual study on this special list, having had it inserted in their regular spelling books for practice with their partners. But I did have the bookshelves in the room stuffed with interesting books written at a primary level and had set aside blocks of time for independent reading. Those books, of course, had repeated those 250 words commonest words over and over and over in the materials the children were reading independently, so most children retained the visual memories of those spellings.

The excuse that these children did so well because they were privileged, suburban children will not pass, however. Bettina Rubicam of Reading Reform Foundation, Scottsdale, Arizona, has data on spelling tests given to first-grade, phonically-taught children in schools in a poor area in Harlem, and those scores were, if anything, even better than my scores. She also has scores for privileged, suburban, first-grade children in Arizona, who had the dubious benefit of sight-word basal readers. The privileged Arizona children were tested on the same list of words that was used in Harlem, but, compared to the Harlem phonic scores, the privileged children who were taught by sight words were rank failures.

Since it is impossible to hear whole, multi-syllable words all at once in oral speech, but only sequential syllables, we should not "hear" whole words in reading, either. We do not hear the spoken words "chocolate" or "strawberry" all at once, because each has three sequential syllables. To hear the first syllable, "choc," does not guarantee that the following syllables will be "o-late." Someone might be describing a new brand of ice cream and say, "I had some choc..." and then finish by saying "o-marshmallow." We process language AFTER deciphering the syllables - or we SHOULD do so if there is nothing wrong with our hearing - or our reading.

So one of the most urgent - and neglected - areas in the

teaching of beginning reading in English, even in most phonics series, is that of teaching children HOW to split print automatically into syllables, which was, not surprisingly, carefully taught by the ancients. This is necessary because vowel sounds are very often dependent on the way in which words are divided. Alpha One does a fine job in this respect, particularly in their film strip series, as I know from using their approach in teaching children to divide syllables, but such drilling on the division of syllables with first graders is relatively neglected in many other English language phonics series.

Gertrude Hildreth, then of Brooklyn College, wrote an article in 1959 for *The Reading Teacher,* carefully describing Russian primers. A well-known reading expert herself and an author on basal readers (the John C. Winston series, *Easy Growth in Reading,* which came out between 1940 and 1950), she was apparently very fair minded. She tacitly acknowledged the superiority of the Russian reading books and recommended that we study their approach. But, in her article, she referred to a 1930 Russian primer she had examined which she found had been divided between syllables. Russian primers in the late 1920's in the Soviet Union, as reproduced in the *Azbuki Ivana Fedorovado Sovremennogo Bukvaria* (1574-1974), a 238-page history of primers in Russia, which lies ignored by reading experts on the shelves of the Library of Congress, were not divided by syllables as earlier ones had been, at least on the few primer examples on which I made photocopies. For a brief period in the 1920's, some Russian primers made modified use of the "global" sight-word method, while still retaining some phonics. As the Great Soviet Encyclopedia states in its article, "Primer," Russia went back to using the analytic-synthetic phonics method in 1932, the same method that had been used by Tolstoy in the primers he wrote in the 1870's. Yet Gertrude Hildreth's comment on that 1930 primer would indicate that the

Russian psychologists had rediscovered the importance of the syllable an appreciable time before 1930, presumably about two years, if enough time were allowed for writing and printing the 1930 primer that she saw.

So Soviet Russia stopped producing sight-word primers about 1930. But America did precisely the opposite and at precisely the same time, although, in the decade before that, 1920-1930, according to Arthur I. Gates, almost all American teachers had taught heavy phonics. Teachers had continued to teach heavy phonics in the 1920's despite the fact that the sight-word method was being heavily promoted at the time. The 1920's phonics, of course, had been supplemental. However, with the advent of William Scott Gray's 1930 Scott, Foresman readers and Arthur Irving Gates' 1931 Macmillan readers, the use of supplementary phonics ceased. Instead, these 1930 and 1931 reading books were supposed to include "intrinsic" phonics, which meant guessing from the context and checking the guesses with only SOME letter sounds.

At the same time that Russia was swinging back to real phonics and syllables, America was swinging, almost silently but wholesale, to sight word, "intrinsic phonics," basal readers, published by only two companies, Macmillan and Scott, Foresman, and edited by the two major "experts," Thorndike's ex-students, Gray and Gates. The hosts of the other beginning reading books that had been published all through the 1920's quietly disappeared, and did so with an astonishing abruptness. See the 1928 *United States Catalog* which lists these multitudinous materials, once so widely used, as an article by Gates in the 1920's confirmed. The entries under "Readers" in the later *Cumulative Book Index, 1928-1932*, seem largely to be story books, foreign books, and Catholic School series. Some few reading series do appear but they were manifestly not influential as no mention seems to appear in the literature about almost any of them, as in Nila Banton Smith's "history, though she did mention fellow-expert Suzzallo's 1930 American Book Company *Fact and Story Readers*, which seems to have died a quick death.

Nila Banton Smith's revised "history" in 1965 implicitly confirms that the Gray/Gates 1930-1931 sight-word materials made an almost immediate clean sweep in the early 1930's of the American primary reading textbook market. Mountains of copies of those two new sight-word reading series must have been published in a huge hurry, because they almost immediately blanketed the country, Coast to Coast. How they were paid for in those deep depression years, when many teachers were being paid in script and not real money, is an intriguing mystery. Yet the record of that massive switch, from multitudinous primary-grade reading series in the 1920's, effectively to only two sight-word series shortly after 1931, has fallen like a dead weight into the sea of oblivion. How can it be that the details of such a massive, massive publishing switch remain virtually untrackable today?

Concerning the conviction that "words" are the atom of reading, the early "greats" in American reading history and psychology about the beginning of the 20th century (E. B. Huey, G. Stanley Hall, Colonel Francis W. Parker, James McKeen Cattell, John Dewey, E. L. Thorndike, and William James) all seemed to accept the existence of pure words in reading, yet some of them played around the edges of the idea a little, that "pure" words were an illusion. Huey said:

"There exist today languages in which the sentences are spoken without differentiation of either words or parts of speech, in a continuum of syllable sounds, or it might be said that the sentence is one long word,"

Huey was elaborating on what the German psychologist, W.

Wundt, had said in his writings. G. Stanley Hall, William James, and James McKeen Cattell had all known Wundt. Huey went on to refer to William James's remarks:

> "To attempt cutting... a sentence in the middle to get a look at it is, in James' figure, like catching a snow flake crystal in the warm hand. The flake is no longer a crystal, but a drop. 'So, instead of catching the feeling of relation moving to its term, we find we have caught some substantive thing, usually the last word we were pronouncing, statically taken, and with its function, tendency, and particular meaning in the sentence quite evaporated.'
>
> "It is like 'seizing a spinning top to catch its motion' or 'trying to turn up the gas quickly enough to see how the darkness looks.'"

Computers have been made which can translate languages, but have not been able to do so using words, and have had to use another route. Research has been done showing that first graders have no clear concept of what is meant by words. Since languages consist of syllables which can generate words and meaning only in syntax, this is hardly surprising. Yet, we do not teach children any longer to read these syllables, but instead to read "words" because we in America share, with much of the Western World, the illusion that it is "words" which are the atom of print and speech, instead of syllables.

So this is the second flat earth fact of the reading experts. Instead of acknowledging the function of the syllable, they teach instead the illusory "fact" that there is such a thing as a pure "word."

The error on Level 1, that there could be such a thing as a pure letter sound, met the error on Level 2, that there could be such a thing as a pure word, for one of the first times in a very strange place. It was the nursery of Johann Bernhard Basedow's little daughter, Emilie, in 1770. She had apparently been named after the hero of Rousseau's book, *Emile,* which had been published in 1762. Yet the connection between the two errors, on Level 1 and Level 2, was not noticed by Basedow, nor did it - THEN - cause any problem.

Rousseau's immensely popular book was actually based on John Locke's work, *Thoughts on Education.* In the 1740's, Rousseau had dinner once a week at the Hotel du Panier Fleuri in Paris with Pere Condillac and Denis Diderot, according to the *Encyclopedia Brittanica.* Angela Medici of France credits Condillac with "anticipating" Rousseau's ideas, which eventually resulted in what we know as progressive education. Condillac published his own book in which he elaborated on Locke's philosophy in 1746, about the same time he was having weekly dinners with Rousseau and Diderot. It is apparent that Condillac would have passed on Locke's points of view to Rousseau and Diderot in conversations over the dinner table. Rousseau later mentioned a small detail from Locke' s *Thoughts on Education,* the use of dice in beginning reading, with letters printed on them. The connection between Locke and Rousseau was apparently recognized by Basedow's group in Germany, however, as Basedow's disciple, Campe, simultaneously translated both Rousseau's and Locke's educational works into German in the late 18th century, and Gedike, who enthusiastically endorsed Basedow's work, also wrote on Locke.

It is strange that true phonics was invented by Pascal, an admirer of a sect preaching predestination, the Jansenists, while the concept of progressive education (and the most powerful defense of civil and religious liberties) were the work of a man, John Locke, who was reacting against such sects. Locke entered Oxford when

Oliver Cromwell's religious wars were still news. But Locke is the very antithesis of Cromwell. His ideas might be called the equal and opposite reaction to the butchering intolerance of that 17th century Jack-the-Ripper. So, in a very real sense, both Pascal's phonics and Locke's progressive education can be said to have grown out of the sects spread across Europe at that time which denied the existence of free will. Phonics was invented by an admirer of such a sect (Pascal) and progressive education by an opponent of such sects (Locke) . Bizarrely, the 20th century problems in reading would come from another group denying the existence of free will. In this case, it was the stimulus-response psychologists coming out of Johns Hopkins, Harvard, Columbia, and the University of Chicago.

The man who grasped Rousseau's ideas and proposed publishing an encyclopedic work, the *Elementary Book* based on Rousseau's philosophy, was Johann Bernhard Basedow, an abrasive German genius. (Comenius had published a somewhat similar book a century before, the *Orbis Pictus*.) Basedow wrote the great of Europe and received the support of Catharine of Russia, the King of Denmark, and many others of the famous. Immanuel Kant even wrote an article attempting to raise funds for the school which Basedow soon founded, December 27, 1774, the Philanthropinum. The wife of the famous Alsatian, Reverend Oberlin, gave up her earrings so that her husband would have some money to send to the new school.

Basedow himself, though persuasive, was extremely disagreeable and peculiar. Goethe was so fascinated with the mental exercise involved in arguing with Basedow that he left home to travel with Basedow for a time. Goethe wrote in his autobiography of Basedow's:

"...heavy, rough voice, his quick and sharp expressions, his somewhat sneering laugh, his sudden changes of the conversation, and his other peculiarities."

Goethe went on to say of Basedow:

"He had the power of speaking in a lofty and convincing way of his plans; and all men readily assented to whatever he argued. But he wounded, in the most incomprehensible manner, the feelings of the men from whom he was asking a contribution, and offended them with no reason, by not being silent upon his opinions and vagaries in regard to religious subjects.... I myself suffered much in private conversation.... and as Basedow was much better read than I, and readier at tricks of disputation, I was obliged to exert myself more and more.... So excellent an opportunity, if not to instruct myself, at least to exercise myself, I could not quickly resign. I prevailed upon my father and friends to give up the most important business, and I left Frankfort again, with Basedow."

Karl Von Raumer, who wrote the article on Basedow translated for Barnard's *American Journal of Education*, 1858, said that Basedow listed the objects of his *Elementary Book* as:

"1. Elementary instruction in the knowledge of words and
   things.
"2. An incomparable method, founded upon experience, of
   teaching children to read without weariness or loss of
   time.
"3. Natural knowledge"
   (and many other points).

The influence of Locke's philosophy on how the mind obtains

knowledge can be seen in Basedow's "elementary instruction in the knowledge of words and things."

This was to grow in the 19th century into the object lessons, the rage on both sides of the Atlantic. Locke had written in his *Thoughts on Education* that "children should receive their first impressions not from words, but from things and the representation of things." Concerning the relaxed, natural approach of Basedow's Philanthropinum, this also was in accord with Locke's comment elsewhere:

"Learning should be made as easy and pleasant as possible for children, as fear hinders their progress."

It is almost impossible to read anything on primary education written in America for the period from 1830 to 1890 without running into heavy references to the Object Lessons given at the time, and Barnard's *Journal* translated a German article with references to them, from 1855-1856. Buisson's *Dictionnaire de Pedagogie et d'Instruction Primaire* of 1887 has an article on "lecons des choses" and reports a model object lesson given by Mme. Pape Carpantier to teachers at the Sorbonne during the Paris Exposition of 1867. In Oswego, New York, the Committee on the Primary Schools made a formal observation of the teaching of object lessons in the schools on February 11, 12, and 13, 1865. The Oswego, New York, report stated, "Pestalozzi, as well as Basedow, desired that instruction should begin with the simple perception of external objects and their relations." This is pure Locke philosophy, of course, and the first purpose of Basedow's *Elementary Book.*

By the mid-19th century, however, point one of Basedow's *Elementary Book* had become mixed with point two, the teaching of reading, but when Basedow wrote his book they were not connected. Basedow's second purpose concerned the teaching of reading only. Basedow had obviously seen French reports of Pascal's sounding and blending phonics. Basedow called his own reading method "incomparable, founded upon experience," of "teaching children to read without weariness or loss of time." Yet it was only Pascal's sounding and blending phonics method, but used at Level Two, syntax-generating- words, instead of Level One, syllables. [Editor's note from 2006: I later learned of Abbe Bertaud's 1744 reading program in France, *Quadrille des Enfants,* which was started with whole words instead of syllables. The article on Abbe Bertaud in the *Dictionnaire de Pedagogie...* said Bertaud's method was used in the 18th century by the King of Prussia who had his son taught by it. It is highly likely that Basedow's beginning with whole words instead of syllables in Germany was because knowledge of Bertaud's method had reached Basedow in Germany.]

Concerning Basedow's method's being founded upon experience, there is an amazingly clear record of precisely what this experience was, as reported in the words of Wolke of the Philanthropinum. Wolke said:

"When I came to Herr Professor Basedow at Altona, at New Year's of 1770, to take part in the labor upon his Elementary Book, in the departments of natural history and mathematics, his little daughter, Emilie, was three quarters of a year old. My inclination to be employing myself about children led me to help her mother, who was instructing her carefully, about an hour a day, in little exercises, which, if made as complete as possible, are much more important than would be supposed.

"I taught her, for example, after a certain order and selection, about things of all kinds and their qualities, by showing them to her, and by clear and accurate descriptions of them.... Both in sport and in earnest, we were very careful to avoid that confusion of ideas which is usual in such teaching. For example, she saw in a looking-glass not herself, but her image; in pictures, not men, trees, beasts, but only their representations.... By such... a method as is now taught in the *Elementary Book*, Emilie had in her third half year learned to form opinions with a correctness which was the admiration of all who saw her...."

This was obviously the first purpose of Basedow's *Elementary Book*, founded on Locke's philosophy on how the mind obtains knowledge. At that point, it had nothing to do with the teaching of reading, but would become part of the 19th century approach when reading began to be taught "meaningfully," at Level 3, consciousness or attention, instead of Level 1, syllables, or Level 2, words-in-syntax.

Wolke had this to say about reading, the second purpose of the *Elementary Book*:

"When she was a year and a half old, she could not only speak much more clearly and correctly than is usual at her age, but, by means of our peculiar method of teaching spelling before the knowledge of the letters, to understand sentences if we only said over the letters of them to her."

As will be obvious, by "letters" he means Pascal's new letter names. In German, words are usually spelled so they are phonically regular. The next sentence, not phonically regular in English, must be so in German:

"If, for example, anyone said to her the letters you shall have a cake, she would say, you shall have a cake. The success of this practice, the facility of which had been foreseen by Herr Professor Basedow, pleased him exceedingly, when Emilie, without further trouble or the wearisome spelling in a book, learned to read in a month, to her own pleasure and to mine. This was at the end of her third year."

Or 1772, and Basedow, in his 1774 *Elementary Book* said that his "incomparable reading method, of teaching children to read without weariness or loss of time had been "founded upon experience," with his own little Emilie, obviously. Basedow's school, the Philanthropinum, did not open until December 27, 1774.

Here, officially, for one of the first times, other than possibly in a few obscure French 18th century primers, was the use of sounding and blending phonics, but to teach words at Level 2, instead of syllables at Level 1. The syllable had been forgotten.

Little Emilie was reported, when she was 6 or 7, to be "snow-white, with coal black hair, and a wreath upon it." The child is reported to have looked at a visitor and said, in Latin, "Salve," and thrown a kiss. She married a minister when she was 19 and passed almost completely out of history, although it was reported later her marriage was not a happy one. Her father, Basedow, broke with the Philanthropinum School in 1778, fighting afterwards with Wolke. Von Raumer said:

"From the year 1778, Basedow taught privately in Dessau, and gave great offense by many vulgarities, especially by drunkenness...."

Basedow was working on the teaching of beginning reading when he died, which was rather suddenly, in the heat of the summer of 1790. Von Raumer said:

"His last words were characteristic: 'I desire to be

273

dissected for the benefit of my fellow-men.'"

He was not - reportedly because of the heat. But this thunderous man did not pass out of history so quietly as his little Emilie, the first child to be taught by the German analytic-synthetic phonics method, which uses whole words to teach phonics.

The influence of Basedow's work has been enormous. Gedike wrote an ode to Basedow:

"Thou North Albion's son, lighted the sparkling torch,
Flung'st it aloft with a Hercules mighty arm,
Many ran toward thee, kindled their lights from thine...."

What was kindled from Basedow's torch, besides progressive education and object lessons, was the teaching of phonics through the use of words, instead of syllables. But, in moving reading up from Level 1, syllables, to Level 2, syntax- generating-words, Germany and the English-speaking countries which were so strongly influenced by German pedagogy in the 19th century lost sight of the once obvious fact that it is the syllable which is the atom of reading, and not the word. We are still beset with this confusion. So, the second flat earth fact in the teaching of beginning reading is that there are such things as pure words which should be taught by their meaning, apart from syllables and syntax. The confusion this has caused is monumental.

THE THIRD FLAT EARTH FACT

The third flat earth fact of the reading experts, their third illusion, is on Level Three, Meaning. It was born right here in America, in Hartford, Connecticut, as a matter of fact, some time about 1814. It began in the garden of Thomas H. Gallaudet's father. Young Gallaudet was a graduate student at Andover, and little Alice Cogswell was a deaf-mute girl who played with Gallaudet's younger brothers and sisters. Alice had already learned to answer Gallaudet's sign language, but, on a particularly fateful day about 1814 in that Gallaudet garden appeared the first sight word in the United States, combined with the first reading comprehension lesson, using "meaning." But it was with the purest of intentions.

Young Gallaudet wrote the word, "hat," and showed it to Alice, indicating that the word on the slip of paper meant the same thing as the hat he held in his hand. Alice understood his sight word and comprehended its meaning, though, of course, it could have no sound at all for the little deaf-mute girl. Alice was obviously operating at Level 2, syntax-generating-words, and then Level 3, consciousness of meaning, with no use whatsoever of Level 1, syllable sounds.

It was with that slip of paper held in Gallaudet's hand, with the word "hat" on it, that the movement began in America to use Level 3, consciousness of meaning, as the primary way to identify printed words. With it was born the third flat-earth fact of the reading experts, their third illusion, but it was on Level 3 this time. It is the illusion that there is a special something called "reading comprehension," which exists apart from general intelligence and acquired knowledge, and that it is possible to TEACH this special something. Yet, if it does not exist, obviously it cannot be taught.

Three experts can immediately be cited to prove that what is called "reading comprehension" is, apart from acquired knowledge, nothing more nor less than native intelligence.

One such expert was Alfred Binet, who wrote the first intelligence tests in France in the early 1900's. Binet used "reading comprehension" as a test of native intelligence and considered it was simply a mirror that reflected how bright or dull the mind of a subject was. Binet's reading comprehension paragraphs are reportedly STILL used to test intelligence.

Another expert is the American psychologist, Edward L. Thorndike, who wrote three famous 1917 articles on reading comprehension, in which he concluded that reading IS reasoning. In Thorndike's view, the mind consists of separate abilities, each of which has to be developed independently, and he concluded that there is no such thing as "transfer of training." With such a view of the mind, obviously, there has to be a special thing called "reading comprehension" that had to be fostered, but its ultimate power would still be dependent on inborn ability. A student of the earlier psychologists, William James and James McKeen Cattell, whose atheistic materialism ruled out the existence of the soul, Thorndike saw the mind simply as a functioning machine.

It is primarily to these three benighted thinkers, William James, James McKeen Cattell, and Edward L. Thorndike, AND their close friend and associate John Dewey, himself an atheistic materialist, that I have traced the origins of our reading problems, as Lance Klass and Paola Lionni, in their book, *The Leipzig Connection*, have traced our other educational problems to them.

R. L. Thorndike, E. L. Thorndike's son, reiterated his father's often-quoted position that reading is reasoning, as reported in Albert J. Harris' and Edward R. Sipay's *How to Increase Reading Ability*. In 1969 and 1971, F. B. Davis had decided, through factor analysis studies on reading comprehension, that there are separate sub-skills which can be identified: word meanings, inferences, details, etc. R. L. Thorndike worked over that data and decided it showed the existence of a word-knowledge factor but that all the rest of the skills could simply be called "reasoning in reading."

Statistical proof also exists that reading comprehension is nothing but native intelligence. Correlation studies have been done comparing intelligence scores to reading comprehension scores. A "perfect" correlation would be 1.0 and one showing no relationship at all would be 0.0. Intelligence quotients and school marks have a correlation of only .40 to .50. Two different forms of an IQ test are considered equivalent with a correlation of 0.90 or more (*Introduction to Educational Measurement*, Victor Noll, p. 50, p. 412). Yet, according to Jean Chall in *Learning to Read, The Great Debate* (1967) , Lennon in 1950 found a correlation between reading ability and intelligence of 0.85 at the eighth grade, almost the same as that of equivalent forms of an IQ test. This should effectively confirm that "reading comprehension" IS intelligence. [Editor's note in 2006: When graphed, "reading comprehension" scores produce the bell-shaped curve of intelligence scores. Bell-shaped curves indicate inborn qualities. However, skills are not inborn, but taught, and skill scores, when graphed (knowledge of number facts, etc.) produce skewed curves, not bell curves, with scores piling up at one end or the other of the graph, depending on whether or not the material has been learned.)

No one has ever said that intelligence can be taught, yet for generations in America we have been trying to teach "reading comprehension" which demonstrably is only a synonym for intelligence. Harris and Sipay concluded in their book, *How to Increase Reading Ability* that methods used to teach reading comprehension were based more on teachers' collected experiences than on proof from research. So how successful have teachers been, then, at teaching reading comprehension (which means its synonym, intelligence)?

H. A. Brown wrote an article in the June, 1914 *Elementary School Journal* on tests on "reading comprehension" he had carried out. In 1914, Brown was Deputy Superintendent (of education) for the state of New Hampshire. The 1914 report was on tests at third and sixth grade in seven school systems, on a total of a little over four hundred children. Brown also said at the end of his 1914 article, on page 55, "A bulletin will be published in the near future giving the results of the application of the test to 12,000 children." This material may never have been published, since only one "bulletin" was ever published. That was in 1916, when Brown published a manual of instructions for giving such tests and said it represented a considerable number of school systems, but it was apparently only on tests given in June, 1915, a full year after Brown's June, 1914, *Elementary School Journal* article. Therefore, it does not seem likely that the 1916 material could have been on the "tests to 12,000 children" that were presumably nearing completion or at least scheduled "in the near future" when Brown wrote in June, 1914, of publishing that data "in the near future." By 1916, when *Bulletin No. 1* was published, Brown was Director of Bureau of Research of the New Hampshire Department of Public Instruction, "In Co-operation with General Education Board" and Brown's manual of directions, *The Measurement of Ability to Read,* was its *Bulletin No. 1.* (It is curious how these "experts" produced No. 1 bulletins, as W. S. Gray did at the University of Chicago. They were certainly trying to set the groundwork for what was to follow.)

However, Bureau of Research of the New Hampshire Department of Public Instruction apparently never issued a *Bulletin No. 2*, because when W. S. Gray issued his *"Descriptive List of Standard Tests, 1917"* in the *Elementary School Journal,* I saw only *Bulletin No. 1* (though it may have been elsewhere in Gray's listings of course.) Gray said further that "Brown's Silent Reading Tests" could be obtained for $0.50 a hundred from H. A. Brown, State Normal School, Oshkosh, Wisconsin. So, by 1917, only a year after issuing *Bulletin No. 1*, Brown had moved on to other pastures (or the "Bureau of Research had been closed down, which the state's possible failure to issue a *Bulletin No. 2* suggests).

The famous (infamous?) "study" reported in the *Elementary*

School Journal by Lillian Beatrice Currier and Olive C. Duguid of Franklin, New Hampshire, "Phonics or No Phonics," in December, 1916, gave no data, just verbal opinions on interest and speed in the no-phonics group. It seems likely that their study in Tilton, New Hampshire, was done in 1915 while Brown was "Director of Bureau of Research of the New Hampshire Department of Public Instruction." However, since Gray's oral reading paragraphs had been published by Thorndike in a preliminary form in September, 1914, in *Teachers College Record*, why did they not test with them, instead of giving a "test" which had no objective data at all, but only anecdotal remarks?

The fact that Currier and Duguid came from Franklin interested me. Thorndike's famous reading comprehension Paragraph J concerns a story about a snowy Franklin where school can be closed when roads are impassable, which undoubtedly happens in Franklin, New Hampshire, and in nearby Tilton, New Hampshire, where Currier and Duguid gave their "tests".

I had the curious feeling that at the time Brown gave his original tests, presumably in 1913-1914 to third and sixth grades, Thorndike gave his original reading comprehension tests, which Thorndike reviewed in his September, 1914, *Teachers College Record* article, along with Gray's oral reading paragraphs that were prepared under Thorndike's direction. It seemed highly likely that Gray's oral reading paragraphs, being developed under Thorndike's direction in 1913-1914, might have been tried out in New Hampshire schools where Brown had a very high official status and in which he could arrange testing programs for those at Columbia Teachers College.

I called the New Hampshire state library to see if they had any data on tests which were carried out in New Hampshire in 1913-1914. They referred me to another office which had bound reports for each year on education in New Hampshire. When the helpful woman on the other end of the phone went to check the shelves, she found the volume reporting 1911-1912, and the volume for 1915-1916, but the volumes for 1912-1913 and 1913-1914 were missing.

In his *Elementary School Journal* article, in June, 1914, Brown wrote with missionary zeal about the need to change teaching methods in first grade, and about the need to use the context-guessing sight-word method he described instead of phonics, in order to protect what we call "reading comprehension." Here is what Brown of the missionary spirit had to say about reading when his "reading comprehension" and sight-word. guessing were not taught, as in one "terrible" class he saw:

> "It is entirely evident that these children are the kind so often seen who can read readily as far as mere word pronunciation goes but who do not apperceive, assimilate and retain the content of what is read in anything like an efficient manner. Reading is about the most deceptive subject in the entire school curriculum.... The writer recently visited a school in which the reading appeared to be highly efficient. The children could stand and read a page with the utmost *apparent* ease and fluency and the casual observer would have said that it was reading of the highest competency. Word pronunciation had been splendidly mastered. It is entirely possible and often happens that reading of this kind is in reality of low grade.... It cannot be pointed out too often that reading is more than mere word-pronunciation. It is feared that some of our prevailing methods of instruction in primary reading are faulty for the reason that undue emphasis is placed on too rapid and too complete mastery of the difficulties of word pronunciation in the earliest stages of reading at the expense of perceptive and assimilative activities and that

this type of teaching produces a pronounced word-consciousness and a confirmed habit of reading words instead of thoughts from the printed page which the pupil never completely outgrows and which proves a real hindrance to real thought-getting in later stages of his reading...."

Most naturally, Brown had received a graduate degree from Columbia Teachers College, on June 13, 1912, which is where he apparently picked up his missionary zeal. His comments belittling good oral reading are almost identical to those of William Scott Gray in a Bloomfield-method classroom about 1940, reported by Mitford Mathews. Gray had been, of course, Thorndike's graduate student at Columbia in 1913-1914.

Here is how Thorndike, himself, put it in one of his three 1917 (famous) articles on reading comprehension:

"In school practice it appears likely that exercises in silent reading to find the answers to given questions, or to give a summary of the matter read, or to list the questions which it answers, should in large measure replace oral reading. The vice of the poor reader is to say the words to himself without actively making judgments concerning what they reveal. Reading aloud or listening to one reading aloud may leave this vice unaltered or even encouraged."

He did not explicitly say so, but he is clearly indicating that oral reading is somehow different from silent reading, obviously because of different "bonds." His research was supposed to indicate that such "bonds" did not transfer. There was no "transfer of training."

Brown's complaint about "terrible" reading in 1914 was

repeated in "Educational Writings" in the *Elementary School Journal* in 1914. In reviewing a book by Paul Klapper, *Teaching Children to Read,* S. Appleton & Co., the reviewer said:

> "When it canes to cultivating silent reading, Professor Klapper is almost helpless.... They ought, as he recognizes, to read more rapidly than they do.... Anyone who is acquainted with the work of schools will agree very heartily with the comment that is made by Professor Klapper in various places that the reading of the upper grades is a blank failure, but why it is a blank failure he does not seem to be able to tell us, and he certainly does not give us the formula by which we could improve the reading...."

Anyone reading this today will be reminded of the reportedly terrible illiteracy problems turned up in World War I when draftees were tested. They were given intelligence tests, and, those reportedly being illiterate, were given Thorndike's non-verbal intelligence test. Obviously, the psychologists were closely connected with the testing movement in 1917. *The Scientific American Reference Book,* Munn & Co., 1921, listed a table for illiteracy results in all the army camps, and also gave the criterion for illiteracy. Seventeen of the 28 used grade level attained in school, from third to eighth. The rest said "read and write" means "ability to read and understand newspapers and write letters home." Who decided whether they "understood" newspapers - the psychologists and men like Brown?

But, for the great bulk of the camps, 17 of the 28, if the draftees had not reached from third to eighth grade, they were "illiterate." That would put our Abraham Lincoln, he of the Shakespearean and Biblical prose, in the group who were "sent to Beta" as the reference book put it. Lincoln never even finished SECOND grade!

The bias against Blacks was prominent in this table. At Camp Sherman, the literacy basis was solely "Sixth grade" with, in parenthesis (negroes, 8 years at school). Literacy statistics for World War I, black or white, based on standards so ludicrous, can be totally disregarded.

In this connection, I want to mention the remark of my dear cousin Duryea Breslin, who died not long ago. She began school in Jersey City, New Jersey, in the 1920's when, as Arthur Gates said, most teachers taught heavy supplementary phonics. I remember Duryeá's remark about the Black children in her class:

"The black kids were always the smart ones."

According to Dr. Hilde Mosse, people fall into dominant perceptual types, auditory or visual, with some mixed. Concerning the talents of so many Black people at music and poetry, it suggests that large numbers of Blacks are the dominant auditory type, the kind most crippled by the sight-word method and most adept with the phonic method. Black children who were auditory types would have made a quicker start at reading with the phonic method, so Duryea saw them as "always the smart ones," even fifty years later. Such dominantly auditory children are tragically handicapped today by the sight-word method. I have such a tiny sample of Black children I tested in European schools with heavy phonic programs in my 1977-1978 oral reading research that I cannot cite the scores as formal research. I do want to say here, though, that NONE of them failed my tests. In one Amsterdam school which had a considerable number of second graders fail the reading comprehension part of my test, the one Black boy in the class passed. Averaging my tiny group of Black European scores against the whole, they did outscore the European average, so they were, like Duryea's classmates, "the smart ones."

All this lamenting of "failure" in reading by reading experts in

1914 appeared about the same time as a review in the *Elementary School Journal* on the 1910 census. It said:

"There has been a notable decrease in illiteracy among children from ten to fourteen years of age, the numbers decreasing from 42 in each 1,000 in 1900 to 22 in each 1,000 in 1910. Most of the illiteracy among children is in the southern states.... (On) the question of what the schools should do to decrease illiteracy in the country... For children between ten and fourteen years of age the problem is relatively simple. Adequate compulsory attendance laws, rigorously enforced, will place such children in the regular schools. For illiterate persons above the compulsory attendance age, the problem is more difficult...."

So, along with a great push on changing methods of primary reading, a great push on teaching silent reading and on reading comprehension tests became the battle cry of the "experts" after 1914. With all their efforts, how well DID they succeed in teaching "reading comprehension"?

In 1923, William A. McCall, another of Thorndike's students, said this in his article in the *Teachers College Record,* "Does It Pay to Measure the Achievement of Pupils?" in which McCall was probably talking about the Horace Mann School:

"Several years ago the highly trained teachers of one of the best-known private elementary schools in the United States decided to make a determined effort to improve their technique of teaching silent reading. The principal of the school divided the teachers into two groups, equal in number and in teaching skill, one a control group, the other an experimental group. The control teachers agreed to continue teaching silent reading by the methods previously used. The experimental teachers agreed to do everything in their power to devise and make use of better means of teaching the subject. They made a careful study of books dealing with methods of teaching silent reading and held many conferences with specialists in the subject and with educational psychologists. (Editor's note: Please carefully note that word: psychologists.) Finally, presumably improved methods were devised and put into operation. In each grade of the school, from grade three through grade eight, there was an approximately equal number of pupils being taught for equal lengths of time by teachers of the experimental group and by experimental methods and by teachers of the control group and their methods.

"To discover whether it was possible for such a group of teachers to improve upon previous methods of teaching reading, the writer was invited to plan and direct the measurement of changes made in the progress of the two groups of pupils. An elaborate series of reading tests was applied. These included such difficulty tests as the Thorndike-McCall, such rate tests as the Starch, such rate-difficulty tests as the Monroe, and such vocabulary tests as the Thorndike. The tests were given both at the beginning and at the end of the year.

"What difference was there in the average growth made by all experimental pupils and all control pupils on all tests combined? The end average difference was almost exactly zero! ... It is needless to say that the disappointment was very keen on the part of all."

McCall then went on to describe his own reading tests, which were given periodically and the pupils tested and marked themselves. With this method (which is what we use now with the SRA cards) scores did rise. What was happening, of course, was that pupils, seeing they were failing, chose freely to pay better attention on subsequent tests. The "reading comprehension" had not improved, but their voluntary attention had. Lack of voluntary attention was the cause for Brown's fluctuating scores, but he had not understood that in 1914 any more than McCall did in 1923. There undoubtedly was a reason they missed an explanation that seems almost self-evident. Since their psychology denied the will, it could not, therefore, include the possibility of VOLUNTARY attention. It was Pascal and Cromwell's "predestination" all over again, expressed in the materialistic psychology of the 20th century.

After William A. McCall, Arthur I. Gates of Columbia Teachers College wrote more test lessons that actually encouraged voluntary attention, but he called it teaching "reading comprehension" in the "skill areas."

So, after all the work on reading comprehension, how did the situation stand in the summer of 1971, when Wayne Otto of the University of Wisconsin reviewed, in the *Reading Research Quarterly*, one of Thorndike's three 1917 articles on reading comprehension? Otto said:

> "...subsequent work has not yielded anything that has been
> very useful in eliminating the kinds of mistakes Thorndike
> found in children's paragraph reading over a half century
> ago."

Dr. Carl Bereiter of the Ontario Institute for Studies in Education told, at the Toronto Reading Reform Conference in 1982, of some interesting work they are doing trying to get children to think logically as they are reading. Actually, it sounded more like training in logical thinking than "reading" and may prove worth while. His group's approach IS different. But his preliminary comment, concerning prior work in reading comprehension up until 1982, was illuminating:

> "....there has not been some technique that could be taught
> to children that would provide them a useful handle on the
> problem of reading comprehension ."

Naturally, because there IS no such thing as "reading comprehension," apart from intelligence (and background knowledge). The existence of a special something called "reading comprehension" is the third flat earth fact of the reading experts.

There they are, the three flat earth facts of American reading instruction: reliance on letter sounds, teaching of whole words, and years of time-consuming instruction in "reading comprehension." Yet none of these three things really exist. In addition, almost all of this so-called instruction is given in reading groups, which means that the teacher's instructional time is divided into splinters. What a hole would be left in the American school day if we no longer taught these non-existent "skills" in time-consuming reading groups! Suppose, instead, that like the Russians, we taught the WHOLE FIRST GRADE CLASS TOGETHER with true phonics and taught virtually ALL of them to read before the end of the winter? Suppose, by the middle of first grade, we were DONE with reading, forever, as the Russians are? We might then, like the Russians, have enough time properly to teach esoteric subjects like geography, history, science, mathematics and literature.

I will return to my charge that academic crimes were committed - the burying, distorting and misrepresenting of facts, which is what George Orwell named in his book, 1984 "unthink." It is a peculiarly 20th century crime, which would have been distasteful to very many earlier societies

In *The Story of the Irish Race* (1921, 1969), Seumas MacManus quoted Dr. Douglas Hyde:

"The numerous Irish annals in which the skeleton of Irish history is contained are valuable and ancient.... The illustrious Bede in recording the great eclipse of the sun which took place only eleven years before his own birth is only two days astray in his date, while the Irish annals give correctly not only the day but the hour.... These annals contain, between the end of the fifth century and the year 884, as many as eighteen records of eclipses, comets, and such natural phenomena - and modern science by calculating backwards shows that all these records are absolutely correct, both as to the day and hour. From this we can deduce without hesitation that from the fourth or fifth century the Irish annals can be absolutely trusted."

MacManus said:

"In history, Ireland's fame stands high. She was justly styled "a nation of Annalists".... Truth and accuracy were regarded as of paramount importance. 'To conceal the truth of history,' ran one saying, 'is the blackest of infamies.'"

In the starker, less elegant language of the 20th century, the English novelist George Orwell has renamed "the blackest of infamies" "Unthink," and it is this which must be dealt with in groping for the truth about American mis-instruction in reading.

The pattern has not changed to the present day. In 1981, Rudolf Flesch published *Why Johnny STILL Can't Read.* It was a careful analysis of the present sight-word phonics controversy and produced unassailable data calling for true phonics in reading instruction.

In 1982, Dr. Patrick Groff reported in the March, 1982, issue of *The Reading Informer* about the April 26, 1982, convention of the International Reading Association in Chicago. Twelve thousand people were expected to attend. A list of 400 separate activities had been given. Yet not ONE of them concerned the teaching of phonics!

Dr. Groff reported in the March-April, 1983 issue of *The Reading Informer* on the upcoming May 2-6, 1983, convention of the International Reading Association at Anaheim, California. Three hundred fifty regular sessions had been scheduled, but only ONE concerned the teaching of phonics. What chance would anyone attending those conventions have to hear Dr. Flesch's carefully constructed arguments on the necessity for phonics?

Dr. Rudolf Flesch turned on the light in America's classrooms, so that we can see what is so plainly wrong. WHY then does the Establishment keep rushing over to the light switch, and turning the light off again?

Most of the material I have included in this paper was pried out of disparate sources, pebble by pebble, and then reassembled into the mosaic that is the history of reading instruction. But how could this be, that these facts were not clearly in the reading record long before I came along, except as the result of that blackest of infamies, Unthink?

www.ingramcontent.com/pod-product-compliance
Lightning Source LLC
LaVergne TN
LVHW011217080426
835509LV00005B/181

* 9 7 8 1 5 8 9 3 9 9 9 5 2 *